STUDIES IN HISTORY, ECONOMICS AND PUBLIC LAW

Edited by the

FACULTY OF POLITICAL SCIENCE
OF COLUMBIA UNIVERSITY

NUMBER 559

THE AUSTRIAN ELECTORAL REFORM OF 1907

BY

WILLIAM ALEXANDER JENKS

THE
AUSTRIAN ELECTORAL
REFORM OF 1907

BY

WILLIAM ALEXANDER JENKS

OCTAGON BOOKS

A DIVISION OF FARRAR, STRAUS AND GIROUX

New York   1974

Reprinted 1974
by special arrangement with Columbia University Press

OCTAGON BOOKS
A DIVISION OF FARRAR, STRAUS & GIROUX, INC.
19 Union Square West
New York, N. Y. 10003

Library of Congress Cataloging in Publication Data

Jenks, William Alexander, 1918-
    The Austrian electoral reform of 1907.

    Reprint of the ed. published by Columbia University Press, New
York, which was issued as no. 559 of Columbia University. Faculty of Political Science. Studies in history, economics, and public
law.

    Originally presented as the author's thesis, Columbia, 1950.

    Bibliography: p.
    1. Elections—Austria.   I. Title.   II. Series: Columbia studies in
the social sciences, no. 559.
JN1991.J46   1974   324'.2'09436   74-4307
ISBN 0-374-94205-6

Printed in USA by
Thomson-Shore, Inc.
Dexter, Michigan

PREFACE

In 1815 the forces of nationalism and democracy which had been propagated in Europe during the Revolutionary and Napoleonic years were halted momentarily by a coalition of European powers which included Metternich's Austria. A hundred years later the Habsburg monarchy found itself involved in its last fateful struggle with these forces. This study has as its purpose the description of one of the last efforts made to reconcile nationalism and democracy with Habsburg tradition in the period preceding the final collapse of the empire.

Essentially, the problem of nationalism in the Habsburg dominions during the nineteenth century had its inception in the privileged position of Germanism in imperial affairs. Since the days of Maria Theresa and Joseph II administration was avowedly dependent upon the German or Germanized elements in the Habsburg territories; in return for services rendered, the Germans were understandably desirous of holding on to their established predominance. That predominance was temporarily challenged in 1848-49, most successfully by the Magyars; thereafter, the favored Germans were increasingly menaced by the well-developed national sentiment of Magyars, Italians, and Poles and by the gradually developing national sentiment of Czechs and other less consciously national groups whose past was being industriously revived by interested intellectuals.

The German position was seemingly strengthened by the Ausgleich of 1867, which surrendered to the Germans' most intransigent rivals, the Magyars, the control of the eastern part of the empire. Theoretically, the Germans could then deal effectively with the less well-organized national movements in the western part of the empire. In reality, the bargain principally increased the resentment of the Czechs, whose aspirations were far more galling to the Germans than the historic aspirations of the Poles and Italians. In the decades which fol-

5

lowed, Czech nationalism exhibited a stubbornness which reached a climax in the wearying and futile parliamentary sessions of the 1890's. At the opening of the new century, government by decree became a normal expedient; in the face of this effective threat to ordinary constitutional procedure, Czech and German leaders finally evinced willingness to attempt a new basis for a compromise. Obviously, the Germans would not accept federalistic schemes which would abandon their brothers in Bohemia, Moravia, and Silesia to Czech control of those areas, but, as pressure for electoral reform increased, some of the German leaders cautiously hinted that a relaxation of suffrage requirements might supply the needed basis for agreement. The nature and extent of the surrender of parliamentary power by the Germans to the other nationalities of Austria is one of the chief themes of this study.

The striking social and economic changes which accompanied the growth of industry in Austria help explain the willingness of some prominent Germans to consider electoral reform. The curial system of representation, with its favoritism towards the landed aristocrats and wealthy leaders of business, had some justification before 1870; after 1896, the mere addition of a fifth curia of seventy-two deputies, to be elected universally by the male citizens of Austria, scarcely met the growing demands of workers in industry and agriculture. The Germans dared not ignore the political demands of the German proletariat, lest international socialism, with its studied contempt for "bourgeois" nationalism, capture the complete allegiance of the laborers and destroy the unity of the Germans of Austria. The aristocracy and the bourgeoisie of the other nationalities shared a like fear of the destructive power of socialistic propaganda among the masses. When absolutism collapsed in the Russian Empire in 1905, the privileged of Austria were forced to reckon with demonstrators in the streets who, if denied their desires, might shatter the shaky Habsburg structure. Concessions to the crowds seemed to be inevitable; indeed, some of the members of the privileged Reichsrat were convinced that universal suffrage might well force a substitution of social and economic questions for the deadly nationalistic bickering which had stultified parliamentary sessions. In the pages which follow, considerable attention is paid to the gradual victory of the idea of universal manhood suffrage and to the controversies which arose over such questions as compulsory voting, vocational representation, etc. An attempt also is made to explain the reasons why a democratically elected Lower House of the Reichsrat failed to better the disappointing record of its privileged predecessors in solving the major Austrian problems.

This discussion will consciously avoid any detailed narration of the abortive plans for electoral reform in Hungary which definitely inspired the renewal of agitation for universal manhood suffrage in Austria in 1905. Such a procedure, it is hoped, will not minimize the importance of those abortive plans. Even if electoral reform had solved the problem of nationalities in Austria after 1907, there is little reason to suppose that this remedy would have been enthusiastically adopted by the Magyars. Unfortunately, the Austrian reform of 1907 failed to eliminate national strife in Austria; at the same time it increased the rising anger of 2,000,000 Slovaks and Czechs and 3,000,000 Croats, Slovenes, and Serbs in Hungary, who looked upon their more fortunate co-nationals in Austria with envy and frustration.

A minimum of attention is paid to Austro-Hungarian foreign policy. Here, too, it is hoped that the reader will remember that Austria-Hungary's membership in the Triple Alliance met with the general disapproval of the Slavic citizens of both parts of the empire. The lack of parliamentary control over foreign policy was a bad omen for any reconstruction of parliamentary bodies; democratic elections would mean little in a state whose foreign policy could not be appreciably influenced by democratic pressure. The Hungarian situation and the problem of control of foreign policy have been mentioned so that the work of the advocates of universal manhood suffrage in Austria may be given some perspective. The progenitors of electoral reform may be justly criticized for their lack of realism and their lack of a sincere spirit of accommodation toward their neighbors of different nationalities; they should be praised at the same time for their dogged fight to find some means of satisfying democratic and nationalistic forces in an empire whose ruler never clearly understood the meaning of either force.

I am deeply indebted to Professor Carlton J. H. Hayes, under whose direction this study was initiated and completed, for his valuable guidance and inspiring qualities as a teacher and scholar. I am also grateful to Professor John H. Wuorinen for his helpful suggestions and personal interest. Among the many persons in library work who were of assistance, I should like to thank particularly Mr. Henry E. Coleman, Jr. and Miss Martha R. Cullipher of Washington and Lee University. I also wish to express my appreciation of the aid and encouragement given me by my friends and colleagues at Washington and Lee University.

LEXINGTON, VIRGINIA, 1949

CONTENTS

9

CHAPTER I

THE DEVELOPMENT OF REPRESENTA-
TIVE GOVERNMENT IN AUSTRIA
1860-1896

THE OCTOBER DIPLOMA OF 1860 AND THE FEBRUARY PATENT OF 1861

THE achievement of universal manhood suffrage in Austria in 1907 was the last step in a series of political developments which went back to the revolutionary disturbances of 1848. In April, 1848 the Emperor Ferdinand I granted a constitution to his peoples and guaranteed full civil and religious rights to all citizens. The disintegration of the liberal movement in Vienna and the military victories of Windischgrätz and Radetzky, however, gave the new Emperor, Francis Joseph, and his authoritarian minister, Schwarzenberg, the opportunity to promulgate a revised constitution in 1849 which appreciably diminished the concessions of the previous year. With the subjugation of Kossuth's Hungarian Republic later in 1849, the Emperor and his advisors were enabled to move gradually toward the suppression of what was left of popular liberties. On the last day of the year 1851, the constitution of 1849 was revoked, and bureaucratic absolutism was resumed. As in Metternich's day, liberalism and nationalism were repressed as much as possible while Austria tried to keep intact her dominant influence in Germany and Italy. For eight years, the Emperor's subjects endured a police regime that was mitigated considerably by the inefficiency of the officials in charge.

Improvement came in 1859, when the defeats suffered in Italy aroused criticisms and resentment at home that forced the Emperor and his chief advisor, Goluchowski, to promise a return to constitutional government. In March, 1860 the Emperor summoned representatives of all of his provinces and informed them that they were to join with the Imperial Council (Reichsrat) in recommending a reorganization of the empire. This consultative body finally decided there should be a central assembly at Vienna selected on a broad national basis and that a certain amount of autonomy should be granted by a revival of the old provincial assemblies, or diets.

On October 20, 1860 Francis Joseph formally recognized the principle of constitutional government in a diploma which promised considerable provincial autonomy. All legislative and financial powers were to be shared by the diets and the Emperor; the central Reichsrat at Vienna would consist of one house whose members would be appointed by the Emperor from nominees suggested by the diets. Bureaucratic centralization was to be scrapped, and most of the nationalities of the empire expressed approval of the new course. However, the experiment was short-lived. The Hungarian Liberals, under Francis Deák, refused to accept the " October Diploma " unless the Emperor first restored to Hungary the complete autonomy that had been abrogated in 1849. Francis Joseph and his ministers had no intention of granting such a concession, and the immediate result of the controversy was the promulgation of a patent on February 26, 1861, which elaborated and essentially nullified the " October Diploma."

The " February Patent " called for the creation of a bicameral legislature which would meet annually. The Upper House, or House of Lords, was to consist of members appointed by the Emperor because of royal or noble birth, possessions and station, or simple merit; the Lower House, or House of Representatives, was to consist of 343 members chosen by the provincial diets from their own membership. Most important of all, the patent severely restricted the powers of the diets and turned over to the central parliament the rights lost by the diets. Centralization was the answer given the recalcitrant Hungarians and the non-German nationalities who had seen much promise in the " October Diploma." Gradually the provincial diets were chosen and began to function, but the Hungarian Diet steadily refused to accept the new arrangements and was therefore dissolved in August, 1861. After four years of sporadic bickering and bargaining, the Emperor temporarily suspended the " February Patent " in September, 1865, to pave the way for a new formula which would be acceptable to the Hungarians. Negotiations were upset momentarily by the war with Prussia in 1866, but the crushing defeat at Sadowa forced the Emperor to treat at once with Deák.

THE FUNDAMENTAL LAWS OF THE STATE, 1867

Practically all of the Hungarian demands for a dual monarchy which would leave Hungary virtually independent were recognized in the compromise which was negotiated in 1867. This compromise, of course, was the famous Ausgleich, which regulated affairs between Austria and Hungary until the collapse of Habsburg dominion in 1918. To gain support for the compromise in Vienna, Beust, the Imperial Minister-President, promised that full constitutional government would be restored in the Austrian half of the Habsburg realm.

Unfortunately for Beust, only the Germans in the Reichsrat in Vienna were in favor of the Ausgleich. The Czechs were enraged that Hungary had attained virtual independence; they controlled the majorities in the diets of Bohemia and Moravia and gave every evidence of refusing to allow their representatives in the Reichsrat to vote for any revision of the " February Patent." A two-thirds vote was required for the necessary amendments, so Beust was forced to order new elections to the diets in these provinces. By using the influence of the court, he persuaded the great landowners to vote for Germans, and the necessary German majority in the diets was secured. The new diets obediently sent a German majority to the Reichsrat, and a revision and extension of the " February Patent " was completed.

The constitutional labors of the revised Reichsrat resulted in the passage of five fundamental laws (*Staatsgrundgesetze*), which were sanctioned by the Emperor on December 21, 1867. Essentially, these fundamental laws, with notable revisions, were the "constitution" of Austria down to 1918. The laws involved: (1) a bill of rights for Austrian citizens, (2) a system of imperial representation, (3) the creation of an imperial court, the *Reichsgericht*, (4) an imperial judiciary system, and (5) the exercise of administrative and executive powers by the Emperor and his ministers. In 1873 an act was passed which permitted changes in the fundamental laws by a two-thirds vote in both houses of parliament, provided at least half of the Lower House's membership was present when the vote was taken.[1]

The second fundamental law, on imperial representation, provided for a bicameral parliament very similar in composition and powers to the parliament created by the patent of 1861. The House of Lords was to be composed of princes of the blood, archbishops and bishops of princely title inherent in their episcopal sees, nobles of high rank and large estates (who received hereditary seats), and persons who had rendered signal service to state, church, or culture (who received appointments for life).[2] No definite limit was placed upon the members in the Upper House. The Lower House was made up of 203 members elected by the provincial diets, a procedure which soon plagued the central administration. The Czechs, for instance, who desired the same degree of independence that the Hungarians had secured, violently denied the legality of the fundamental laws, and they refused to elect representatives to the Reichsrat when they secured control of the diets of Bohemia and Moravia. In 1868 the Reichsrat passed a law which presumably would eliminate such tactics; should any provincial diet fail to elect its quota of deputies to the Lower House, direct elections were to be held. This law was a poor

1 For the text of the fundamental laws before the amendments of 1907 (in German) see A. Lawrence Lowell, *Governments and Parties in Continental Europe* (Boston and New York, 1896), II, 378-404. An English translation, including the amendments of 1907, is to be found in Walter F. Dodd, *Modern Constitutions* (Chicago, 1909), I, 71-89.

2 Frederic A. Ogg, *The Governments of Europe* (New York, 1913), p. 465.

remedy, for the diets usually complied by voting for representatives who then refused to take their seats. When the Bohemian and Moravian diets refused to comply, they usually were dissolved, and the electoral campaigns which ensued created continual disturbance of public order. Nor did the members elected by direct vote always take their seats in Vienna.[3]

THE REFORM OF 1873

The Liberal ministry, presided over by Prince Adolf Auersperg after 1871, decided to bring an end to this situation by an electoral reform. The reform, which was recommended to the Reichsrat by the ministry in February, 1873, substituted direct elections to the Lower House in place of the previous system of elections of deputies by the diets. In retrospect, it seems quite clear that the ministry was chiefly interested in eliminating the obstructionist tactics of the diets, for direct elections did not mean an increase in the number of Austrians who enjoyed the franchise. Direct voting for members of the diets had been the rule since 1861, but only certain parts of the provincial population had the right to vote for their representatives. The law of April 2, 1873 merely adopted the provincial electoral arrangements by creating a system of " class representation."

According to this system, the population of Austria was divided theoretically into four classes, for the purpose of choosing representatives. Each class, or curia, was to be allotted a certain number of representatives within each province. The classes were: (1) the great landowners who paid taxes ranging from 50 to 150 florins on estates usually held by noble or feudal tenure; (2) the male inhabitants of cities who were twenty-four years of age and who paid at least ten florins in direct taxes annually; (3) members of chambers of commerce and industry; and (4) male inhabitants of rural communes who met the same qualifications expected of members of the

3 Lowell, *op. cit.*, II, 85-86, 102-103.

second, or urban, curia. In some of the smaller provinces, the urban curia and the curia of the chambers of commerce were combined; otherwise, the different classes voted within their own curias. The great landowners received 85 seats, the cities received 118 (19 of which were shared with the curia of the chambers of commerce), the chambers of commerce, 21, and the rural communes, 129, making a grand total of 353. Elections were direct, save in the rural communes, where electors were chosen for every 500 inhabitants. Any male who had possessed Austrian citizenship for at least three years, who was thirty years old, and who had the general right to vote could be elected to parliament by any curia in any province, despite his membership in a particular curia or his residence in a particular province.

Obviously, the system adopted in 1873 was a curious mixture of traditional representation of medieval estates and of new classes which had arisen with the gradual industrialization of Austria. Petitions from workers begged that the franchise be extended, but the ministry insisted that self-sustaining men of the community, whether rural or urban, alone should be entrusted with the right to vote. The new proposals elicited the hearty disapproval of the Czechs, Poles, and Slovenes; yet the obstructionist maneuvers of the Czechs literally secured the passage of the reform. The Czechs had consistently refused to sit in the Reichsrat, lest they thereby recognize the fundamental laws which they declared to be illegal, while the Polish deputies refused to take any part in the voting. As a result, the Germans easily secured the necessary two-thirds vote for the passage of the bill. Had the Czechs been present, 134 affirmative votes in the Lower House would have been needed; the law actually was secured by 114 favorable votes. The Polish abstention was generally believed to be due to promises made to the Poles by the Emperor, and this abstention, coupled with Czech intransigence, spelled victory for the ministry.[4]

---

4 Alois von Czedik, *Zur Geschichte der k. k. österreichischen Ministerien 1861-1916* (Teschen, Vienna, Leipzig, 1917), I, 256-270.

THE REFORM OF 1882

Disparities in the importance of the individual voter in each curia were great; by 1879, there was one deputy for every 63 voters in the landed curia; in the chambers of commerce, 27 voters elected a deputy; in the cities, one deputy represented some 1,600 voters; in the rural communes, a deputy represented some 7,900 voters.[5] However, a modification in the direction of fairer representation did not come for nine years, and then its appearance was largely the result of the activities of politicians who made little effort to disguise their distaste for a comprehensive reform. The elections of 1879 had cost the German Liberals their majority in the Lower House, and, after some preliminary attempts at a true coalition cabinet, the new Minister-President, Count Taaffe, picked colleagues from representatives of the Poles, Czechs, Clericals, Conservatives, and South Slavs—groups which were collectively known as "the Right." The parties of the Right were united only in their determination to keep the German Liberals out of power, and the coalition did fairly well in defying the disgruntled German Liberals for several years.

In 1881, however, the various factions within the German Liberal party composed their differences and entered upon a policy of parliamentary obstruction that worried the parties of the Right considerably. Roll-call votes demonstrated that the Right's majority was none too secure; practical strategy demanded some means of increasing the coalition's power, and electoral reform was the palliative decided upon. It was quite clear that no sweeping amendments to the fundamental laws could pass the Reichsrat, for the necessary two-thirds vote would be lacking. Indeed, the Clerical-Conservative-Slavic bloc scarcely desired any wide extension of the suffrage; only a few "radicals" spoke up for universal manhood suffrage and the abolition of the system of curias. New supporters for the

5 *Stenographische Protokolle über die Sitzungen des Hauses der Abgeordneten des Reichsrates*, XVII Session (1901-1907), *Beilagen*, No. 2552.

Right could be found more easily among the small landowners and lower bourgeoisie who did not pay a direct tax of ten florins annually. Such groups had become quite anti-Liberal as a result of the financial panic of 1873 and its scandals, and many were becoming ardent followers of the intense nationalism that was on the increase among all of the non-German nationalities. Opponents of economic liberalism and friends of a federal scheme for Austria had everything to gain by enfranchising such men.

Before the Right could prepare proposals reducing the tax qualifications in the rural and urban curias, some deputies of "radical" tendency in the German camp introduced a bill which called for direct suffrage for all Austrian males at least twenty-four years old. The German Liberals and the Right united in rejecting this bill. The "radicals" then offered another plan, which would permit every man who was thirty years old and who paid a direct tax to vote in the urban or rural curia; elections in the latter curia were to be direct. On the same day (January 28, 1882), the Right introduced its own plan; its most important clauses provided for the extension of the franchise to men in the rural and urban curias who paid at least five florins in direct taxes annually. In the sessions of the committee of the Lower House which considered the two plans, the "radical" plan never had a chance of approval. The Poles and Czechs expressed general approval of the five-florin reform, but the latter demanded a price for their support. The curia of the great landowners in Bohemia was to be remodeled so that Czech landowners would have greater power in selecting deputies to parliament in the future. The German Liberals had remained fairly quiet on the subject of the five-florin plan, but they energetically protested the concession extorted by the Czechs. They did not dare oppose a limited extension of the suffrage; in fact, a few Liberals favored it as a check upon incipient socialism. But a change which would increase Slavic strength would not be endured, and the Liberal spokesmen rebuked the Rightist bloc for attempting to balance votes for the less wealthy classes with new privileges for Bohemian landowners.

Count Taaffe had already expressed his approval in principle of the reform, and he was forced to defend all of its provisions in the Lower House. On March 23, 1882 the proposals were accepted by a vote of 162 to 124. Later in the year the Upper House likewise agreed to the plan, and the Emperor sanctioned the law on October 4, 1882.[6] At least 400,000 more votes were cast in 1885 than in 1879; even so, the reform still ignored great numbers of Austrians.

THE TAAFFE ELECTORAL BILL OF 1893

In the decade which followed the reform of 1882, German Nationalists, Young Czechs, and the increasingly noisy Christian Socialists and Social Democrats continued to agitate for a further liberalization of franchise requirements. Their arguments anticipated many of the controversial questions which were to come in 1905-1906, and the debates which resulted from their recommendations revealed rather clearly party alignments which did develop in the later period.

In April, 1891 Young Czechs, German Liberals, German Radicals, and Christian Socialists submitted to the Reichsrat motions which provided for the abolition of indirect elections in the rural curia. The Young Czechs also championed universal manhood suffrage in the sessions which followed, while workers' demonstrations in the streets of Vienna underlined the Young Czech proposal. A committee was elected by the Lower House to study the motions which had been made, but it showed little interest in its task until the Young Czechs prodded it into greater activity. In the autumn of 1891 the committee asked Taaffe to deliver his opinion of the motions, but the Minister-President avoided committing himself, with the excuse that he had more pressing affairs to consider. The

6 Gustav Kolmer, *Parlament und Verfassung in Österreich* (Vienna and Leipzig, 1902-1914), III, 137-162.

Lower House seemed to lose interest in the proposed changes, and the committeee, continually lacking a quorum, did nothing. The year 1892 passed with only occasional references to the need for reform, but the next year witnessed tumultuous sessions that were ended only momentarily by Taaffe's resignation.

The Young Czechs had been much chagrined by the impotence of the parliamentary committee, and in March, 1893 the group discussed future tactics. Some members feared that universal suffrage would merely strengthen the centralizing tendencies of the fundamental laws, but a majority finally accepted a plan which would give every Austrian male, twenty-four years old, who had been a citizen at least three years, the right to vote. The curial system would be replaced by electoral districts which would include 50,000 to 70,000 inhabitants; the Slavic nationalities would receive 240 seats, the Germans, 245, the Italians, 11, and the Rumanians, 4. The ballot would be secret, and the provinces were to have preponderant power in creating the boundaries of the electoral districts and in enforcing clean elections. The plan enlisted little enthusiasm among the German Liberals and the representatives of the landed curia, but it did stimulate street demonstrations. On July 9, 1893 there was a huge demonstration of workers at the Rathaus in Vienna in behalf of universal direct suffrage, and another open-air meeting of similar proportions and intent in August. The agitation spread to other cities, and the political groups in parliament spent a good amount of time trying to work out counter-proposals during the summer.

Meanwhile, Taaffe maintained an attitude of indifference toward the demonstrations. His prestige with the Emperor was very low, for parliament had refused to assent to very important financial and military needs, particularly a new law on the Landwehr, which the Emperor impatiently awaited. Taaffe undoubtedly was weary and in poor health as a result of his long tenure of office, and his actions prior to the opening of parliament in the autumn of 1893 betrayed a lack of preliminary planning which was surprising in a person noted for shrewd political manipulation. Since 1879, Taaffe had generally carried on in the face of determined German Liberal opposition, but on too many embarrassing occasions, he was forced to make bids for their support. Under the influence of his new Minister of Finance, Dr. Steinbach, Taaffe suddenly decided to wreck the German Liberals by overwhelming their middle-class support with 4,000,000 new voters. A plan was evolved in great secrecy; not a single party leader was consulted or even informed.

When parliament reopened in October, 1893, Taaffe astounded the assembly by recommending proposals that smacked of the demands made by street agitators and socialists. To be sure, the curial system was left intact, but the existing tax requirements for voting in the rural and urban curias were to be done away with. Any adult male who could read and write, who had resided in his electoral district six months before the election, who paid some direct taxes or could prove he had a vocation, or who had served against the enemy in time of war, was to be given the franchise. With a good deal of truth, Taaffe justified his proposals with the remarks that state interest demanded the fuller participation of citizens in elections and pointedly asked that parliament also favor him with decisions on the budget and the Landwehr.

Reaction was quick and intense. The leaders of the Clerical-Conservatives and of the German Liberals bitterly declared that Taaffe's failure to consult them gave them ample excuse to refuse to consider his plan. Both groups had reason to fear a reform that would enfranchise urban laborers and the " hired hands " on the farms; other political groups found different flaws in the proposals. The Poles dreaded an increase in Ruthene representation, the Young Czechs denounced the retention of the curial system, and the Social Democrats (outside of parliament) condemned the measure because it did not go far enough. The Ruthenes and the Christian Socialists seemed to be the only supporters Taaffe could get, and their adhesion was not unconditional. Almost overnight, the Polish Club, the German Liberals, and the Clerical-Conservative bloc formed a working coalition to destroy the proposed reform and Taaffe with it. The latter realized his impossible situation and went to Budapest to offer the Emperor his resignation. While the Emperor delayed accepting the resignation, Taaffe returned to Vienna and tried to justify his proposals during a first reading of several plans which were being considered. The three great parties did not yield an inch; only the Young Czechs seemed willing to join Taaffe's few supporters. On October 28 both houses of parliament were adjourned, and on November 2 the leaders of the anti-reform coalition were asked to form a new cabinet. Taaffe was formally relieved of his duties as Minister-President on November 11, and Prince Alfred Windischgrätz formed a cabinet supported by the German Liberals, the Poles, and the Clerical-Conservatives.[7]

THE FIFTH CURIA REFORM OF 1896

Windischgrätz, in his speech to parliament on November 23, 1893, promised an electoral reform which would retain the curial system and yet give the vote to a considerable number of Austrians who were disfranchised by existing regulations. Moreover, he promised that the political groups in parliament would be consulted in making the necessary changes. The leaders of the coalition parties, however, were not informed of the specific proposals Windischgrätz had in mind until February 26, 1894, just before the Minister-President presented them to parliament. Windischgrätz recommended the creation of a new curia which would control forty-three new seats, divided along urban and rural lines in all of the provinces. Voting requirements in this curia were to include Austrian citizenship, attainment of the age of twenty-four, six months residence in an electoral district, and graduation from an in-

---

7 Kolmer, *op. cit.*, V, 333-364.

termediate school or its equivalent. The last requirement could be waived if the prospective voter had served a year in the army, or had attended a trade school, or had contributed to the laborers' sick fund for three consecutive years, or had paid direct taxes for two years.

The coalition parties showed little enthusiasm for the plan, while the Social Democrats at their annual Party Day in Vienna (March 27, 1894) demanded a general strike in order to attain universal suffrage. An electoral committee of the parliament was elected to consider Windischgrätz's preliminary plan, but its members were averse to upsetting the accepted system of curias and accomplished practically nothing before the summer recess. The reopening of parliament in October, 1894 was the signal for a demonstration of workers demanding universal suffrage in front of the parliament building, and another group of demonstrators on October 18 clashed with the police in an attempted march on the Hofburg. Windischgrätz condemned this pressure from the streets and warned that future excesses would be repressed. Meanwhile, the coalition parties wranged continually over the proposed fifth curia. The German Liberals in December, 1894 finally agreed to accept the fifth curia as proposed by the ministry, but the Clerical-Conservatives stubbornly insisted that the new curia should be formed along professional or vocational lines. The electoral committee turned over the conflicting plans to a subcommittee which was to iron out the differences between the Liberals and Conservatives. The subcommittee reached a compromise solution in June, 1895, by recommending forty-seven new seats, thirteen of which were to be controlled by laborers who were enrolled in the health-insurance funds. The ministry meanwhile had fallen into great difficulties on another issue. It had recommended that Slovene be taught in certain grammar schools in Styria (the famous Cilli controversy), and the German Liberals had withdrawn their support from the government as a consequence. On June 19, 1895 Windischgrätz and his cabinet resigned,[8] to be succeeded by an interim cabinet headed by Count Kielmansegg. The Polish governor of Galicia, Count Badeni, succeeded Kielmansegg in turn on October 4, 1895 and promised a settlement of the electoral controversy.

On February 15, 1896 Badeni acquainted the Lower House with his version of electoral reform, which called for the creation of a fifth curia of seventy-two seats, based on universal suffrage. Every male citizen twenty-four years of age could vote for the deputies of the new curia if he had resided in a given district at least six months prior to the election. There were to be no changes in the existing curial system, and provincial legislation would be decisive in the question of direct or indirect voting. It was estimated that the total number of voters would be increased from 1,732,000 to 5,373,000, but many who already had the right to vote in the four older curias now would also have the vote in the fifth curia. In effect, the program encouraged plural voting on the part of the " established " classes so that the entire program would be more palatable to doctrinaire opponents of universal suffrage. The Lower House exhibited a spirit of accommodation for once in the debates, for the Poles, Conservatives, and Liberals had decided that reform was well-nigh inevitable and desired consequently to surrender as little as possible of the old system. The Christian Socialists were critical but expressed willingness to approve a step " in the right direction," while more radical deputies once again moved the introduction of universal, equal, and direct suffrage.

The committee elected to review the ministry's plans returned a favorable report in April, and the Lower House finished its general debate on April 23. The motion for universal, equal, and direct suffrage was voted on and defeated, 173 to 61, with the German Radicals, the Young Czechs, some members of the German *Volkspartei,* and some Slovenes and Croats on the losing side. On May 7 Badeni's plan was ac-

8 For Windischgrätz's electoral program, see Kolmer, *op. cit.,* V, 493-511.

cepted by a vote of 234 to 19, and the Minister-President tele-
graphed the good news to the Emperor. His reward was the
usual laconic message: "*Ich gratuliere.* Franz Joseph." The
Upper House accepted the bill unchanged, and on June 14,
1896 the law received imperial sanction.

During the 1890's, the land tax in Austria had been subjected to a reappraisal that meant general reductions in taxation for most citizens. It will be remembered that the payment
of a direct tax of five florins was required for voting in the
rural and urban curias, and several Christian Socialists and
Young Czechs had demanded that some modifications be made
for men who might lose their vote as a result of tax reform.
Consequently, the tax requirement for voters in the curias mentioned was lowered to four florins by parliament late in 1896.[9]

The elections of 1897, the first to be held under the new
electoral system, brought some interesting results.[10] In the first
place, the electoral districts created for the fifth curia were unusually large and unwieldy, and electioneering of an almost
terroristic nature marred the campaign. The Germans returned
to parliament with about 200 deputies, but they were divided
into eight groups; the German Liberals had only forty-seven
representatives. The Social Democrats captured fourteen seats,
while the Young Czechs, with sixty-three seats, and the Polish
Club, with fifty-nine seats, became the strongest individual
political groups in the Lower House. The Germans were forced
to go on the defensive, and they resorted to outright obstruction to block any concession to the Czechs. Badeni soon was
compelled to give up, to be followed by four similarly unsuccessful cabinets. If the Czechs were favored by the government,
the Germans would turn parliament into a shambles, and
vice versa. The most vital legislation was ignored by the jeering and sometimes violent deputies. From the summer of 1898
through the end of 1904, the Austrian parliament was almost
consistently deadlocked, and the Emperor and his ministers
were forced to take a drastic step.

9 Kolmer, *op. cit.*, VI, 152-172.

10 See Table I, Appendix.

The solution to the parliamentary crisis could not be found in concessions to the parties, save for short periods of time, nor could it be found in the ordering of new elections. The final resort was the employment of the much-condemned Article 14 of the Fundamental Law on Imperial Representation, which permitted the Emperor, in case of urgent necessity, to issue ordinances with the temporary force of law when the Reichsrat was not in session. During the winter months, a Minister-President would submit his pleas for urgent state necessities to the Reichsrat, which usually ignored the pleas. When the unruly members went home for the summer, the Emperor issued ordinances taking care of governmental needs; technically, either house of parliament could reject the ordinance when it reassembled, but the Lower House never could unite to exercise this prerogative. The Upper House, of course, was generally averse to adding to imperial embarrassment and gave the ministry little trouble over the use of Article 14.

By the end of 1904, both Germans and Czechs gave indications that they were weary of strife which merely made a joke of parliamentary government at Vienna. The Koerber ministry (1900-1904) had proved that the central administration might be embarrassed, but not crushed by parliamentary obstruction. When Gautsch became Minister-President on December 31, 1904, he was virtually assured by Czechs and Germans that they would cooperate in reaching compromises in Bohemian and Moravian affairs. The sessions of the Lower House calmed down appreciably, and the important leaders of the two opposing nationalities were persuaded to sit down together at private conferences. The deputies of the Lower House sensed the need to drop obstruction for the moment, if only to regain their old power of extracting concessions from the ministries. The return to prosaic bargaining was short-lived, for, as the year 1905 progressed, a new and powerful movement for universal manhood suffrage pushed all other issues into the background.

CHAPTER II

THE CHRONOLOGICAL DEVELOPMENT
OF THE REFORM OF 1907

THE RESURGENT DEMAND FOR REFORM, AUTUMN, 1907

THE advent of universal manhood suffrage in Austria in 1907 can be ascribed to several factors. In the first place, the reform of 1896 stimulated the advocates of equal rights for the masses to a continuing effort in behalf of their beliefs; after 1896 the Austrian press was never free of discussion which aimed at universal equal suffrage for all Austrian males. Yet the factor which compelled Austrian politicians to pay attention to the issue was not to be found in Austrian affairs; it emerged from one of the greatest crises which developed between Francis Joseph and his Hungarian subjects.[1]

During the last decade of the nineteenth century, Hungary witnessed the remarkable development of a separatist, ultra-nationalistic political party which called itself the " Party of Independence." Under the leadership of Louis Kossuth's son, the group demanded complete separation from Austria in all matters save common allegiance to the Emperor; the Ausgleich of 1867 was cited as a betrayal of true Magyar interests, while the laws of the Hungarian Republic of 1848-49 were praised as an ideal constitution for Hungary. In the election of 1901, Kossuth's party had made considerable gains and used its increased strength to block a definitive modification of the financial arrangements with Austria and to deny a slight increase in the number of recruits which Hungary was to furnish the common army. Obstruction was the technique employed to embarrass the Hungarian cabinet, and, by 1903, parliamentary activity was deadlocked. The Party of Independence made it-

---

1 Czedik, *op. cit.*, III, 14-16, 19-20; William E. Lingelbach, *Austria-Hungary* (Philadelphia, 1907), pp. 439-446, based on Paul L. Léger, *L'Histoire de l'Autriche-Hongrie* (Paris, 1895).

self particularly obnoxious to Francis Joseph by demanding that Magyar be adopted as the language of command in all Hungarian regiments of the common army and that all Hungarian officers be transferred to these regiments. Unfortunately for the Emperor, these terms were welcomed by a majority of the deputies in the Lower House of the Hungarian parliament, who continued to refuse to vote the recruit bill. Consequently, the Hungarian cabinet was forced to promulgate a special decree which kept soldiers whose period had expired in the army for an indefinite period. Because of the military issue, the cabinet was finally forced to resign in October, 1903.

The Emperor gave indications of a desire to placate the majority in the Lower House, and Count Stephen Tisza, the new Hungarian Premier, offered the opposition a compromise. German was to be retained as the language of command, but all Hungarian officers were to be transferred to Hungarian regiments, the term of military service was to be reduced, and increased facilities for the training of Hungarian cadets were promised. After violent parliamentary sessions, the recruit bill was passed in conjunction with the new provisions, but only after the Party of Independence had forced through a resolution declaring that "in Hungary the source of every right and in the army the source of rights appertaining to the language of service and command is the will of the nation expressed through the legislature." [2] The cooperation between Tisza and his opponents was short-lived. In an attempt to end obstructive tactics, the Premier resorted to a revival of strict closure rules; the opposition responded with a country-wide series of demonstrations that had as a climax the physical destruction of the furnishings of the Lower House in December, 1904. Tisza's only recourse was the ordering of general elections for January, 1905.

Tisza's Liberal supporters in the Lower House were decisively rejected at the polls, obtaining fewer seats than did

2 Lingelbach, *op. cit.*, p. 444.

the Party of Independence. Tisza resigned, and the Emperor summoned the leader of the opposition, Kossuth. As might have been expected, the two men failed to reach any agreement, and the Hungarian premiership remained vacant for several months. The new Lower House, in April, composed an address to the crown which " demanded the appointment of a responsible government supported by the majority; the reform of the parliamentary and electoral system; the commercial and financial independence of Hungary, and the nationalizing of the Hungarian army by the introduction of the Magyar language and emblems." [3] Francis Joseph's answer, in June, 1905, was the appointment of Baron Geza Fejerváry, a member of the minority, as Premier. The majority in the Lower House issued a manifesto on July 18, declaring that the new ministry was unconstitutional and asking all Hungarians to refuse to obey its decrees.

The Minister of the Interior in Fejerváry's cabinet, Kristoffy, realized that there was no chance of a rapprochement between the Emperor and Kossuth's party. However, he felt that a solution to the constitutional crisis could be found in introducing universal manhood suffrage, and he proposed this fundamental change in July, 1905. At once, the united weight of the great Hungarian magnates was thrown against Kristoffy's plan, which promised to end their domination of Hungarian government. On August 22 Fejerváry was summoned to Ischl by the Emperor to discuss the proposed reform, in the presence of the Austrian Minister-President, Gautsch. The Hungarian Premier seconded Kristoffy's plan, but Gautsch was quite worried about the reaction which could be expected in Austria in the event of electoral reform in Hungary. He doubted that public order could be maintained by the army in the face of the inevitable commotion which would be aroused; one might well wonder, said Gautsch, whether a simple separation of the two states might not be the lesser

3 *Ibid.*, p. 445.

evil.[4] Another crown council was held in Vienna on September 10, and Hungarian affairs were again on the agenda. Count Goluchowski, the Minister of Foreign Affairs of Austria-Hungary, and Gautsch were present, and the latter again sharply attacked the idea of electoral reform in Hungary. Two days later, the Fejerváry cabinet resigned; the Social Democratic press erupted with violent condemnations of Gautsch, " the enemy of the people," who was blamed for Fejerváry's fall. Significantly, a united conference of Social Democrats [5] ten days later demanded universal, equal, and direct suffrage for Austria as well as Hungary. Meanwhile, the Emperor had turned once again to the leaders of the opposition in Hungary, but no reconciliation seemed possible after a stormy five-minute audience at the Hofburg on September 23.

Rumors and surmises of a possible Hungarian reform filled the columns of the Austrian newspapers during the summer of 1905, and the possibilities of a similar reform in Austria were explored and exploited rather completely. Party leaders sensed a new issue which might blot out the sorry record of parliamentary turmoil and obstruction; they seemed ready to take full advantage of the opportunity of " serving the people " when parliament reassembled in September, 1905.

Another factor was the revolutionary disturbance which convulsed the Russian Empire, 1905-1907. Loyal supporters of the Habsburg monarchy were able to discount the effect of Pan-Slav propaganda upon the Slavic nationalities of the Dual Monarchy as long as Russia was the synonym for repression. Should Russian liberals achieve a really constitutional mon-

4 Rudolf Sieghart, *Die letzten Jahrzehnte einer Grossmacht* (Berlin, 1932), p. 82.

5 The Social Democrats of Austria dated their existence from their first party-day, held at Hainfeld, December 30, 1888. At first, members of all nationalities in Austria were integrated within one organization, but by 1905, there were separate leaders and party-days for each nationality. In 1905, they controlled about 10 seats in the Lower House. Richard Charmatz, *Deutsch-österreichische Politik* (Leipzig, 1907), pp. 185-187.

archy, with the trappings of universal suffrage, then Pan-Slavism might regain the attraction it once had for Czechs, Slovaks, Slovenes, and others. Such a possibility was seldom mentioned in the great debates on reform, yet it undoubtedly gave the Germans in Austria much to think about.

The factors already mentioned implicitly suggest what was probably the most convincing argument of all for universal manhood suffrage. That argument was to be found in the full-grown European vogue for constitutional governments elected by all of the citizens of a modern state. The entire nineteenth century had been a period of growing respect for universally elected parliaments; France, Great Britain, and the German Empire were models of propriety and stability in 1905. Although Austria indubitably had little reason to congratulate herself on a sane or efficient parliamentary life, yet the *institution* of parliament was seldom questioned. Rather, the question was: How can Austria attain the blessings of parliamentary life which seemingly are enjoyed by Britain, France, and Germany? To many sincere men, universal manhood suffrage was the obvious answer. The masses, they felt, had developed tremendously economically, while universal literacy, another great panacea of the nineteenth century, was on the threshold of reality, even in relatively backward Austria. The spirit of the times called for a recognition of Austria's position as a modern industrialized state, with a sensitive proletariat; the most conservative gentlemen in the Upper House admitted the impact of the present while bemoaning the loss of the past. The realization of democratic rights for all was an aspect of contemporary European culture that the most hardened devotees of caste and privilege could not ignore. Renewed political agitation or the possibility of Russian and Hungarian reform would have meant little without the general feeling in Austria that universal manhood suffrage would be salutary and " progressive " and that it was in any case inevitable.

Dr. Paul Gautsch, Minister-President of Austria,[6] alluded to the growing agitation for reform when parliament reopened in September, 1905. In his speech outlining future policy, he turned to the problem of universal suffrage in Hungary, a question which, he complained, had been the occasion for attacks against his own person. Amid cheers and interruptions, he declared that he had no idea of interfering in internal Hungarian affairs, but that there were situations which required his advice. Since his conferences with the Emperor and the Hungarian Premier on Hungarian reform had given rise to speculation concerning his stand on a similar reform in Austria, he wanted to make very clear his attitude in the matter.

He announced that he was not fundamentally opposed to the extension of the franchise on very broad bases; his record showed that he had repeatedly stood for suffrage extensions. Indeed, all developments in Europe pointed in the direction of gradual extensions of suffrage, as he well knew. But difficulties stood in the way of such a far-reaching reform in Austria; for instance, would the rights of all nationalities be effectively secured by supplanting the age-old recognition of cultural interests by the mechanical principle of numbers? When Gautsch implied that the proposed reform would be a violation of legal developments that would lead to contempt for legal forms for

6 Baron Gautsch (1851-1918) was rather typical of the stop-gap bureaucratic ministers who struggled with Austrian problems after Taaffe's retirement in 1893. At 33, he was appointed Minister of Education in Taaffe's cabinet (1885). His work in the cabinet elicited imperial favor and a decoration, though there were occasions when his vigorous activity contrasted strangely with the astute lethargy of Taaffe, who seemed to believe that a minimum of activity meant a minimum of criticism or embarrassment. Gautsch was not retained in the ministry which succeeded Taaffe's in 1893, but he was recalled by Badeni to serve in his old post during the years, 1895-1897. When Badeni was dismissed in 1897, Gautsch became Minister-President but resigned in 1898 in the face of violent Czech opposition. On December 31, 1904, he was again named Minister-President, and during the first nine months of his second ministry, he worked hard to reestablish working relationship between Germans and Czechs in Bohemia, with considerable success. Czedik, *op. cit.*, I, 342-50.

generations, the Lower House interrupted him so noisily that its president had to ring for order. Leaving one thorny problem for another, Gautsch concluded by saying that his government hoped to do its best to restore good relations between Czechs and Germans in Bohemia.[7] It was obvious to the members of the Lower House that Gautsch preferred to ignore electoral reform and concentrate his efforts on reconciling the nationalities which had contributed so effectively to the sad state of parliamentary affairs in Austria.

On the same day, following Gautsch's speech, four separate motions demanding the immediate preparation of a law providing for universal, equal, direct, and secret suffrage were introduced by various political groups: (1) Young Czechs and various Czech associates; (2) Polish, Czech, and German Social Democrats; (3) South Slav deputies, many from clerical groups; and (4) Czech National Socialists combined with Croatian, Slovene, and Polish deputies.[8] Reform clearly was to be sponsored at the beginning, at least, by Socialists and Young Czechs, with considerable support from moderate and left-wing Slavic groups. On September 29 Polish Independent Socialists and their Polish Democratic allies underlined the Slavic-Socialist interest in reform by introducing a motion similar to those of September 26.

The debate on Gautsch's statement of policy took seven sessions to complete (through October 5, 1905), with two interruptions by Gautsch which made clear his refusal to favor the preparation of an electoral reform.[9] The question of extending the franchise was discussed by most of the deputies who com-

---

7 *Stenographische Protokolle über die Sitzungen des Hauses der Abgeordneten des Reichsrates*, XVII Session (1901-1907), XXXV, 31420-5, Sept. 26, 1905. Hereafter, references to the stenographic reports of the Lower House will be abbreviated as *S. P. A.*, with the appropriate volume, pages, and date.

8 For the texts of the motions, see *S. P. A.*, XXXV, 31446-7.

9 *S. P. A.*, XXXV, 31685-9, Sept. 29, 1905, and 32010-11, Oct. 4, 1905.

mented on Gautsch's stated policy, and the most interesting development of the sessions was a motion introduced by Dr. Alfred Ebenhoch, a German Clerical,[10] on October 5, which requested the government to hold investigations and make studies with the idea of introducing universal, secret, and direct (but not equal) suffrage.

The arguments advanced by the friends and enemies of reform prefigured those which were to appear in the more important debates of 1906; the speeches are chiefly interesting as evidence of the developing party alignments in regard to reform. German parties offered anything but a united front, a manifestation of the decades of political disagreement and splintering over economic and social problems. A spokesman of the German *Volkspartei*,[11] a party which had arisen in the 1890's to preach a strenuous protection of Germanism that stood midway between the German Progressive[12] and the

10 Technically speaking, Ebenhoch was a leading member of the *Katholische Volkspartei*, which he had founded on Nov. 25, 1895, as a result of a conflict with his German Clerical colleagues. For several years, some German Clericals had flirted with the demagogic Christian Socialists, despite the frowns of the higher clergy; in 1894, Ebenhoch and some friends signed a Christian Socialist motion of urgency, denouncing the Emperor's refusal to confirm Karl Lueger as mayor of Vienna. The result was the schism mentioned; between 1895 and 1907, Ebenhoch worked in close cooperation with the Christian Socialists and played a leading role in uniting his fraction with the latter late in 1907. Charmatz, *op. cit.*, pp. 178, 182-3.

11 For a discussion of the origins of the *Deutsche Volkspartei*, see Paul Molisch, *Geschichte der deutschnationalen Bewegung in Oesterreich* (Jena, 1926), pp. 175-82, and Charmatz, *op. cit.*, pp. 178-9. In reality, the members of the party could not unite on a common program; the friction between Alpine and Sudeten members was particularly noticeable. The term, "German Populist," when used in this study, denotes a member of the *Volkspartei*.

12 The German Progressive Party (*Deutsche Fortschrittspartei*) was the successor of the once-great German Liberals. Its program, as of April 7, 1897, stressed security for Germanism in Austria, complete parliamentary control of nationalistic problems, freedom of education from clerical influence, special protection of trade and industry, and protection of labor. Charmatz, *op. cit.*, p. 180.

Pan-German [13] positions, was embarrassed by the return of an issue whose rejection would cost the party support among the German masses and whose adoption would seemingly give Slavs the control of Austria. He advocated a " generalization " of political rights while declaring that an unreserved support of reform would be an act of treason.[14] German Progressive spokesmen were equally cautious; one felt that electoral reform would be no solution to nationalistic quarrels,[15] while another was willing to support reform to quiet the Socialist clamor.[16] Karl Lueger, the grand old man of the Christian Socialists, hinted at his party's stand by asking that minorities be protected, that voting be compulsory, and that residence qualifications be required in case of the adoption of universal manhood suffrage.[17] As mentioned previously, Dr. Ebenhoch summarized his party's stand on October 5 with a motion which studiously avoided equal suffrage, presumably to leave open the question of extra votes for heads of families or for representative leaders of communities. Social Democrats of German background were avowed proponents of reform and bitter critics of Gautsch's stand. Bourgeois agitation was the cause of nationalistic strife in Austria, they argued. The reform of 1896 had been negative in its results; now, they claimed, it

13 After the election of 1901, the Pan-Germans under Georg von Schönerer split into two groups; the more moderate faction, under Karl Hermann Wolf, rejected Schönerer's leadership and called itself *freialldeutsch*. These Independent Pan-Germans still desired the closest bonds possible with the German Empire, but, unlike Schönerer's group, they were more cautious in discussing the Jews, Catholicism, and the dynasty, and played a relatively minor role in the debates on electoral reform. Charmatz, *op. cit.*, pp. 181-2.

14 Speech of Paul Hofmann von Wellenhof, *S. P. A.*, XXXV, 31681-5, Sept. 29, 1905.

15 Speech of Leonhard Demel von Elswehr, *S. P. A.*, XXXV, 31670, Sept. 29, 1905.

16 Speech of Baron Heinrich d'Elvert, *S. P. A.*, XXXV, 31904, Oct. 3, 1905.

17 *S. P. A.*, XXXV, 31783, Oct. 2, 1905.

was imperative to have thoroughgoing reform of political life.[18]

The Slavic deputies also were divided in their approach to Gautsch's speech. Polish and Bohemian nobles praised the Minister-President's vigilance in rejecting rash schemes and stressed the need for loyalty to existing institutions.[19] Yet Count Sternberg, the doughty Independent from Moravia, ridiculed the idea that reform would mean a dictatorship of "numbers" and optimistically expected cleaner politics if the franchise were extended.[20] Non-noble Slavic deputies were generally in favor of reform, though a Slovene Liberal felt that reform was a threat to the middle classes and would merely benefit clericalism.[21] A Slovene Clerical, Šusteršič, demanded immediate reform,[22] and his views were echoed by Young Czechs and Czech National Socialists.[23] The latter cited parliamentary anarchy, German "oppressions," and simple social justice for all as reasons for reform.[24]

18 Speeches of Engelbert Pernerstorfer, *S. P. A.*, XXXV, 31577-82, Sept. 27, 1905, and of Franz Schuhmeier, *S. P. A.*, XXXV, 31689-99, Sept. 29, 1905.

19 Speeches of Count Ernst Sylva-Tarouca, *S. P. A.*, XXXV, 31582-3, Sept. 27, 1905, and of Count Adalbert Dzieduszycki, *S. P. A.*, XXXV, 31678, Sept. 29, 1905.

20 *S. P. A.*, XXXV, 31508-15, Sept. 26, 1905.

21 Speech of Ivan Tavčar, *S. P. A.*, XXXV, 31590-1, Sept. 27, 1905.

22 *S. P. A.*, XXXV, 31679, Sept. 29, 1905.

23 In March, 1900, the Young Czechs agreed to confer with Germans on a possible compromise of the controversy over the language to be used in administrative offices in Bohemia and Moravia. At once, a coalition of violent Czech nationalists, generically known as "Czech National Socialists," attacked the Young Czechs and frightened the latter into breaking off negotiations with the Germans. This group's "socialism" was almost completely hidden by their nationalism. See G. L. Jaray, "L'Autriche Nouvelle: Sentiments Nationaux et Préoccupations Sociales," *Annales des Sciences Politiques*, XXIII (1908), 304.

24 See speeches of Adolf Stránský, *S. P. A.*, XXXV, 31915, Oct. 3, 1905; of Václav Choc, *S. P. A.*, XXXV, 31894-5, Oct. 3, 1905; and of Václav Dvořák, *S. P. A.*, XXXV, 31793-4, Oct. 2, 1905.

When the debate on Gautsch's address was completed on October 5, the Lower House turned its attention to the various motions which had been introduced for the purpose of initiating universal suffrage. In order to obtain " urgent " or priority treatment at the hands of the ministry, a motion introduced by deputies had to receive the approval of two-thirds of the Lower House. Consequently, the discussion, which lasted until the next day, found the friends of reform making strenuous efforts to obtain the necessary votes in spite of renewed cautions from Gautsch. The latter still declared that peace among the nationalities should be the prerequisite for reform and warned that all sorts of political wares were being offered under the flag of reform.[25]

The lively speeches also marked further splits in the German ranks. The German Progressive deputy Dr. Max Menger declared that the groundwork for universal suffrage was lacking in Austria and predicted that violence would threaten Germanism as a result of reform.[26] His party colleague, Dr. Otto Lecher, refused to believe that the tactical power of German parties in the Lower House would be impaired by reform and asserted that pleas for special studies of reform and settlement of nationalistic strife were merely stupid delays.[27] The *Volkspartei* continued its ambiguous attitude, which was delineated by a spokesman, Dr. Julius von Derschatta, who insisted on thorough study of all proposals and asked for guarantees that Germans would receive full consideration in those proposals. He admitted the necessity of a reform which would protect all minorities.[28] The German Clerical and the Christian Socialist who entered the lists, Ebenhoch and Dr. Ämilian Schöpfer, differed on the detail of compulsory voting, but the latter sup-

25 *S. P. A.*, XXXV, 32239-40, Oct. 6, 1905.
26 *S. P. A.*, XXXV, 32244-45, Oct. 6, 1905.
27 *S. P. A.*, XXXV, 32249-55, Oct. 6, 1905.
28 *S. P. A.*, XXXV, 32259-62, Oct. 6, 1905.

ported the passage of Ebenhoch's motion, which would compel an adequate study of reform proposals. Ebenhoch clearly sympathized with the German reluctance to agree to reform,[29] while Schöpfer pointed out that Germans still would retain the supremacy they had gained thanks to their historical and cultural tradition in Austria.[30] The Pan-German deputy from Eger, Franz Stein, expressed the extreme partisanship of his group by asking that a reform be passed which would give Germans one-half of all the seats in the Lower House, the other half to be elected by professional and vocational bodies.[31]

Undoubtedly the most influential speech of the preliminary debate was Dr. Karel Kramář's. The acknowledged leader of the Young Czechs reported that his party needed no reform to increase its strength; it wanted reform because the masses could no longer be denied their rights by privileged groups which had failed to live up to their obligations. Radicalism and anti-militarism were the logical results of the denial of popular participation in government, and even nationalistic bitterness was caused by the unfair German hegemony in parliament. Of course, there were possibly difficulties in achieving completely a system of universal equal manhood suffrage; the problems of illiteracy and residence requirements would have to be taken up at length.[32] With this speech, Kramář in effect linked his party with the Christian Socialists in an effort to obtain a reform which would destroy the old curial system while taking into account the cultural and economic differences which existed in Austria. The pattern of reform now needed the active cooperation of the ministry; for the moment, Gautsch refused to budge, taking some comfort from the moderate tone of Kramář's speech. The Polish Club's chairman, Count

29 *S. P. A.*, XXXV, 32231-8, Oct. 6, 1905.

30 *S. P. A.*, XXXV, 32262-4, Oct. 6, 1905.

31 *S. P. A.*, XXXV, 32249, Oct. 6, 1905.

32 *S. P. A.*, XXXV, 32107-16, Oct. 5, 1905.

Dzieduszycki, had also made it clear that Gautsch could depend on his party's support in rejecting these proposals, which Dzieduszycki felt would only increase the warfare among the nationalities.[33]

On October 6, 1905 the five motions which asked the government to prepare an electoral reform on the basis of universal, equal, direct, secret manhood suffrage were voted upon. In favor were 155 deputies; opposed were 114. The president of the Lower House announced that the vote had failed to reach the necessary two-thirds required to force the ministry to act. Dr. Ebenhoch's motion failed as well, by a vote of 137 (in favor) to 124. An analysis of the voting is worthy of some attention. Only some 63 per cent of all of the deputies chose to vote, and on a percentage basis the deputies of the landed property curia outdid the deputies of the fifth curia in expressing their convictions. Only one member of the former group voted for the motions, while six deputies of the latter group voted against the preparation of a reform bill.

Among those who voted for the motions were many members of the German *Volkspartei* (including Derschatta), a large number of Christian Socialists (including Lueger and Schöpfer), some German Progressives, and the backbone of the Pan-German groups. The bulk of the vote came from Social Democrats of all nationalities, Young Czechs, Slovene Clericals, and a heterogeneous group of Slavic deputies (including Poles) of moderate tendencies. The men who voted against the motions included for the most part members of the powerful Polish Club, under Dzieduszycki, Bohemian representatives of the landed curia, a goodly number of German Clericals under Ebenhoch's lead, and some German Progressives.[34] The first test of electoral reform seemed to indicate that Pan-Germans and Young Czechs could unite on an issue

33 S. P. A., XXXV, 32240-3, Oct. 6, 1905.
34 The list of deputies who voted is given, *S. P. A.*, XXXV, 32272.

which failed to unite more friendly groups. Ostensibly, the question of reform was not solely an issue of national sensibilities.

GAUTSCH'S ACCEPTANCE OF REFORM

Discussion of reform did not cease with this initial setback; in fact, it increased considerably with the news that Fejerváry had been asked by the Emperor to reassume the post of Hungarian Premier on October 16, with imperial approval of electoral reform in Hungary. Gautsch, however, gave no sign of a change in point of view and devoted most of the month of October to long discussions with Germans and Czechs in Brünn. The purpose of these discussions was a nationalistic compromise for Moravia, and the Minister-President finally evolved a plan which seemed to satisfy both groups in the Moravian diet.[35]

Meanwhile, the Social Democrats kept up a constant demand for electoral reform. On October 30 their party-day got under way in Vienna, and, during the first session, the Reichsrat deputy Dr. Wilhelm Ellenbogen began to read a report on "The Austrian Crisis and the Franchise." He was interrupted by the sensational news that the Czar of Russia had issued a manifesto to the Russian people, promising that all previously disfranchised classes would be permitted to take part in elections for the Duma. The conference was overjoyed by the report, and another Reichsrat deputy, Daszyński, called upon the proletariat to demonstrate in the streets of Vienna, so that Austria might have universal suffrage.[36] The workers jubilantly obliged on the following evening, filling the Ringstrasse in orderly fashion; there was a similar demonstration in Brünn on the same day.[37] On November 1 the Social Demo-

35 See Alfred Fischel, *Die mährischen Ausgleichsgesetze* (Brünn, 1910).

36 Richard Charmatz, *Österreichs äussere und innere Politik von 1895 bis 1914* (Leipzig and Berlin, 1918), pp. 72-73; *Neue Freie Presse, Morgenblatt,* Nov. 1, 1905, p. 7.

37 *Neue Freie Presse, Morgenblatt,* Nov. 1, 1905, pp. 11-12.

crats of Prague organized mass meetings in celebration of the news from Russia,[38] but the great events were still to come. So far, there had been a minimum of disorder or conflict with the police in any city.

On November 2 the Social Democrats scheduled a monster "promenade" of workers along the Ringstrasse, which the police attempted to prevent. The demonstrators resisted, and a number were wounded. Luckily, simultaneous processions in Prague and Graz were calm in comparison with the Viennese disturbances.[39] Unknown to the public, which merely read that the ministry was taking precautions against a recurrence of the disorders, the Emperor decided to intervene personally. On November 3 he summoned Gautsch to an audience and informed him that universal manhood suffrage was to be introduced in Austria as well as Hungary.[40] The Minister-President then went to Goluchowski to acquaint him with the news; the latter was astounded by Gautsch's complete change of heart but soon realized that the Emperor had been able to persuade the avowed foe of reform to undertake the new policy.[41] The Emperor had acted none too soon, for the Social Democrats had already ordered new demonstrations in Vienna for November 5, and the news of the "bloodbath" of November 2 in Vienna had unleashed new disorders in Prague on November 4, in which the police were stoned by demonstrators.[42]

38 *Ibid., Morgenblatt,* Nov. 2, 1905, pp. 5-6.

39 *Ibid., Morgenblatt,* Nov. 3, 1905, pp. 8-10.

40 Sieghart, *op. cit.,* p. 83.

41 W. Beaumont, "Le Suffrage Universel en Autriche: la Loi du 26 Janvier 1907," *Annales des Sciences Politiques,* XXII, 620, declares that Gautsch's conversion is explained by his character; too correct a bureaucrat to have any ideas of his own, the Minister-President was ambitious enough to change his mind, rather than suffer ignominious dismissal.

42 *Neue Freie Presse, Abendblatt,* Nov. 4, 1905, p. 5; *New York Times,* Nov. 5, 1905, p. 6.

The Emperor's decision [43] was communicated to his subjects by the semi-official *Wiener Abendpost* of November 4, 1905. The text of the communique asserted that the recent sessions of the Lower House had been almost entirely consumed by discussions of a possible electoral reform and that there was a general impression that previous opposition in the parliament and among the people to such a reform had weakened considerably. As a result, the ministry felt itself compelled to canvass at once the possibilities of a universal, equal, and direct franchise; popular desire for reform, it was frankly admitted, had been strengthened appreciably by events in other states. However, the ministry sternly warned that violence and disorder had to cease; it was determined to repress with all legal means a repetition of offenses against public order. Parliament, not the street, was the place where the decisions had to be reached.[44] Despite the article, demonstrations were reported in all parts of the empire on November 5 and 6; among the cities and towns affected were Vienna, Prague, Brünn, Trieste, Salzburg, Lemberg, Krakov, Linz, Graz, Klagenfurt, Pilsen, Karlsbad, Innsbruck, Budweis, St. Pölten, Teplitz, Teschen, and Mährisch-Ostrau. Luckily, the crowds, predominantly laborers incited by Social Democrats, were in the mood for celebrating

43 No clear explanation of Francis Joseph's reasons for recommending electoral reform has been advanced. Baron Beck, who completed the work of reform in 1907, later wrote that the Emperor never expressed himself on the subject, in an article entitled "Der Kaiser und die Wahlreform," in the collection of memoirs edited by Eduard von Steinitz, *Erinnerungen an Franz Joseph I* (Berlin, 1931), p. 223. Sieghart, who was intimately connected with the preparation of Gautsch's plans, wrote that the Emperor's motives stemmed only from his conception of duty; Sieghart resolutely condemned the notion that the Emperor desired to "socialize" the empire in order to restore parliamentary activity. As proof, he quotes Francis Joseph as saying at the ministerial council at Ischl on Aug. 22, 1905, that Kristoffy's designation of electoral reform as a conciliation of socialist principles was an error (*op. cit.*, p. 218.) One may assume that Francis Joseph's ability to yield to popular pressure at the right moment best explains his action of Nov. 3, 1905.

44 Reprinted in the *Neue Freie Presse, Morgenblatt*, Nov. 5, 1905, pp. 3-4.

the news of Gautsch's adherence to the idea of reform, and there was a minimum of casualties.[45] Indeed, for a few weeks, street demonstrations ceased, though it was well known that the Social Democrats were planning tremendous mass meetings and parades for November 28, the day scheduled for the resumption of the sessions of the Lower House.

The ministry had a short respite from pressure from the streets but on November 9 a " passive resistance " strike of railway workers began.[46] The workers undoubtedly were actuated by a desire for higher wages, but there were rumors that the interruption and delay of traffic might be aggravated by a general strike in Prague in behalf of universal suffrage. Troops were prepared for possible disorders, the ministry took a firm line with the representatives of the strikers, but in a few days it granted most of the demands of the workers employed on the state railways and urged the privately owned railways to do likewise.[47] Gautsch dared not give the Social Democrats further chances to embarrass his government.

The Lower House was due to reassemble on November 28, at which time the Minister-President was expected to outline what plans he had for electoral reform. On November 27 the Christian Socialists held a large mass meeting in Vienna, at which their leader, Karl Lueger, described the terms which the party hoped to obtain in the preparation of a reform.[48] But the Christian Socialist clamor did not compare with the impressive demonstrations prepared by the Social Democrats on

45 *Ibid., Abendblatt,* Nov. 6, 1905, pp. 1-5, and *Morgenblatt,* Nov. 7, 1905, pp. 5-6.

46 The railway men did not cease work. They merely observed to the letter all of the existing regulations imposed by the government; the complexity and absurdity of the regulations automatically delayed or stopped traffic. The workers, of course, continued to receive their pay and argued that their activities were perfectly legal. *New York Times,* Nov. 10, 1905, p. 2.

47 Ernst von Plener, *Erinnerungen* (Stuttgart and Leipzig, 1921), III, 353.

48 *Neue Freie Presse, Abendblatt,* Nov. 27, 1905, p. 8.

the following day. The latter had urged all Austrian laborers to celebrate the reopening of the Lower House as a day of rejoicing, and in Vienna there was almost complete cessation of work. An hour before the Lower House began its session, the first of a remarkable procession of workers marched past the parliament building. By three o'clock in the afternoon, an estimated quarter of a million had passed the building, marching in complete silence, each person wearing a red arm-band which called for the enactment of universal equal suffrage. No incidents marred the demonstration.[49] At noon, Gautsch announced to the Lower House that the ministry hoped to bring in definite proposals for universal manhood suffrage early in 1906. On the same day, the Social Democrats also sponsored demonstrations in Prague, Brünn, Olmütz, Salzburg, Linz, Graz, Innsbruck, Laibach, Trieste, Troppau, Lemberg, Krakov, Czernowitz, Pilsen, Budweis, Pola, Cilli, St. Pölten, Austerlitz, and other towns. In Austerlitz, disorders were reported; there the troops fired on allegedly disorderly demonstrators, killing two and wounding thirty.[50]

How did the Minister-President account for his about-face? The near passage of the motions at the voting on October 6 had persuaded him, he said, that reform should be undertaken jointly by the ministry and parliament. The Lower House was to settle questions of the extent and execution of the reform; the ministry would not, however, fail to take the leading role in recommending provisions which would guarantee the cultural and national rights of all Austrians. Gautsch remarked rather sternly that street demonstrations could not increase the tempo of deliberation. More specifically, his cabinet was prepared to guarantee the rights of all Austrians who enjoyed the franchise at that moment; it dared not countenance the deprivation of the franchise already enjoyed by illiterates who voted

49 *Neue Freie Presse, Abendblatt,* Nov. 28, 1905, pp. 1-2; *Morgenblatt,* Nov. 29, 1905, p. 5; *New York Times,* Nov. 29, 1905, p. 2.

50 *Ibid., Morgenblatt,* Nov. 29, 1905, pp. 5-7.

in the fifth curia. Nor would an independent, self-sufficient economic status be set up as a prerequisite for voting. Possibly residence requirements might be extended, if only to prevent radical upsets in nationally mixed districts. Proportional and plural voting, he felt, would simply add to the complexity of the Austrian scene, but his ministry would be willing to consider such schemes. Seats definitely were not going to be divided on a percentage basis among the national groups or parties, nor would mere numerical ratios be decisive in all instances. Minorities had to be protected in Austria and the historic rights of the provinces could not be ignored; the constitution demanded that seats be apportioned according to crownlands. Electoral districts would be smaller in the future and would conform as far as possible to ethnic boundaries; it would be the task of the Lower House to decide where to compromise with this principle. Gautsch made it very clear that the modern trend toward truly representative government forced his ministry to demand the abolition of the curial system in Austria. Yet "interests" which had significance for the state would not be completely destroyed; perhaps a rearrangement of the Upper House would do justice to these "interests" and the state they served. Gautsch also declared that a reconstituted Lower House certainly would require a new order of procedure, lest obstruction nullify the effects of the desired reform.[51]

The Lower House devoted six sessions to a discussion of Gautsch's new policy. As a generalization, it can be said that most of the speakers were pleased by the new turn of affairs, though several of the Minister-President's suggestions were deemed to be too conservative or too pro-German by Social Democrats and by Slavic representatives, respectively. Dr. Julius Sylvester, the German Populist, promised that his followers would cooperate fully with Gautsch;[52] his colleague, Richard Herzmansky, revealed the true split in the party by

---

51 *S. P. A.*, XXXV, 32315-23.

52 *S. P. A.*, XXXV, 32443, Nov. 30, 1905.

painting a drab picture of a reform which might be forced through as a result of Social Democratic demonstrations.[53] German Progressives who spoke resigned themselves to electoral reform, but testified that they would insist on protection of the German middle class.[54] The Independent Pan-Germans expressed astonishment at Gautsch's tardiness in accepting reform and boasted that Germans had no fear of changes.[55] The Christian Socialists refrained from offering comment. Speaking for the Constitutionalist deputies of the landowners' curia,[56] Count Stürgkh expressed great surprise at the ministry's unwarranted change of front. Parliamentary freedom to discuss this momentous event was lacking, thanks to outside pressure. He felt that there should be some development in the direction of universal suffrage, but he especially feared mechanical principles of equality.[57] Far to the left of Stürgkh, Dr. Viktor Adler, leader of the Social Democrats, humorously admitted that Gautsch had developed well in a few months but warned against any provisions in the new law which would hamper the free expression of the masses.[58]

Practically all of the Slavic speakers were cordial to the idea of reform, though several merely regarded it as a step

53 *S. P. A.*, XXXVI, 32600-1, Dec. 5, 1905.

54 See speeches of Artur Skedl, *S. P. A.*, XXXV, 32444-5, Nov. 30, 1905, and of Konstantin Noske, *S. P. A.*, XXXV, 32517-25, Dec. 1, 1905.

55 See speeches of Adolf Glöckner, *S. P. A.*, XXXV, 32459-64, Nov. 30, 1905, and of Josef Herold, *S. P. A.*, XXXVI, 32660-4, Dec. 6, 1905.

56 With the creation of the German Progressive Party in 1897, the German Liberal deputies of the landowners' curia formed a party of the *verfassungstreu Grossgrundbesitz*. Their program stressed defiance of clericalism, insistence upon a centralized empire, and protection of the upper middle class. On most occasions, they worked in concert with the German Progressives. Some were true aristocrats, some were simply rich middle class men who had acquired noble land, but most belonged to the class of recently ennobled functionaries. Under the leadership of Stürgkh and Baernreither, they numbered about 30 in the Lower House. For convenience, they are referred to as " Constitutionalists " in this study. See Charmatz, *Deutsch-österreichische Politik*, p. 181 and Jaray, *op. cit.*, p. 662.

57 *S. P. A.*, XXXVI, 32613-14, Dec. 5, 1905.

58 *S. P. A.*, XXXV, 32446-59, Nov. 30, 1905.

closer to autonomy for their particular national group. Kramář promised that the people of Bohemia would be in the front ranks of reform,[59] and equally friendly remarks came from Rumanian, Ruthene, Slovene, Jewish Nationalist, Italian and Polish (People's Party) deputies. Each had some reservations as to the machinery of reform, as was to be expected. The great Slavic dissent came from Count Dzieduszycki, arbiter of the votes of the Polish Club. Gautsch's reversal of policy and impatience for reform amazed him; did not the government realize that the entire social order would be jeopardized by sudden change? Provincial autonomy (a threat which was consistently used by the Polish Club to extract concessions from Francis Joseph's harassed ministers) should come before any revision of the constitution; Dzieduszycki alleged that universal suffrage would function only in conjunction with a system of provincial autonomy.[60] The debate on Gautsch's second declaration on electoral reform closed on December 6; the Lower House was promised that concrete proposals would be submitted by the ministry for its inspection in February, 1906.

Gautsch faced a much more hostile group when he carried his proposals to the Upper House on December 1, 1905. Anticipating resentment, he clothed his message in conciliatory and flattering phrases which did little to mollify his listeners. The ministry appealed to the rich political experience and the independent judgment of the gentlemen of the Upper House and asserted that in the future these gentlemen would play a significant role in checking the rash impulses of a reconstituted Lower House. Moreover, it was hoped that special interests which might lose their representation in the Lower House would be transferred to the Upper House. Surely the honored gentlemen realized that growing social and economic cleavages among the inhabitants of Austria demanded constitutional revision. Is it not better to grant today what cannot be denied tomorrow?

59 *S. P..A.*, XXXV, 32467, Nov. 30, 1905.

60 *S. P. A.*, XXXVI, 32569-74, Dec. 4, 1905.

No member of the Upper House on December 2 positively denied the necessity of a reform of some nature, but the reaction to Gautsch's attitude was distinctly unfriendly. The ministry was censured for its passive attitude toward street demonstrations, and great emphasis was placed on the need for thorough study and long deliberation before decisions were to be made. There was no optimistic feeling that nationalistic bitterness would be ameliorated by reform, and there was a good deal of alarm over reports that the Upper House would be reconstituted. Gautsch, answering demands for further clarification of his statement of policy, denied that he had yielded to street demonstrations and expressed determination to continue with reform. He desired the Upper House's co-operation or its passive non-cooperation. No definite plan for a reconstitution of the Upper House had been made, but, as a member of the Upper House, he felt certain he could deny the statement that the Upper House had always completely fulfilled its duties. Gautsch's tone was quite sharp in answering the complaints of the princes, barons, elder statesmen, and bureaucrats; reform might well be inevitable, but the Upper House gave little evidence of accommodating its will to the wishes of the Minister-President. The first encounter made very clear the ministry's predicament; how could any group of parliamentarians concoct a plan that would reasonably satisfy the conservatives in the Upper House and the radicals, economic and nationalistic, in the Lower House? [61]

THE INTRODUCTION OF PROPOSALS OF REFORM, FEBRUARY, 1906

On February 23, 1906 Gautsch acquainted the Lower House with his plans for universal equal suffrage.[62] The system of representation by curias was to be abolished, and the right to vote was not to depend on the payment of taxes. With insig-

61 For a convenient summary of the proceedings in the Upper House, see Czedik, *op. cit.*, III, 314-31.

62 *S. P. A.*, XXXVIII, 34657-61, Feb. 23, 1906.

nificant exceptions, every Austrian male twenty-four years of age who had resided in his particular district one year was given the franchise. New electoral districts were to be created, as ethnically homogeneous as possible; in addition, the previous line of demarcation between urban and rural voters was to be retained. One deputy was to be elected from each district, with the exception of Galicia, where special provision was made to protect the Polish minority settled in the eastern part of the province. In that area, two deputies would be elected from each district; should one of the candidates receive at least one-third of the votes cast in the election, he would receive the mandate. The ministry's recommended delimitation of electoral districts, Gautsch claimed, would remedy injustices which existed in the past. In the nine crown-lands which had mixed populations, about four million inhabitants had previously been represented by deputies of " foreign " nationalities; the new plan would give these inhabitants representatives of their own nationality.

The new Lower House would have 455 members in place of 425. Each province would receive a certain percentage of the seats, and each nationality in a particular province would receive its percentage of the provincial total in accordance with its numbers and its taxpaying ability. Gautsch felt that the one-year residence requirement would help in stabilizing these ratios created by his plan, but he refused to recommend compulsory voting because of the administrative difficulties involved. Special legislation to penalize intimidation at elections was to be introduced, and parliamentary procedure was to be revised so that greater discipline would prevail in the new house. The Upper House, Gautsch admitted, was not inclined to accept any far-reaching modification of its present composition; he merely proposed that a rule be made which would prohibit any person from being a member of both houses simultaneously. Should a member of the Upper House be elected to the Lower House, he would be forced to relinquish his privileges of participating in the deliberations of the Upper House as long as he held a seat in the Lower House.

Gautsch justified his proposals by declaring that the vitality of the system of curias had waned, as the record of parliamentary obstruction amply proved. A restoration of parliamentary efficiency could come only through a guarantee of equal suffrage for all. The ministry would appreciate cooperation in attaining necessary compromises, but it would resign rather than give up its demand for the abolition of the privileged parliament. Even so, the fall of a ministry would not mean the defeat of reform.

The first reading of the ministry's proposals was scheduled for March 7, 1906, when the Minister of the Interior, Count Artur Bylandt, made further explanations.[63] No doubt there would be complaints about the demarcation of electoral districts, but he warned that changes would not be effected without the consent of all political groups involved. The general increase in population since 1896 accounted for the figure of 455 mandates recommended for the new house, and the one-year domiciliary clause was the result of compromising with all of the suggestions made by various groups. The ministry rejected all accusations of a pro-Slav bias; it realized that the Germans in Austria were strong supporters of the state and promised to respect the position of Germanism in Austria. All parties should recognize the definite steps taken in the ministerial program which would forward the just representation of all nationalities in Austria. The first reading of the proposals then began, taking up seven sittings and ending on March 23, 1906.

The first reading revealed no change in the attitude of the various parties. Many of the avowed supporters of Gautsch's plan criticized certain portions of the plan, but Christian Socialists, Young Czechs, Social Democrats, and South Slav Clericals were generally pleased and willing to pledge support. The most impassioned protests came from the representatives of

63 S. P. A., XXXVIII, 34825-29. Bylandt was chiefly responsible for the elaboration of the proposals. Ironically, in May, 1907 he was rejected by the electorate which he had helped to enfranchise.

the landowners and from members of the Polish Club. The former doubted that electoral reform could cure nationalistic strife unless it could come about gradually; they fully expected that a rash change essentially would profit demagogues.[64] Dr. Josef Baernreither eloquently defended the conservative position by arguing that constitutional reform should be gradual, well-planned, and subject to necessary checks and balances.[65] Count Sylva-Tarouca suggested that a type of professional representation be adopted and that the nationalistic problems be removed from the competence of a parliament so chosen.[66] The members of the Polish Club expressed great dismay at the " unjust " treatment meted out to Galicia in the apportionment of mandates.[67] Dzieduszycki pointedly remarked that Gautsch had not only reduced the Germans to a minority but also had fatally insulted the other nationalities.[68]

Numerous German deputies—Progressives, Constitutionalists, and Pan-Germans—were very critical of the increase in Slavic mandates, though the leader of the Independent Pan-Germans, Wolf, asked that a mere ten seats be added to the German quota.[69] German complaints found ready answers in the Czech camp. Kramář declared that the Slavs were the people suffering from discrimination,[70] while a spokesman for

64 For instance, see speech of Karl von Grabmayr, S. P. A., XXXVIII, 34829-39, Mar. 7, 1906.

65 S. P. A., XXXIX, 35480-91, Mar. 21, 1906.

66 S. P. A., XXXVIII, 34980-1, Mar. 9, 1906.

67 Galicia was scheduled to receive 88 mandates in contrast to 78 under the old system. Of these 88, 28 were to go to the Ruthenes, who previously controlled only 8 of the Galician mandates. In sum, the Poles would control only 60 Galician seats in a Lower House of 455 members, in place of 70 Galician seats they had controlled in a house of 425 members. Beaumont, op. cit., p. 625, footnote 1.

68 S. P. A., XXXVIII, 34891-4, Mar. 8, 1906.

69 S. P. A., XXXIX, 35564, Mar. 22, 1906. Of the proposed 455 mandates, only 205 were to fall to the Germans, who already controlled approximately that number. The Slavs were to receive 230 mandates, the Rumanians and Italians combined, 20. Beaumont, op. cit., p. 622.

70 S. P. A., XXXVIII, 35251, Mar. 15, 1906.

the Czech National Socialists bitterly reprimanded Gautsch for "favoring" the Germans.[71] Gautsch answered his critics on March 14 with denials that he favored Germans, that he had a bias against conservative groups, or that reform would create more demagoguery. He reiterated his willingness to make compromises on the allotment of mandates, while rejecting the idea of a possible representation by professions or vocations.[72]

On March 22 an obviously weary and impatient Lower House voted to conclude the debate, though about 100 deputies still were to be heard from. Dr. Ebenhoch made the final summation in behalf of the ministerial plan, while Count Stürgkh was elected general spokesman *contra*. Ebenhoch's speech was a masterful defense of Gautsch's program; the speaker recognized the fact that there had been brilliant speeches condemning the proposed reform, but he could discern no concrete alternate plan.[73] Stürgkh scathingly rebuked Gautsch for claiming that the vote of October 6, 1905 had forced him to change his mind. The government obviously had no set political convictions but was tossed about like the fragments of a ship on top of the waves. By insinuation, Stürgkh bewailed the lack of appreciation shown the deputies of the landed curia. Now who would vote for military expenditures and other essential state needs? The ministry should realize that its proposals threatened the real interests of the monarchy.[74]

Ebenhoch had moved, at the conclusion of his speech, that the ministry's program be turned over to a committee for further discussion. The motion was adopted on March 23, as were motions which set the membership of the committee at forty-nine and which turned over to the jurisdiction of the committee the preparation of clauses which would protect electoral rights. The committee's chief task was to delimit the boundaries of electoral districts and increase mandates where

71 Speech of Karel Baxa, *S. P. A.*, XXXIX, 35574-80, Mar. 22, 1906.

72 *S. P. A.*, XXXVIII, 35141-5.

73 *S. P. A.*, XXXIX, 35581-93, Mar. 22, 1906.

74 *S. P. A.*, XXXIX, 35629-42, Mar. 23, 1906.

necessary. On March 27 voting for the members of the committee took place, and the results were announced on March 28.

Before the electoral committee could begin its work, the opponents of electoral reform had another chance to register their disapproval of Gautsch and his plans. On March 27 the two Pan-German fractions introduced motions of urgency calling for special status for Galicia, which was to be granted in conjunction with electoral reform. The Polish Club was especially pleased to have another means of delaying reform, but the debate on the motions lasted only two days. At the balloting, the motions failed to obtain the necessary two-thirds of the votes cast, but 153 deputies did favor special status for Galicia. Probably only 20 per cent of these men really desired special status; the vote was primarily a demonstration against Gautsch and his version of electoral reform.[75]

The Achievements of the Electoral Committee of the Lower House, 1906

The deputies elected to the committee represented a good cross-section of the Lower House. More than twenty parties had at least one representative on the committee; by nationality, there were twenty-six Germans, eight Czechs, seven Poles, four South Slavs, two Italians, one Rumanian, and one Ruthene. Nine were representatives of the landed curia, twenty-two were from urban districts, twelve were from rural communes, and six had been elected by the fifth curia. Of the forty-nine, thirty-three had voted on October 6, 1905, when the original motions for reform had failed to pass. Of those thirty-three who voted, seventeen had voted against the motions.[76]

Meanwhile, Gautsch had made little or no progress in persuading the members of the Upper House to adopt a more favorable view of reform. About a month after the heated debates of December 1-2, 1905 in the Upper House, Gautsch

75 Beaumont, *op. cit.*, pp. 623-4.

76 For the complete list of the members chosen, *S. P. A.*, XXXIX, 35747.

asked the president of the Upper House to give him a chance to confer confidentially with the leaders of the three great parties (Right, Center, and Left) in the Upper House.[77] In order to make arrangements for such a conference, the presidents and the executive committees of the parties met and participated in an informal general debate on the entire issue of reform. Some who were present expressed limited approval of Gautsch's plans, but the majority wished to reserve opinions until the Minister-President revealed his precise program. On January 20, 1906 the conference with Gautsch took place; the representatives of the Upper House merely listened to Gautsch's and Bylandt's exposition without comment.

The Minister-President informed his conferees that the government did feel that the Upper House was susceptible to change, to correspond to the revision of the composition of the Lower House. A new category of members might be created— mayors of larger towns, presidents and officials of the provincial diets, etc.[78] The government, he implied, might agree, in return, to a provision which would limit strictly the number of men who might be appointed to the Upper House. Moderates in the Upper House had already argued that such a *numerus clausus* was the best basis for a compromise with Gautsch and his supporters in the Lower House. Finally, the government asked members of the Upper House to agree to give up their seats in the Upper House while fulfilling the duties of a deputy in the Lower House. At the end of the conference, Prince Alfred Windischgrätz, spokesman for the members of the Upper House, promised to arrange for another meeting with Gautsch, in order to come to some decision.

77 Information concerning Gautsch's *pourparlers* with the Upper House is detailed by a contemporary member of the Upper House in Czedik, *op. cit.*, III, 330-1.

78 Specifically, Gautsch suggested the appointment of 120 to 140 new members: the 16 governors of the provinces, the 17 mayors of the provincial capitals, 30 representatives of chambers of commerce, 40 to 45 great landowners, representatives of the proposed agricultural chambers, and a number of men to be elected from the provincial diets. Plener, *op. cit.*, p. 358.

The feelings of the members were obviously upset by Gautsch's disclosures, for all three parties decided to refuse to consent to the cabinet's general propositions. After much argument, the parties did decide to accept Gautsch's plea for a new rule which would prevent the simultaneous enjoyment of seats in both houses of parliament, but that was the only concession. No party was willing to agree to any other part of the reform as long as there was a possibility that the cabinet would attempt a reorganization of the Upper House. Some members were so embittered by Gautsch's attitude that they demanded that an answer be sent to him by letter, instead of meeting with him once again, as promised. Moderate opinion finally prevailed; there was a second conference with Gautsch a few days later. Not all who were present at the first meeting appeared at the second; those who did come simply delivered the abrupt refusal of practically all of Gautsch's points.

In February, it will be remembered, Gautsch made known to the Lower House the cabinet's plan for reform. Behind the scenes, the parties of the Upper House carried on brisk conferences, if not intrigues. In March and April, certain members of the Center group met in confidential gatherings, but no decisions were reached.[79] When Gautsch resigned in May, 1906, the new Minister-President, Prince Hohenlohe, tried to enlist the support of the Upper House for reform. Discussion of the entire program was about to be renewed, when Hohenlohe resigned in favor of Baron Beck. Private discussions continued until the beginning of the summer recess of 1906, but the Upper House definitely was awaiting the report of the electoral committee of the Lower House before renewing its activity in the matter.

The electoral committee of the Lower House on March 28, 1906 held its first meeting, at which the German Progressive, Dr. Gustav Marchet, was elected chairman, and the Slovene

Clerical, Dr. Ploj, elected deputy chairman.[80] Marchet served until he was called upon to enter Beck's cabinet (June 2, 1906); Ploj was elected chairman on June 12.[81] The conferences of the committee totalled sixty-three plenary sittings, lasting through October, 1906. Full conferences gave way to individual discussions during part of the summer months,[82] and the changes in the cabinet also distracted the committee's labors somewhat. The minutes of the proceedings of the committee made up a volume of more than 500 pages; here is to be found the real core of the reform, namely, the apportionment of mandates by provinces and nationality. Had not compromises been reached on this point, the entire reform would have been delayed or wrecked.

A general debate which would permit every member of the committee to deliver his particular critique of reform and Gautsch's version thereof was scheduled first. It became obvious that the speakers were repeating most of the arguments already heard in the Lower House's debates, and in the fifth meeting (April 26), Albert Gessmann appealed to Marchet to bring the general debate to a close or else see to it that every party state its views as quickly as possible. Marchet refused to limit the right of every member to speak, and the discussion continued.[83] At the end of the meeting, Dr. Adler likewise requested that the general debate cease "in the interest of the people," but Marchet curtly replied that he had every intention of preventing any miscarriage or delay of reform.[84]

---

80 *Beilagen, S. P. A.*, XXVII-XXVIII (1906-1907), 189. Hereafter, references to this appendix will be cited as *Beilagen*, with the appropriate pages and date. Unless otherwise stated, all citations will refer to Vol. XXVII-XXVIII.

81 *Beilagen*, p. 239.

82 Czedik, *op. cit.*, III, 378.

83 *Beilagen*, p. 212.

84 *Beilagen*, p. 218.

When the committee reassembled three weeks later, on May 18, it was confronted with some major changes. First of all, there was a new Minister-President, Prince Konrad Hohenlohe-Schillingsfürst, the governor of Trieste.[85] On April 29 the deputies of Galicia had issued an ultimatum to the effect that they would not vote for reform unless Galicia received 110 deputies under the new plan; Gautsch and Bylandt were consequently forced to resign on May 2.[86] Gautsch, however, picked his successor, who retained Gautsch's cabinet, with the exception of the Interior portfolio, which he took over himself. Hohenlohe immediately declared that the fight for universal equal suffrage would continue and made an eloquent appeal for the Upper House's support on May 16.[87] In his first meeting with the committee, Hohenlohe disclosed that he was in the midst of working out compromises with various groups; should a search for compromise be unsuccessful, then he would be prepared to submit his own proposals to the committee.[88]

85 Hohenlohe (1863-1918) was born in Vienna, the son of a "court" noble, and educated at the university there. He began his state service in the provincial administration in Salzburg, and later held other posts in Bohemia. He was appointed *Landespräsident* of Bukovina in 1903 and governor of Trieste in 1904, in which position he was noted for his surveillance of irredentist activity. Czedik, *op. cit.*, III, 58-67.

86 Czedik, *op. cit.*, I, 349-50. During the month of March, Gautsch had tried to conciliate the Poles and Germans, who seemed to be most opposed to his apportionment of mandates, by proposing to take representatives of the various nationalities into his cabinet. In addition, Gautsch proffered twenty-four new mandates: twelve for the Germans, ten for the Poles, one for the Czechs, and one for the Italians. Neither Germans nor Poles reached for the bait, and Gautsch's position steadily deteriorated. Beaumont, *op. cit.*, p. 626.

87 *Stenographische Protokolle über die Sitzungen des Herrenhauses des Reichsrates*, XVII Session, pp. 1233-5. Hereafter, references to the stenographic reports of the sessions of the Upper House will be abbreviated as *S. P. H.*, with the appropriate pages and date. In his speech, Hohenlohe stressed the fact that great landowners still could be elected to the new Lower House.

88 *Beilagen*, p. 219, May 18, 1906. The Young Czechs had received Hohenlohe with unconcealed dislike, for they regretted the departure of Gautsch, who had promised them great concessions. The Germans and Poles adopted

A member of the committee, in view of Hohenlohe's remarks, proposed adjournment, but his motion was defeated. The general debate was finally brought to a conclusion at the same sitting, and the committee voted to proceed to a special debate on individual parts of the ministerial proposals.

At the seventh meeting, on May 25, Marchet informed the committee that it would have to decide what particular article in the proposed new reform was to be discussed first. His own suggestion, that the article dealing with the apportionment of mandates and the demarcation of districts be put first on the agenda, was finally accepted.[89] Hohenlohe then offered the members a new plan, which called for 495 seats in the Lower House, including 102 for Galicia. He realized that he had not pleased all parties with his plan, but he hoped that his proposals would form a basis for eventual compromise and settlement of the reform issue.[90] The committee, at the close of the meeting, decided to have Hohenlohe's plan printed so that it might be studied before the next sitting.

Meanwhile, Hohenlohe got into difficulties with the Hungarian Premier, Wekerle, over tariff arrangements. The latter had persuaded the Emperor to permit the official use in Hungary of the term "Hungarian tariff" in describing the "common tariff" which had been put into effect by decree by the former Premier, Fejérváry. The Austrian Minister-President considered this step a violation of the Ausgleich of 1867 and refused to countenance it. To clear the air, Hohenlohe resigned on June 2 and returned to his post in Trieste, which, realistically, he had kept open.[91] In spite of his brief tenure as Minister-President, he did a great deal to effect necessary compromises among the parties, and a contemporary observer declared

---

a cool and reserved attitude; only the Social Democrats heartily welcomed the man popularly known as "The Red Prince." Beaumont, *op. cit.*, p. 627.

89 *Beilagen*, p. 225.

90 *Beilagen*, pp. 226-8.

91 Hohenlohe was accused of using the Hungarian tariff controversy as a pretext for getting out of the uncomfortable post of Minister-President and thereby preserving his general popularity. Beaumont, *op. cit.*, p. 628.

that Hohenlohe, with Marchet's able assistance, worked out plans which were the basis of the provisions which were finally adopted.[92]

Baron Max Vladimir Beck, the new Minister-President, was one of the trusted advisors of the heir-apparent, Archduke Francis Ferdinand.[93] In his first meeting with the electoral committee on June 8, he reaffirmed the government's pledge to secure electoral reform but refused to add new proposals to those already made by previous ministries. Naturally, he said, the cabinet would be happy to facilitate any further compromises that were deemed necessary.[94] The majority of the committee seemed pleased that the latest switch in cabinets would not mean another program which would require study, and at the next meeting on June 12, the discussion of mandates for Dalmatia began the great task of assigning mandates for all of the provinces of Austria. On October 9 the final apportionment of seats was decided upon; as a result of various compromises, Austria was to have a new Lower House of 516 members—233 for the Germans, 259 for the Slavs, and 24 for the Italians and Rumanians.

The theoretical distribution of seats in each province by nationality was as follows: Bohemia, fifty-five German, seventy-five Czech; Dalmatia, eleven Serbo-Croat; Lower Austria,

92 Czedik, *op. cit.*, III, 60-63. For an unfavorable estimate of Hohenlohe, see Sieghart, *op. cit.*, pp. 90-91.

93 Beck (1854-1941) was born in Vienna and educated at the University of Vienna. He entered the bureaucracy as a young man and served with particular distinction in negotiating trade treaties in the Ministry of Agriculture. His friendship with Francis Ferdinand stemmed from the latter's youthful days, when Beck was his tutor in law and politics. See Czedik, *op. cit.*, III, 142-7; Sieghart, *op. cit.*, p. 96.

94 *Beilagen*, pp. 233-4. Francis Joseph made it quite clear that he expected the committee to expedite Beck's pledge, in a special audience with Marchet, who had just resigned the chairmanship of the committee to join Beck's cabinet. On June 11 the Emperor received the Austrian members of the Delegations and pointedly told Kramář that a reform had to be passed before the elections scheduled for 1907. In similar vein, the Emperor admonished other delegates who would give the necessary publicity to the imperial utterances. Steinitz, ed., *op. cit.*, p. 209.

sixty-four German; Upper Austria, twenty-two German; Bukovina, five Ruthene, five Rumanian, four German; Silesia, nine German, four Polish, two Czech; Tyrol, sixteen German, nine Italian; Voralberg, four German; Istria, three Italian, two Serbo-Croat, one Slovene; Gorizia, three Slovene, three Italian; Styria, twenty-three German, seven Slovene; Carinthia, nine German, one Slovene; Carniola, eleven Slovene, one German; Trieste, four Italian, one Slovene; Salzburg, seven German; Moravia, thirty Czech, nineteen German; Galicia, seventy-eight Polish, twenty-eight Ruthene.[95]

The committee also busied itself with making necessary changes in the Election Law of the Reichsrat (*Reichsratswahlordnung*) and in recommending to the attention of the Lower House changes which would have to come in the Fundamental Law on Imperial Representation. Many of the wrangles which ensued hinged on the connotation of words or the clarity of the phrases found in the ministerial plans. Even so, the committee was able to hammer out a new regulation for imperial elections and spent some time discussing compulsory voting, plural voting, and the competence of provincial diets. It was finally decided to recommend that compulsory voting be left to the discretion of the diets of the individual provinces,[96] but plural suffrage based on education, tax-paying capacity, and age was defeated by a small majority.[97] A slight change was made in the Fundamental Law on Imperial Representation, in order to clarify the competence of the provincial diets.[98] These

95 This distribution was generally validated in the elections of 1907, *if* one counts Social Democrats of German background as German, Social Democrats of Czech background as Czech, etc. In Silesia, however, the Czechs captured a seat destined for the Poles, while in Galicia, Jewish Nationalists obtained two "Polish" mandates and one "Ruthene" mandate. In Bukovina, the Jewish Nationalists also secured a "German" mandate.

96 *Beilagen*, p. 616, Oct. 5, 1906.

97 *Beilagen*, p. 610, Oct. 4, 1906.

98 *Beilagen*, p. 724, Oct. 29, 1906. The clarification of provincial competence was agreed to by Beck in order to obtain the Polish Club's ap-

problems, and many others concerning the machinery of elections, were handled with considerable dispatch, so that the committee was able to wind up its work on October 31. Its report was submitted to the Lower House early in November, and on November 5 Gessmann moved that the report be considered at once.[99]

Two days later, the committee's report was accepted by a vote of 227 to 46, as a basis for a second reading, which began with a statement from Julius Löcker, reporter for the electoral committee. His speech reviewed the principles which had guided the committee in completing its task, and he stressed the composite nature of the final form of the committee's proposals. Reckless and unsound deviations had been avoided, he declared, and he closed with a fervent appeal for the support of the German middle class.[100] On November 8 Baron Beck justified the committee's work as essentially conservative and expressed pleasure that its deliberations had taught many lessons in the art of composing nationalistic quarrels. He warned that the Rubicon had been crossed; the miscarriage of electoral reform would be as significant as a defeat in battle.[101] The special debate (in reality, the second reading of the committee's proposals) again found Sylva-Tarouca and Stürgkh lamenting the sudden change from representation of interests to universal equal suffrage, but both clearly expected little result from their complaints. More than 200 deputies spoke in the second and third readings, and Löcker did a commendable job in reproaching those who would have upset the apportion-

---

proval of reform. The Poles also were won over by the state's purchase of the Nordbahn, whose private owners had exacted high rates on Galician products. As a result of this purchase, which was voted on Oct. 17, 1906, Galician products were able to compete with Bohemian and Moravian products on the Viennese markets. Beaumont, *op. cit.*, p. 629, footnote 3.

99 *S. P. A.*, XLIII, 39438.

100 *S. P. A.*, XLIII, 39559-61.

101 *S. P. A.*, XLIII, 39617-21. In Budapest, during November, the Emperor added his weight to Beck's pleas by telling Austrian members of the Delegations that reform was imperative and by expressing outspoken regret at the delays in both houses of parliament. Steinitz, ed., *op. cit.*, p. 213.

ment of seats decided upon by the electoral committee. Very few changes were made in the recommendations of the committee; they concerned almost exclusively the machinery of elections. On December 1, 1906 the proposed changes in the Fundamental Law on Imperial Representation and in the Election Law of the Reichsrat were accepted by a vote of 194 to 63.[102] The result of the voting was greeted with cheers, and Beck, Löcker, and Bienerth, the Minister of the Interior, were congratulated by many of the satisfied deputies.

THE COMPROMISE WITH THE UPPER HOUSE :
Numerus Clausus

Electoral reform, however, had won only half of the battle. The consent of the Upper House was mandatory, and Gautsch and Hohenlohe had done little to make reform palatable to the gentlemen of the Upper House. Discussion of reform among the latter had continued on an informal basis during the early autumn months of 1906, and on November 23 a special commission was elected to deal with the proposals which the Lower House seemed likely to pass. The bad humor of the Upper House was demonstrated in this election by its refusal to choose Count Bylandt, a nominee of the Center group, as a member of the commission, despite precedent. Undoubtedly his work in furthering reform while a member of Gautsch's cabinet caused his defeat at the hands of his colleagues. After some half-hearted attempts to smooth over this rudeness, the Upper House scheduled the first meeting of the commission for December 10.[103]

---

102 *S. P. A.*, XLIV, 40708. Beck's concessions to the Polish Club paid off handsomely. Without the seventy-two favorable Polish votes, the reform would have failed to pass; after the balloting, Beck took pains to visit the members of the Polish Club to thank them for their cooperation. Beaumont, *op. cit.*, p. 630, footnote 2.

103 Czedik, *op. cit.*, III, 400-1. The Upper House found unexpected support for its unyielding attitude in the person of the new Austro-Hungarian Minister of Foreign Affairs, Baron Alois Aehrenthal, who vainly attempted to persuade the Emperor to give up his notion of universal manhood suffrage. Steinitz, ed., *op. cit.*, pp. 218-19.

The debates which followed (December 10, 11, and 12, 1906) revealed that a small number of members were willing to accept the reform as passed by the Lower House, while another group was determined to reject the reform completely. A majority supported a plan originated by Dr. Heinrich Lammasch and Prince Alois Schönburg-Hartenstein, who pointedly proposed that universal suffrage be accepted with the proviso that all voters, thirty-five years of age or above, be given a second vote. In addition, the commission voted to demand compulsory voting and a limitation of the number of men who could be appointed to the Upper House for life. Beck wanted to allow a maximum of 180 life-members, but the commission insisted that the total be not more than 170 and not less than 150. After some negotiations, Beck, with the Emperor's permission, consented to this *numerus clausus* but made very clear his opposition to plural suffrage. The commission also accepted the rule which permitted members of the Upper House to accept mandates in the Lower House by leaving their seats in the former.[104] The report of the commission, published on December 16, aroused warm criticism because of its demand for plural suffrage, and the united front of the members of the Upper House wilted visibly in the face of the public protests. Individual members who had ties with deputies in the Lower House campaigned for a compromise which would amalgamate *numerus clausus* with the reform accepted by the Lower House. Preliminary balloting in meetings of all three parties of the Upper House on December 18 indicated that a substantial majority would accept the suggested compromise. On the same day, Count Franz Thun, chairman of the special commission, conferred with Beck,[105] and on December 20 the cabinet proposed a supplementary law to the Fundamental Law on Imperial Representation, calling for *numerus clausus*. A reconstituted special commission met to consider this development and recommended that the Upper House agree to univer-

104 Czedik, *op. cit.*, III, 401-2.

105 *Ibid.*, p. 406; Plener, *op. cit.*, p. 364.

sal equal suffrage *after* the Lower House voted to accept *numerus clausus*. On December 21 twelve hours were consumed in debating, followed by the summation of the commission's reporter, Alois Czedik. After midnight, the weary members decided to abandon plural suffrage and to accept universal equal suffrage after the Lower House confirmed the proposed *numerus clausus*.[106]

Christmas recess intervened for both houses, and the progress of reform was again delayed briefly. On January 9, 1907, the first day of the reconvening of the Lower House, Gessmann moved that *numerus clausus* be accepted for the sake of the entire reform.[107] The debate on January 10 indicated plainly that the medicine prescribed by the peers was hard to swallow, but Beck threw his weight behind the compromise and *numerus clausus* was accepted on the same day. On January 21 the Upper House fulfilled the bargain by voting for the Lower House's version of universal manhood suffrage. Francis Joseph approved the new legislation, and it received formal imperial sanction on January 26, 1907. Austria, by reputation a stronghold of privilege, had joined the ranks of countries which enjoyed universal manhood suffrage.

---

106 Czedik, *op. cit.*, III, 409-14. The ministry packed the Upper House with every member who could be relied upon to vote favorably for the compromise. Peers who seldom bothered to attend sessions were present, a messenger was dispatched to Rome to bring back one agreeable member, the clerical members were won over, and even the dignitaries of the imperial court put in an appearance. Among them was the *Oberststallmeister*; a wit thereupon asserted that the Imperial Stable had to be mobilized to effect electoral reform. Sieghart, *op. cit.*, p. 99.

107 *S. P. A.*, XLV, 41265.

CHAPTER III

THE MAJOR PROBLEMS OF ELECTORAL REFORM

UNIVERSAL EQUAL SUFFRAGE: COMPLETE OR RESTRICTED?

OF all the questions facing the members of the Austrian parliament in the debates on electoral reform in 1905-06, none was greater than the definition of universal equal suffrage. As long as Gautsch refused to consider an abolition of the curial system in the autumn of 1905, the issue was academic; with Gautsch's approval in principle of an entirely new system of representation in Austria in November, 1905, the discussion of the bases for the new system began in earnest.

In the beginning, there were political leaders who warmly recommended unrestricted manhood suffrage because it partially fulfilled what they considered to be an inevitable triumph of democracy. Austria, they felt, had lagged behind France, Great Britain, and the German Empire in political development, but the evidences of industrialization in Austria no longer permitted any retention of vestiges of the feudal system. If the empire was to be saved, its citizens would have to be given a just share in the government. Such arguments were reiterated throughout the entire course of the debates, and in some instances they were undoubtedly sincere expressions of an optimistic belief in the general efficacy of a democracy working its will through parliamentary institutions. Less idealistic parliamentarians soon revealed the true nature of the controversies on universal equal suffrage, however, and eventually forced the discussion of concrete issues. Completely equal, direct, secret, universal manhood suffrage would have created a veritable revolution in Austrian affairs. In the first place, the Germans no longer would have been in a position to control parliament. In the second place, the nobility would have lost much of the great influence it had exerted for centuries.

65

In the third place, the Poles might well be stripped of their ability to gain concessions for their well-to-do classes, should a vigorous parliamentary life replace the previous record of bargaining with imperial bureaucrats.

The brief chronology of the progress of the reform of 1907 has already indicated that the great landowners and nobles remained in general opposition, that the Poles were quieted only by more seats for Galicia, and that the Germans, though divided, fought many rear-guard actions which left the Slavs with a very small majority of the seats in the new Lower House. It would be incorrect to assume that all Slavs fought for complete universal manhood suffrage and that all Germans were determined to deny it because of the expected increase in Slavic strength. Many Slavic deputies feared socialism, while many Germans feared antagonizing the disfranchised German rural and urban laborers. Yet the question of Slavic strength versus German strength was undoubtedly the greatest single aspect of the struggle for a definition of universal manhood suffrage. Confronted with this open struggle of nationalities, the exponents of liberty and equality for all were forced to find concrete justifications for thoroughgoing democracy. Appeals to " progress " and to the natural rights of man were not enough.

Three definite justifications for unrestricted manhood suffrage were found to replace the theoretical philosophy of political rights. Austrian males were universally liable for taxes, for military service, and attendance at schools, and various speakers vigorously asserted that such civic duties clearly called for comparable civic rights (that is, the enjoyment of the franchise). In the debate on the motions for reform on October 5, 1905, Karel Kramář alluded particularly to the military and tax burdens of the masses. Recruits drawn from the unrepresented masses were beginning to wonder what they were supposed to fight for. Kramář expressed no great surprise at such an attitude; the masses, after all, were simply asked to pay the bills without having any voice in the approval of expenditures. Certainly no confidence between state and subjects could exist on such a basis of relationship. Moreover, the tremendous financial expenditures of the state, he claimed, were being met by taxes on necessities used by the masses, particularly beer, coffee, tobacco, sugar, and spirits. Conscription and taxation without representation were the very causes of the radicalism and anti-militarism which infected the people. Let the state allow the people to bear part of the responsibility of government and the future would be far calmer.[1] In the same debate, the Polish Social Democrat Ignacy Daszyński bitterly contrasted increases in taxation and in the term of military service with the continuing denial of civic rights for all.[2] On the following day, Dr. Alfred Ebenhoch expressed agreement with Kramář's views that military service should be sufficient reason for universal suffrage. Was it not true in past centuries that independence and freedom were synonymous with ability at arms? Ebenhoch felt that universal compulsory education was another argument for extending the franchise; maturing youth should be acquainted with public affairs, as part of the educational process.[3]

Gautsch readily admitted that universal military and educational obligations had strengthened the demand for reform in his speech of November 28, 1905, which revealed that the ministry was prepared to work for greater equalization of electoral rights. Concerning universal taxation, the Minister-President carefully pointed out that the provinces had considerable variations in their ability to pay direct and indirect taxes; to ignore such disparities in tax-incidence would create new injustices in place of old injustices. Tax receipts had to be considered in the allotment of seats to provinces, even though such a procedure might seem to limit complete equality

1 *S. P. A.*, XXXV, 32108-10.
2 *S. P. A.*, XXXV, 32129.
3 *S. P. A.*, XXXV, 32231-2.

in voting. The ministry had no intention of advocating tax-requirements for the individual citizen, but it did insist on using tax receipts as a basis for assessing the representation of particular provinces.[4] This reservation was repeated when the ministry's plan was submitted to the Lower House on February 23, 1906, and it caused some complaints. Dr. Schlegel, the German Clerical, felt that it was unfair to use indirect taxes as partial basis for the division of new mandates. Taxes on sugar, for instance, were paid at the place of production, such as Bohemia, while consumers in the Alpine areas had to absorb the taxation in the price they paid for the sugar.[5] Kramář also was critical of the ministry's use of tax figures in apportioning seats. The city of Vienna had been favored with new seats because of its high tax receipts; did not the ministry realize that much of Vienna's prosperity was due to the profits made from the provincial sources? Equalities in voting disappeared as a result; the ministry was playing the ancient game of protecting German influence in Austria.[6]

Obviously, the concept of universal taxation as a basis for universal suffrage was being twisted to suit the needs of the ministry, the nationalities, and the parties. Where provincial taxation was largely indirect, politicians representing that province called for indirect taxes as a basis for representation. Representatives of areas which contained large numbers of small independent landowners preferred representation on the basis of payment of direct taxes. In the final apportionment of seats, it was clear that taxation still remained a factor, though the Poles and other Slavs had done much to make other factors equally decisive.[7]

---

4 S. P. A., XXXV, 32318-20.

5 S. P. A., XXXVIII, 34842, Mar. 7, 1906.

6 S. P. A., XXXVIII, 35250-1, Mar. 15, 1906.

7 Theoretically, a province's percentage of the total Austrian population and the percentage of the total direct and indirect taxes it contributed to the treasury were to be added together and then divided by two to ascertain

The arguments for universal suffrage deduced from universal payment of taxes, universal military duty, and universal compulsory education did not go unchallenged. Defenders of Germanism in Austria and defenders of the nobility maintained there were other great factors which had to be taken into account.

First of all, differences in cultural and literacy standards among the provinces and nationalities had to be considered, maintained the deputies who desired checks on universal equal suffrage. The empire, it was admitted by all, had many subjects who could not read or write despite compulsory education laws. But there was much dispute as to whether or not these illiterates should be deprived of the right to vote, or, more practically, whether or not provinces having a large number of illiterates should be penalized in the apportionment of seats.

Slavic deputies were particularly anxious to avoid a loss of seats in a new universally elected parliament because of low literacy standards, and several expressed great chagrin when Karel Kramář, in the debate on his motion for universal suffrage, admitted that illiteracy might be a difficulty standing in the way of reform. Their disappointment was not especially relieved by Kramář's additional comment that political interest was not necessarily predicated on ability to read and write.[8] Daszyński expressed fear that the Polish Club would accept the idea of literacy requirements, in order to keep the Polish

---

the percentage of seats due the province. For instance, on June 25, 1906 a government spokesman declared that Galicia was due 140.7 seats on the basis of population, 64.8 seats on the basis of tax-recipts in a proposed house of 495 members. The average of the two figures was 102.8; consequently, the government at that time insisted that 102 mandates were sufficient. *Beilagen*, p. 281. It should be pointed out that Lower Austria contributed about 27.5 per cent of the total tax-receipts and composed about 11.9 per cent of the total population in 1906. Its share of the seats in a house of 516 should have been 19.7 per cent, or about 102 seats. It actually received 64. Beaumont, *op. cit.*, p. 623, footnote 1.

8 *S. P. A.*, XXXV, 32114, Oct. 5, 1905.

masses from voting.[9] Romanczuk, leader of the Ruthene deputies, felt it would be unjust to punish any Austrian subject because there was no school in his district where he might learn to read and write. Moreover, illiterates already were voting in the fifth curia and in other curias. How could a " reform " take away established rights? [10]

Gautsch effectively ended much of the Slavic alarm in his speech of November 28, 1905, in which he promised a reform which would not exclude illiterates from future elections.[11] Viktor Adler expressed approval of Gautsch's stand and added that it would be a poor principle to exclude anyone from voting because of inability to read or write; culture did not in any way depend on literacy.[12] The Slovene Šuklje was equally pleased with the ministry's decision. The state alone was to blame for illiteracy; recalling his own school days, he asserted that the amount of knowledge taught was no guarantee of culture, anyway.[13] Gautsch's definite proposals of February, 1906 clearly permitted illiterates to vote,[14] and this redemption of his pledge of the previous year enlisted commendation generally from the Slavic deputies.

Deputies of German nationality were particularly fond of stressing culture and literacy as necessary prerequisites for representation. Dr. Alfred Ebenhoch declared there were grave hindrances in the way of complete and immediate universal

9 S. P. A., XXXV, 32140-1, Oct. 5, 1905.

10 S. P. A., XXXV, 32229, Oct. 6, 1905.

11 S. P. A., XXXV, 32319. According to the census figures of 1900, about 35 per cent of all Austrians were illiterate. There was considerable variation in the provinces: in Dalmatia, 76 per cent illiteracy; in Bukovina, 70 per cent; in Galicia, 63 per cent; in the Littoral, 44 per cent; in Carniola, 34 per cent; in Carinthia, 31 per cent; in Styria, 25 per cent. Richard Charmatz, Der demokratisch-nationale Bundesstaat Österreich (Frankfurt a. M., 1904), p. 69.

12 S. P. A., XXXV, 32457, Nov. 30, 1905.

13 S. P. A., XXXVI, 32557, Dec. 4, 1905.

14 S. P. A., XXXVIII, 34657, Feb. 23, 1906.

suffrage, in defending his motion which conspicuously omitted a demand for equal suffrage, on October 6, 1905; the existing variation in levels of culture was one great hindrance. He could not agree with Kramář that political interest was not necessarily a matter of literacy.[15] Dr. von Derschatta, the German Populist, adopted the attitude that the passage of equal suffrage would be the negation of equality. Unless provisions were made for cultural attainments, educated groups would be overwhelmed by impressionable illiterates. How could one demand "equality" when the last census figures gave the following percentages (by nationality) of men over twenty-four able to read and write: German, 95 per cent; Czech, 95 per cent; Ruthene, 24 per cent; and Rumanian, 20 per cent? One could speak of a truly equal franchise only if such cultural differences were respected in the apportionment of seats.[16] Evidently, Gautsch's system of apportionment of seats reassured many German deputies when it was submitted in February, 1906. Dr. Schlegel admitted that Ebenhoch's motion of the previous October had omitted a demand for equal suffrage simply because of the illiteracy issue. Now, with Gautsch's plan to work with, the German Clericals were willing to consider an equal franchise.[17] The Pan-Germans, however, continued to denounce the ministry for failing to keep illiterates from voting. Their representative on the electoral committee of the Lower House declared that the scheme was planned to aid either socialist or clerical candidates.[18]

The easy assumption by some German deputies that their nationality was superior culturally and in the matter of literacy evoked strenuous protests from the Czechs. Kramář indignantly refused to accept such German claims; if Czechs were inferior in any cultural matters, the blame should be put on

15 S. P. A., XXXV, 32234, Oct. 6, 1905.

16 S. P. A., XXXV, 32260, Oct. 6, 1905.

17 S. P. A., XXXVIII, 34843-4, Mar. 7, 1906.

18 Speech of Franz Stein, *Beilagen*, p. 199, Apr. 24, 1906.

the policies of past German regimes. If the Germans were afraid that in the future the Czechs would retaliate by retarding the growth of German schools, they should put aside their fears. The Czechs never had opposed the development of German culture.[19] In March, 1906, during the first reading of Gautsch's proposals, Kramář again showed considerable resentment over renewed German claims for more seats because of "cultural superiority." Did not the Germans realize that the Austro-Hungarian state originated with the union of Bohemia with the Habsburgs in 1526? For a century thereafter, Bohemia was the cultural model for central Europe and in later centuries her wealth was the mainstay of the Habsburgs. Despite the state's failure to do anything for Czech culture, his people had few illiterates, and Czech literature and art were on a par with that of the German Austrians! Admittedly, there could not be apportionment solely on the basis of population, but the Germans should beware of trying to perpetuate old injustices by flimsy pretensions.[20] Czech National Socialists and Agrarians were equally vehement in rejecting the German claims, and the Old Czech representative on the Lower House's electoral committee, Jan Žáček, warned that repeated German emphasis on their cultural position would seriously endanger the passage of the entire reform.[21]

Several German deputies agreed with their colleagues that German culture was superior to any other culture in the realm, but they did not consequently believe that Germans should receive special treatment. The Viennese Independent Julius Ofner assured the Germans that the source of German strength lay in their economic and cultural predominance in Austria. They already were a minority in the present parliament, yet their cultural and economic attainments outweighed

19 S. P. A., XXXV, 32112-14, Oct. 5, 1905.

20 S. P. A., XXXVIII, 35252-6, Mar. 15, 1906.

21 Beilagen, pp. 210-11, Apr. 25, 1906.

political considerations.[22] Schöpfer was likewise certain the Germans would retain their place in the empire; thanks to their history, culture, and hoped-for unity, they would be able to get whatever they needed from the state and, in return, contribute whatever the state needed.[23] Dr. Viktor Adler, speaking as a German Social Democrat, ridiculed the idea that the only indication of German political power was the number of parliamentary mandates held. Could the totals of parliamentary seats take precedence over the material culture of Germanism, over the development of the German masses?[24] At the end of the first reading, Dr. Alfred Ebenhoch summarized these arguments very ably in defending Gautsch's proposed reform. He asserted that the economic and cultural position of the Germans was so great that electoral reform could not injure them. Anyway, there were only two foolproof means of safeguarding Germanism. First, the Germans had to be fair to all other nationalities; secondly, there must be unity among the Germans. If the Germans lacked either safeguard, their position would be tremendously weakened.[25]

The second great argument advanced against unrestricted universal suffrage was a spirited defense of the functions of the historical nobility of Austria. "Rabble-rousers" might claim that universal compulsory military service, taxation, and education were sufficient reasons for universal equal suffrage, but, according to the defenders of the nobility, they showed little historical sense in making such claims. Who could dare propose that "a mechanical principle of population figures "[26] supplant the balanced wisdom and unquestioned patriotism of the feudal aristocrats? Here, of course, one finds the second

22 *S. P. A.*, XXXV, 32247, Oct. 6, 1905.

23 *S. P. A.*, XXXV, 32264, Oct. 6, 1905.

24 *S. P. A.*, XXXVIII, 34995, Mar. 9, 1906.

25 *S. P. A.*, XXXIX, 35588, Mar. 22, 1906.

26 The phrase was Gautsch's, appearing in his speech of Sept. 26, 1905, *S. P. A.*, XXXV, 31423.

great conflict in defining universal suffrage. The German noble and middle-class deputies had put forth claims of cultural supremacy in an effort to prevent a Slavic parliamentary majority; now many of the same deputies would unite to defend the curial system of interest-representation against the masses who so easily might fall victim to demagogues. The German aristocrats were ably seconded by their Polish and Bohemian counterparts, and both houses of parliament witnessed the development of a defense of paternalism that took up more time in debate than did the cultural argument.

In early debates in the Lower House, the nobles who were deputies made little effort to extol their own worth to the state, probably because Gautsch had already warned that he did not favor a reform based on mere population figures. Titled gentlemen who did speak referred vaguely to the necessity for loyalty to institutions and the need for lengthy study of any reform. On October 4, 1905, however, the problem of assessing the true worth of the aristocracy was brought into general discussion by one of those tragic-comic episodes typical of parliamentary behavior in Austria. Some days earlier, Dr. Lecher, a German Progressive from Brünn, had shown considerable independence of party discipline by supporting the motions for universal suffrage. In his remarks, Lecher had derided the cultured classes, the priests, the traditional aristocracy, and the military caste as pillars of the State.[27] In doing so, he irritated Count Sternberg, a picturesque writer and soldier who represented a Moravian rural district. Sternberg had previously expressed approval of universal suffrage, but he was not the man to permit a slander of the aristocracy. He declared that Lecher had no right to say that the noble-republican was the worst curse that befell Hungary and Poland; who, other than nobles, had protected Poland from three avaricious empires? Perhaps, Sternberg continued, Lecher had been judging all aristocrats by his colleague, Baron Ludwigstorff, who was one

27 *S. P. A.*, XXXV, 31574, Sept. 27, 1905.

of those people who always bargain with whatever ministry is in power. The president of the Lower House immediately called Sternberg to order because of the personal attack on a colleague, but the Lower House itself practically dissolved in uproar. Sternberg threw a glass of water at a jeering deputy, and the president finally adjourned the meeting. An hour later, the meeting resumed, but Sternberg's apology to Ludwigstorff was deemed insincere by the president, who then dismissed the entire house for the rest of the day.[28]

Not a bit deterred, Lecher renewed his attack on the aristocracy two days later. Let there be universal suffrage, he said, so that the privileged and cultured classes would be forced to go to the people for support. At present, the former rest on their privileges while demagogues profit from public misery. The aristocracy had entered into a liaison with business interests that led to its betrayal and misuse by the shrewd bourgeoisie. Was not almost all of the *Almanach de Gotha* enjoying positions in the administration of stock exchanges, insurance, railroads, and banks? The French aristocracy once sought *le roi soleil* and thereby failed in its historic duties; Austrian nobles were likewise deserting duty to serve other masters.[29] Lecher's phrases, one can well imagine, made his Progressive colleagues, the avowed defenders of business and the bourgeoisie, writhe.

In the Upper House in December, 1905, aristocrats both of long standing and of recent title defended by implication the great worth of the Austrian nobility. Baron Plener, the erstwhile leader of Austrian Liberalism, ardently defended the large landowners' curia as an artificial support in an obviously artificial empire. In Austria, the clash of disparate nationalities and the troubled international situation resulted in contradictions that could only be solved artificially; the landowners' curia had been used to support governmental policies, and it

28 *S. P. A.*, XXXV, 32025-6, Oct. 4, 1905.

29 *S. P. A.*, XXXV, 32252, Oct. 6, 1905.

had served its purpose well. It would be foolish to toss away this nucleus of imperial strength.[30] Prince Karl Schwarzenberg bitterly assailed Gautsch for approving universal suffrage, but he boasted that the aristocracy would be less pained by reform than would cultured, serious members of the agricultural and urban middle classes. The latter would scarcely dare offer themselves as candidates under the new system when they realized how much brimstone they would be forced to spout in order to be popular.[31]

As the debates on reform continued, the representatives of the aristocrats and landowners in Austria made various proposals which, in their opinion, would protect Austria from radicalism and disorder. Their proposals were not always ill-received by the proponents of simon-pure universal suffrage, but Kramář probably spoke for all of their respectful friends when he simply recommended that the aristocrats get out and campaign for a seat in the new elections. Representatives of privileged groups should not retire to a corner but should mingle with the people. Ideally, universal equal suffrage meant that the men best fitted by education and intelligence should represent the people. Men far less worthy than the representatives of the land-owners would campaign for parliament, and the latter should have no hesitancy in opposing them.[32] Ebenhoch also urged the representatives of privilege to return as representatives of the people; looking back upon their service in behalf of social reforms, he could not believe that they would disappear from the Lower House.[33] The general spokesman for

30 *S. P. H.*, pp. 1130-1, Dec. 2, 1905.

31 *S. P. H.*, p. 1144, Dec. 2, 1905.

32 *S. P. A.*, XXXVIII, 35248, Mar. 15, 1906. The Emperor also felt that the great landowners should become candidates, though he admitted the practical difficulties involved. See Count Oswald Thun's letter of Dec. 13, 1905 in Paul Molisch, ed., *Briefe zur deutschen Politik in Österreich von 1848 bis 1918* (Vienna and Leipzig, 1934), pp. 374-5. Hereafter, this collection will be cited as *Briefe*.

33 *S. P. A.*, XXXIX, 35587, Mar. 22, 1906.

the members of the landed curia, Count Stürgkh, was not con-
soled by such possibilities. Never directly, but by insinuations,
he bewailed the lack of appreciation shown for the sacrifices of
the gentlemen of his curia. Could one forget that deputies of
the various nationalities had voted against military appropri-
ations, fearing the displeasure of their constituents? Others,
more conscious of state needs, had voted the credits and had
earned the unpopularity; their reward, presumably, was to be
ejection from the Lower House.[34]

The defenders of the curial system had little hope of with-
standing the demand for abolition of interest-representation
after Gautsch's speech of November 28, 1905. As indicated
above, their resentment occasionally revealed itself in veiled
allusions to the lack of appreciation shown their patriotic endeavors over the years. With no real chance of saving the
curias, the conservative landowners and aristocrats adopted
other tactics which they hoped would prevent somehow the
adoption of unqualified universal suffrage. In certain instances,
their efforts and recommendations were heartily seconded by
various other political groups in the Lower House, who feared
either a flood of Slavic or socialist votes. The conservatives
and aristocrats had their way, finally, in only one question; the
restriction on the number of members who could be appointed
to the Upper House by the Emperor. But their insistence on
plural voting and on a clause requiring long residence for voting caused lengthy discussions in parliament and in the electoral committees of both houses which almost resulted in
substantial modifications of the ministerial plans. Again, the
demand of the Polish nobles that diets be given more autonomy
was accepted by the electoral committee, though the consequent
change in the Fundamental Law on Imperial Representation
did little or nothing to change the essentially centralizing
aspects of Austrian administration.

34 *S. P. A.*, XXXIX, 35638, Mar. 23, 1906.

PLURAL SUFFRAGE

The question of a plural franchise in place of universal equal suffrage received little direct attention in the Lower House prior to the sessions of the electoral committee, nor did the Upper House explicitly demand plural suffrage until the autumn of 1906. Implicitly, however, scores of members of both houses had suggested some limitation on universal equal suffrage from the very beginning of the debates, so that no great surprise was occasioned by the full-blown discussion of plural voting late in 1906. To be sure, Gautsch had promised in November, 1905 that the ministry would give careful consideration to proposals of plural suffrage which aimed at greater protection of the nationalities of Austria, but his tone revealed little enthusiasm for such schemes.[35] The Minister-President's reference to plural suffrage evoked no immediate comment, save from Dr. Adler, who expressed amazement that Gautsch would bother studying a system that had worked so poorly in Belgium and which gave rise to widespread fraud.[36] Early in December, 1905, the Upper House's debate on Gautsch's espousal of reform practically ignored the question, and Gautsch's concrete proposals of February, 1906 clearly rejected the idea of plural suffrage.[37]

The omission did not go unnoticed, though only a few deputies gave indication that the issue was not dead. Dr. Schlegel pointed out that an equalization of political rights for farmers and their helpers might be hard to endure, particularly in the case of farmers who previously had voted in two curias.[38] Dr. Karl Beuerle, the German Populist, pointedly asked for the plural franchise, citing as his reason the necessity of eliminating friction in the large cities; the curial system was obviously

35 S. P. A., XXXV, 32320, Nov. 28, 1905.

36 S. P. A., XXXV, 32456, Nov. 30, 1905.

37 See above, p. 49.

38 S. P. A., XXXVIII, 34843, Mar. 7, 1906.

outmoded, but there had to be some guarantees of respect for Germanism.[39] Dr. Alfred Ebenhoch, in his summation and defense of Gautsch's proposals at the end of the first meeting, answered the friends of plural suffrage. Men who complained that propertied groups would become a minority as a result of reform should remember that the present electoral system had made the non-propertied groups a minority. The time for schemes which would discriminate against farm-laborers and which would favor landowning farmers had passed; after all, labor created property, and a continuing denial of laborers' rights would destroy peace in Austria.[40]

As expected, Gautsch made no changes in his proposals when they were turned over to the electoral committee in March, 1906, but there were definite signs that plans for plural suffrage would be introduced in the committee meetings by some of the members. Dr. Johann Tollinger, representative of rural communes in the Tyrol, asserted that he favored universal suffrage but considered equal suffrage a campaign phrase, in an introductory statement of policy on April 24, 1906. The middle classes were being threatened by the rash ideas of the ministry, and he was prepared to demand plural suffrage as a token of respect for the property-owning family man.[41] Leo Pastor, the Polish Centrist, agreed with Tollinger that pluralism should be used to dam the floods of radicalism; citizens who carried the heaviest burdens in the state should have a preponderant influence in state affairs. He recommended that a second vote be given to every man who paid eight kronen or more in direct taxes or to every man who had a family to rear.[42] The Tollinger-Pastor partnership, which was to spearhead the drive for plural suffrage in later sessions of the committee, aroused

---

39 *S. P. A.*, XXXVIII, 35162-3, Mar. 14, 1906.

40 *S. P. A.*, XXXIX, 35584-5, Mar. 22, 1906.

41 *Beilagen*, pp. 201-2.

42 *Beilagen*, p. 209, Apr. 25, 1906.

some comment with its proposals. Dr. von Grabmayr, the Constitutionalist representative of the landed curia, pessimistically said that plural suffrage should be adopted only if a better system could not be found. Undoubtedly the device would remove the threat of the non-propertied classes, but, if its provisions were too vague, the middle class would scarcely be protected. On the other hand, a stiff requirement would injure the just demands of labor.[43] Dr. Adler sharply denounced plural suffrage as a practical injustice; eight kronen in direct taxes meant a great deal more in some provinces than in others, for one thing.[44]

Nothing more was heard of plural suffrage until the electoral committee of the Lower House reassembled in September, 1906. However, the opponents of equal suffrage had not been idle in the interim. Early in September the leaders of the great German landowners in Bohemia met in Prague and passed a resolution instructing their parliamentary colleagues to support plural suffrage. One of these leaders, writing to a friend, doubted that any scheme for plural suffrage would pass the Lower House, particularly in view of the settlement of the thorny problems of assigning mandates. The group merely hoped that enough parties in the Lower House would rally to the cause of plural suffrage to strengthen the Upper House's desire to curb egalitarian notions. Sabotage was not intended; an honorable compromise which would spare the fatherland the worst evils of radicalism was the goal.[45]

When the time came for the electoral committee to discuss Article 5 of the new Election Law of the Reichsrat on September 19, Tollinger asked for a postponement of discussion on the ground that he planned to introduce changes along the lines of plural suffrage in the near future. Adler and

43 *Beilagen*, p. 215, Apr. 26, 1906.

44 *Beilagen*, p. 217, Apr. 26, 1906.

45 Count Erwein Nostitz-Rieneck's letter of Sept. 10, 1906, in Molisch, ed., *Briefe*, pp. 376-77.

Šuteršič, the Slovene Clerical, argued that the proponents of the device should be given no more time to concoct intrigues against equal suffrage, but the committee voted to postpone the discussion by a vote of twenty-one to ten.[46] In the days which followed, one may assume, from a letter written by Grabmayr,[47] that Tollinger labored to find a formula which would enlist the approbation of as many members of the committee as possible. By September 28 the formula had been found and could be expected to attract some twenty votes. According to Grabmayr, there was no real chance of a favorable majority in the Lower House; nevertheless, a strong minority vote there would possibly encourage the Upper House to insist upon a second vote for some men, if not a third vote. On October 2 Tollinger finally submitted to the committee his own wording of Article 5.

According to Tollinger's plan, an extra vote was to be given to any male who already was entitled to vote if he fulfilled certain qualifications. First, a second vote was to be granted any male who had reached the age of thirty-five who was married or widowed and the father of at least one legitimate child, and who had a definite place of residence, whether as an owner, usufructuary, or tenant. Secondly, an extra vote was to go to any male who had passed his matriculation examination at a secondary school or teachers' training school or to any male who had finished successfully a special or professional school equal in status to a secondary school while fulfilling his military service. Thirdly, a second vote was to be given to any male who carried on an independent business or who owned real estate on which he paid at least twenty-five kronen annually in direct taxes in the tax year preceding a given election, providing the tax had been paid at the time of the election. The last requirement, calling for the payment of at least twenty-five kronen annually in direct taxes, might be modified

46 *Beilagen*, p. 473, Sept. 19, 1906.
47 Letter of Sept. 28, 1906, in Molisch, ed., *Briefe*, pp. 377-8.

by the diets of particular provinces as long as the minimum annual amount did not drop below eight kronen. Should any voter be able to qualify in at least two of the three categories mentioned above, he was to be granted the right to cast three votes. In short, special credit was to be given Austrian voters who were mature and settled, or who had a superior educational background, or who enjoyed an independent economic status.[48]

In introducing his version of the proposed Article 5, Tollinger elaborated his reasons for desiring plural suffrage. An equal franchise, according to his reasoning, meant equal rights for those who bore equally the burdens of the state. Naturally, all citizens should vote, but some citizens of superior talents or position should have extra votes. His plan admittedly was not ideal by any means, but it did grant special political influence to citizens who were most interested in a well-ordered functioning of the state. Tollinger defended the large amount of discretion permitted the diets as necessary in view of the varying economic levels in the provinces. His motives, he asserted, were not "capitalistic," for laborers could qualify for extra votes if they were family men over thirty-five. The sole purpose of his plan was the protection of the middle classes, particularly rural landowners.[49]

Other supporters of plural voting in the committee advanced similar arguments. No one would admit anything save affection for the laboring masses, but everyone seemed agreed that the masses should be saved from socialism (or clericalism, as the case might be) by giving good solid citizens extra votes. A Polish Centrist blandly asserted that the scheme was compatible with the encyclical, *Rerum novarum*,[50] while a Slovene Liberal felt sure that pluralism would keep reactionary clericals

48 The text of Tollinger's original motion is to be found in the *Beilagen*, p. 570.

49 *Beilagen*, pp. 570-2, Oct. 2, 1906.

50 Speech of Leo Pastor, *Beilagen*, p. 576, Oct. 3, 1906.

from obtaining control of state schools and from securing a new concordat.[51] Kaiser, the sole German Populist who endorsed plural suffrage, stressed the need for redressing the " wrongs " inflicted upon rural voters in general by the apportionment of mandates. So far, he said, the agrarian class had remained calm, in contrast to its counterpart in Russia, but it could not endure everything. It would be fine to find a new home for the lost power of the rural areas in the Upper House, but the new Lower House might well abolish the Upper House. So, to protect the agrarian class and to avoid a repetition of obstruction and government by means of Article 14, he would vote for plural suffrage.[52] Hagenhofer, the German Clerical, claimed that farmers had no desire to accept their hired help as equals. If the crown really wanted an equal suffrage, the ministry would have fought plural voting openly. Again, it would be well to remember that Tollinger's plan could be modified by future parliaments; once universal equal suffrage was adopted, there could be no modifications.[53] Other speakers emphasized the need to avoid the domination of public affairs by the uninformed, the necessity of electing a parliament which would be able to reach non-partisan decisions and vote necessary military credits, and so forth; the impulsive Slovene Liberal Ivan Tavčar bluntly admitted that he would be glad to vote for any controversial issue which would wreck the whole "terrible" reform.[54]

Baron Beck, the Minister-President, seemed embarrassed by the plans advanced by Tollinger and his supporters and tried to refute them on the grounds of inexpediency. He revealed that the ministry had been unable to work out any satisfactory system of plural suffrage; Tollinger's plan did not seem to be satisfactory, either. Already the ministry and the committee

51 Speech of Ivan Tavčar, *Beilagen,* p. 583, Oct. 3, 1906.

52 *Beilagen,* pp. 585-8, Oct. 3, 1906.

53 *Beilagen,* p. 608, Oct. 4, 1906.

54 *Beilagen,* p. 583, Oct. 3, 1906.

had taken pains to respect peculiar and special conditions in creating and delimiting electoral districts; a switch to plural voting would mean beginning all over again, without any reliable statistics to go by in assessing the future results of such a change. At any rate, he could not see how the results of pluralism could justify a modification of one of the fundamental bases of reform. The argument for special treatment of family men thirty-five years of age had some justification, but the other arguments were insignificant or unjust. Beck ended his contribution to the debate equivocally by declaring that the ministry only wanted peace among all factions.[55]

Far from equivocal were the speeches of the deputies who denounced Tollinger's motion, point by point. Concerning the extra vote for men thirty-five years old, some deputies felt that this concession would favor every class, so why have it? Others argued that physicians could testify that the laboring class, with a high death-rate among its younger members, would be discriminated against by the same provision. Adler crisply remarked that age was no protection from stupidity and agreed that in effect the provision would be injurious to the relatively short-lived laborers.[56] As for the bonus for education, there were various retorts. One deputy agreed that the better educated man had more influence than his less favored brothers; why increase his influence?[57] Others asserted that culture had been paid sufficient respect already in the reform, that an average intelligence was adequate to cope with national affairs, and that, after all, radicals were often well-educated.

The proposed tax requirement for a second vote aroused the loudest protests. Many deputies felt that it was a denial of rights granted by the reform of 1896, while others claimed that direct taxes were insignificant in comparison with the indirect taxes which the broad masses were forced to contribute to the

55 *Beilagen*, pp. 581-2, Oct. 3, 1906.

56 *Beilagen*, p. 593, Oct. 3, 1906.

57 Speech of Ludwig Vogler, *Beilagen*, pp. 579-80, Oct. 3, 1906.

upkeep of the state. One objector asked what would happen to a farmer who had a bad year and was unable to pay twenty-five kronen in direct taxes; [58] another stoutly denied that the minimum eight kronen prerequisite would protect small land-owners in Tollinger's own Tyrolean district, where, " according to an informal census," only five persons desired plural suffrage—two half-wits, two peasants, and one deputy. [59] Ivčevič, the Croatian deputy, humorously recommended that an extra vote be given for every increase in taxation; then Rothschild would have more votes than anyone. [60] Löcker, the German Populist, was particularly angry that the diets were to be permitted to modify the twenty-five kronen requirement. He was convinced that this concession was an attempt to enlist the support of Slavic autonomists. [61]

The verbal duels over tax requirements, educational require-ments, and " maturity " requirements were window-dressing for the real problem which seemed to obsess proponents and opponents of plural suffrage alike, Adler excepted. The prob-lem was simple: How many Social Democrats will be elected if universal equal suffrage is granted, or, what will the Social Democrats do if universal equal suffrage is denied? Almost to a man, the proponents of pluralism felt that socialism could be checked only by granting " responsible " citizens extra votes. They had no hope of restraining socialism once universal equal suffrage was accepted. How did their opponents, who were often of the same nationality and sometimes of the same politi-cal party, hope to contain the threat of socialism with a system of universal equal suffrage? The collective reply was uniformly fatalistic, if not pessimistic. The disfranchised classes were re-sentful, and a continuance of privileged voting of a plural

58 Speech of Otto Lecher, *Beilagen*, p. 574, Oct. 2, 1906.
59 Speech of Josef Schraffl, *Beilagen*, pp. 598-9, Oct. 4, 1906.
60 *Beilagen*, p. 601, Oct. 4, 1906.
61 *Beilagen*, p. 580, Oct. 3, 1906.

nature would goad them to disagreeable tactics; only a fair reform could keep them under control. In the future, warned Albert Gessmann, bourgeois parties would need all the support they could get from the masses; should plural suffrage be adopted, this potential support indubitably would go to the Social Democrats.[62] In less serious vein, his Christian Socialist colleague Schraffl feigned surprise that Adler did not support pluralism, which would make such wonderful material for a campaign, even among Tyrolese peasants.[63] Kramář was somewhat more optimistic in his appraisal of the situation; he was confident that the Social Democrats would change their tactics for the better when they had secured numerous seats in the new parliament. Passage of plural suffrage, on the other hand, would simply increase their revolutionary tendencies.[64]

The devil of the plot, Dr. Adler, answered the hopes and fears of his many colleagues in masterly fashion. At first, he airily dismissed the possibility of having plural suffrage. Beck had admitted that he had toyed with the idea with no success; if the ministry had failed to appease the enemies of reform, how could a mere committee hope to do so? Dispassionately, Adler went on to say that, of course, the calm of the last six months was due to the feeling among the masses that equal suffrage had been guaranteed. He was glad to confirm implications that revolution was a scant possibility among the rural classes; their deputies, with their demands for plural suffrage, reminded him of lonely swimmers in a vast ocean. He confessed that he was forced to smile at his nervous colleagues who should know very well that they had made a big socialist victory impossible. Electoral geometry was one thing, however, and an attack upon equal suffrage was quite another. Tavčar had admitted the real purpose behind plural suffrage—destruction of the entire reform. Adler reminded his listeners that the

62 *Beilagen*, p. 603, Oct. 4, 1906.

63 *Beilagen*, p. 599, Oct. 4, 1906.

64 *Beilagen*, p. 589, Oct. 3, 1906.

adoption of pluralism would definitely be the best opportunity in the world for agitation. It was true, as Gautsch had said, that equal suffrage was the best weapon to combat socialism. Social Democrats were eager to place the class struggle on a plane of action where the possessors and the dispossessed of the earth could trade fair blows; equal suffrage would provide such a plane of action. His party would never limit its efforts to protection of labor. It was a state party in that it had a vital interest in the cultural development of the empire and in the progress of the empire toward a firm foundation of political peace. Those who described themselves as props of the state were really the men who threatened it, not the Social Democrats.[65]

A short while before the committee ended its debate, Tollinger made two changes in his motion. He eliminated the requirement that men thirty-five years of age had to be fathers of at least one legitimate child in order to receive a second vote and also the requirement that direct taxes had to be paid up at the time of an election before a second vote could be granted. In spite of these changes, those parts of his motion which created a plural suffrage were defeated; the " maturity " provision by a vote of twenty-six to twenty, the educational and tax provisions by a vote of twenty-seven to nineteen. Arrayed in favor of plural suffrage were all of the members of the Polish Club (Conservatives, National Democrats, and a Centrist), Czech and German deputies of the landowners' curia, the Pan-Germans and the German Clericals, a Slovene Liberal, and single members of the German *Volkspartei* and the Ger-

---

65 *Beilagen*, pp. 590-5, Oct. 3, 1906. For an incisive critique of the Social Democrats as a prop of the Habsburg monarchy, see Oscar Jaszi, *The Dissolution of the Habsburg Monarchy* (Chicago, 1929), pp. 177-84. The Social Democratic program to ameliorate nationalistic troubles is summarized in Karl Gottfried Hugelmann, ed., *Das Nationalitätenrecht des alten Österreichs* (Vienna and Leipzig, 1934), pp. 242-3, and is evaluated in Virginio Gayda, *Modern Austria, Her Racial and Social Problems* (London, 1915), pp. 323-6.

man Agrarian group. The Old Czech deputy voted for the " maturity " clause, but against the educational and tax clauses. The victorious opposition included the Young Czechs, four Christian Socialists, five members of the German *Volkspartei,* the German Progressives, and the single representatives of the Social Democrats, Czech National Socialists, Italian Clericals, Independent Pan-Germans, Italian Liberals, Czech Agrarians, Slovene Clericals, Ruthene National Democrats, the Croatian Party, and the Rumanian " Club." Article 5 of the Election Law of the Reichsrat, as recommended by the committee, would simply specify that every enfranchised person had the right to one vote and that the franchise had to be exercised personally. Tollinger immediately announced that he would submit his defeated motion to the entire Lower House as a minority recommendation.[66]

The special commission elected by the Upper House on November 23, 1906 to consider electoral reform also was concerned with the problem of plural suffrage. A second reading of the report and recommendations of the electoral committee of the Lower House had been in progress for several weeks and a vote was expected momentarily; consequently, the members of the special commission had to come to some decisions of their own quickly. Count Franz Thun, well aware of the probable decisions of the commission, felt compelled to advise Beck of the sentiment in the Upper House. In an exhaustive interview late in November, he warned the Minister-President that *numerus clausus* and some provisions for plural voting were imperative. Beck did not dismiss either demand lightly, but he absolutely refused to consider Tollinger's formula, which, in his opinion, was impossible and nonsensical. He warned Thun that it would be difficult to reopen discussion in the Lower House, because of the welter of motions of urgency already scheduled, and insisted that the Upper House reach

---

66 The roll-call vote of Oct. 4, 1906, on Tollinger's motion, is given in the *Beilagen,* p. 610.

some decision before the Christmas holidays. Thun, in turn, warned Beck not to use any pressure on the Upper House, even from the highest quarters, but at heart he was not at all confident that a solid majority against universal equal suffrage could be maintained in the Upper House. In a letter, describing this interview, he was much perturbed by the question of strategy; he feared that the Upper House, by insisting on *numerus clausus* and double votes, would end up with neither. With Thun, the loss of the former would have been the greater tragedy, and his desire to secure its passage foreshadowed the eventual compromise.[67]

Thanks to the scandal surrounding the non-election of Bylandt to the special commission, the sessions of the latter did not begin until December 10, ten days after the Lower House had decisively accepted its own committee's recommendations, which excluded plural suffrage. Just prior to the meeting, two members of the Center Party, Dr. Heinrich Lammasch and Prince Alois Schönburg-Hartenstein, elaborated a proposal which accepted universal " equal " suffrage when accompanied by a second vote for men thirty-five years of age.[68] In spite of some determined opposition, this proposal was accepted by the commission by a vote of fourteen to four. The morning newspapers on December 12 announced the result to the public, despite the fact that all members of the commission were pledged to secrecy. The official report of the commission, published a few days later, justified the double vote for men thirty-five or over on the usual grounds of the need for mature consideration of public affairs. It added that comparisons of this plan with the Belgian device were unfair, for plural franchise in Belgium had been complicated by tax qualifications, which the commission had not recommended.[69] Public opinion at once turned against the Upper House's plan for pluralism,

67 Letter of Nov. 28, 1906, in Molisch, ed., *Briefe*, pp. 278-80.

68 Czedik, *op. cit.*, III, 401.

69 Czedik, *op. cit.*, III, p. 404.

and many members of the Upper House began to waver. On December 20 a new special commission was asked to report on a possible compromise, and in its report, it declared that the majority of the commission would favor a renunciation of plural suffrage.[70]

The Upper House debated the commission's report on December 21. Count Franz Thun still felt that double votes for older men was desirable, but admitted that the Lower House would never accept such a device. Prince Schönburg and Dr. Lammasch continued to defend their creation; the latter alleged that the plan had foundered because of the efforts of " that corporation for the mutual protection of mandates." Baron Plener was hardly pained by the loss of plural suffrage but, rather, grieved by the surrender of the Upper House to the pressure exerted by the Lower House. Baron Chlumecky, at the end of the session, moved that plural suffrage be stricken from the commission's report, and his motion was accepted by a large majority. Plural suffrage was dead; the price of the Lower House's acceptance of *numerus clausus* had been paid.[71]

RESIDENCE REQUIREMENTS

Residence requirements for voters in Austria were well established by the time reform was discussed in 1905-06. The reform of 1896 had specified six months' residence as a prerequisite for voters in the fifth curia, and the question of retaining, abolishing, or increasing this requirement received a good amount of attention in parliament. In a sense, the conflict over domiciliary provisions was another aspect of the general apprehension aroused by the specter of the masses entering into political life. Yet the representatives of the landowners' curia in the Lower House and the members of the Upper House paid relatively little attention to the controversy; the conflict, such as it was, developed primarily between the

70 *Ibid.*, p. 408.

71 For a résumé of the debates, *ibid.*, pp. 409-414.

Christian Socialists and the Social Democrats, the latter allied with various independents and radicals.

Karl Lueger, the leader of the Christian Socialists, had touched off a discussion of domiciliary requirements before Gautsch had ever decided to sponsor a general reform by asserting that any reform should adequately protect the settled elements of the population from the fluctuating elements.[72] His German Clerical colleague Ebenhoch was less sympathetic toward domiciliary requirements, which, he felt, should be required only at communal elections.[73] In the manner of a man clutching at straws, Gautsch, who still was opposing reform, solemnly warned that the question of residence requirements was of tremendous importance and needed much study. With his conversion to the cause of reform in November, 1905, the Minister-President still balked at recommending a specific residence requirement. Though he adamantly refused to disfranchise illiterates who had voted in the fifth curia, he did believe it would be permissible to extend the period of residence required by the law passed in 1896. An extension of the requirement might enhance the chances of an increased rapport among the new voters and help avoid calamitous changes in the relationships of the nationalities.[75]

This hint of a possible change aroused scattered critical comments. Adler disliked the idea of denying rights which already had been granted in 1896 and requested that the ministry consider the plight of seasonal workers who had to move about the country. Even a requirement of six months would keep them from voting.[76] The Ruthene deputy Romanczuk agreed with Gautsch that voting should not be casual and haphazard, but migrant workers at least should be permitted to

72 S. P. A., XXXV, 31783, Oct. 2, 1905.

73 S. P. A., XXXV, 32237, Oct. 6, 1905.

74 S. P. A., XXXV, 32239, Oct. 6, 1905.

75 S. P. A., XXXV, 32319, Nov. 28, 1905.

76 S. P. A., XXXV, 32458, Nov. 30, 1905.

vote with their own nationality and not be subjected to onerous domiciliary rules.[77] The Jewish Nationalist deputy from Bukovina, Straucher, asked that the requirements remain at six months,[78] while the Independent Socialist from Lemberg, Breiter, indignantly denounced the rumored Christian Socialist demand for a five-year requirement. In a business age, very few persons died where they were born and travel was no longer rare, said Breiter. Even a two-year requirement would be senseless.[79] Ofner could understand why commune or diet elections required domicile provisions, but imperial citizenship should be ample proof of the right to vote in national elections. A residence requirement was only a subterfuge being used by politicians who hope to sabotage the entire reform; as proof, he pointed out that no one had dared to criticize openly the maximum requirement of six months in the reform of 1896.[80]

The definitive electoral program introduced in February, 1906 specified a one-year domicile for all potential voters. Gautsch again declared that his motive was the stabilization of the relationships of the nationalities, and, despite a few criticisms, his recommendation remained intact in the final reform. Richard Weiskirchner, speaking for the Christian Socialists, expressed a wish for a longer term of residence,[81] but his colleagues did not press the issue. They did refuse to consider modifications of the one-year requirement, which were urged anew by Adler and Klofáč, the Czech National Socialist. The Social Democratic leader predicted that 6 per cent of all Austrian laborers would be disfranchised by a ruling that the German Empire and other countries disdained.[82] Klofáč argued that the domiciliation clause would be particu-

77 S. P. A., XXXV, 32509-10, Dec. 1, 1905.

78 S. P. A., XXXVI, 32568, Dec. 4, 1905.

79 S. P. A., XXXVI, 32594, Dec. 5, 1905.

80 S. P. A., XXXVI, 32617-18, Dec. 5, 1905.

81 S. P. A., XXXVIII, 34883, Mar. 8, 1906.

82 S. P. A., XXXVIII, 34986, Mar. 9, 1906.

larly injurious to Czech labor, and he assailed Adler for betraying labor by a general acceptance of Gautsch's plan.[83]

The question of a domiciliary requirement reappeared briefly in the autumn sessions of the electoral committee of the Lower House. Once again, the Social Democrats and the Czech National Socialists, through their respective spokemen, Adler and Choc, vigorously condemned the one-year residence requirement. The former moved that all domiciliary requirements be abolished, declaring that labor had already surrendered too much for the sake of reform. He estimated that 9.6 per cent of all Viennese men between the ages of twenty-four and thirty would be deprived of the vote should the ministry's formula be adopted. However, in case his motion were defeated, he also moved that voters be permitted to cast their ballots in their electoral district rather than in their commune, or, if their commune was divided into several electoral districts, to cast their ballots in any one of these electoral districts. This plan, of course, would have helped migrant laborers who were unable to be in their own particular commune on election-day.[84] The Minister of the Interior, Bienerth, refused to consent to either plan, and Adler's motions were defeated.

Baron Oskar Parish asked that the ministry clarify the phrasing of the proposed Article 7 of the Fundamental Law on Imperial Representation so that candidates for the Lower House clearly would be excused from domiciliary provisions.[85] A spokesman for the ministry, Haerdtl, declared that a one-year domicile was a stipulation for active rather than passive suffrage, and that, of course, no such requirement would interfere with the eligibility of a prospective deputy.[86] Parish, nevertheless, moved the addition of a phrase which left no loophole for misunderstandings, and his proposal was agreed to by

83 S. P. A., XXXVIII, 35180-1, Mar. 14, 1906.

84 Beilagen, pp. 436-8, Sept. 13, 1906.

85 Beilagen, p. 431, Sept. 12, 1906.

86 Beilagen, pp. 431-2, Sept. 12, 1906.

the ministry and accepted by the committee. Deputy Kaiser also asked for a definition of the term " *Wohnsitz* " (domicile) and suggested that the definition employed in Article 66 of the Law of August 1, 1895 (*Jurisdiktionsnorm*), be specified. Bienerth agreed, and domicile was accordingly defined: " A person's domicile is established at the place in which he has settled himself with the purpose, demonstrable or circumstantially deduced, of making his permanent abode there." Kaiser also suggested that mayors be ordered to make up a list every January 1 of all men who had resided in their districts for at least one year; elections, according to Kaiser, were never announced far enough ahead of time to eliminate a great deal of confusion about eligibility.[87] Bienerth saw little value in this proposal, for the suggested article specified a domicile of one year prior to the announcement of elections. Dr. Pergelt then suggested that the proposed article require that voters have an established domicile dating from the first of January of the year preceding the announcement of elections, but this unsubtle attempt to extend the period of domicile was rejected by Bienerth and the committee.[88] Pergelt also asked if a voter just released from military service would be forced to reside a full year in his own locality before being able to vote. Bienerth replied that a soldier's domicile was his "station "; in order to vote, a soldier just released from service would have to remain at his last station. After all, said Bienerth, circumstances always deprived some persons temporarily of the right to vote.[89]

On September 13, 1906, the committee decided to prescribe that every male citizen, otherwise eligible to vote, be a resident of a commune in which the election was to take place at least one year before the announcement of the election. More explicit directions as to how the vote was to be exercised were

87 *Beilagen*, p. 434, Sept. 13, 1906.

88 *Beilagen*, p. 439, Sept. 13, 1906.

89 *Beilagen*, p. 441, Sept. 13, 1906.

incorporated into Article 6 of the proposed new Election Law of the Reichsrat, which was discussed briefly on September 19, 1906. According to the phraseology adopted, a voter who had several residences was to vote in the district in which he held a public office; failing this, he was to vote in the district in which he plied his trade or practised his profession; failing this, he was to vote in the district in which he had his principal residence (*Hauptwohnsitz*) during the specified one-year period. Should no decision in accordance with the above provisions be possible, then the voter was to be free to decide in which district he would vote.[90]

The Upper House made no effort to modify the decision reached by the electoral committee of the Lower House concerning residence requirements, and the one-year rule became part of the general reform of 1907.

VOCATIONAL REPRESENTATION

The idea of vocational representation in the Austrian legislative bodies, as a partial substitute for the doomed system of representation of interests by curias, figured briefly in the speeches of a few of the enemies of unrestricted universal suffrage. The defenders of the *status quo* in both houses expended most of their influence and energy in championing plural suffrage, but Plener, in the Upper House, and Sylva-Tarouca, in the Lower House, suggested vocational representation as a fair and "modern" means of recognizing the disparate economic conditions existing in Austria. This device was nothing new in Austrian political discussions, for it had been warmly espoused by Vogelsang, the recognized leader of Catholic Socialism in the last decades of the nineteenth century, some of whose ideas, at times mangled, were popularized by the Christian Socialists. Moreover, Hohenwart, leader of the Conservatives and Clericals in the Lower House in the 1890's, had

90 The debate on Article 6 of the Election Law of the Reichsrat is to be found, *Beilagen*, pp. 474-77, Sept. 19, 1906.

published an elaborate scheme of vocational representation in the *Vaterland* in 1895, but he eventually agreed to the fifth curia reform in the following year. The recurrence of the issue in 1905-1906 indicated that the issue, though not dead, was incapable of arousing much enthusiasm.

Baron Plener, during the debates on electoral reform in 1891, had suggested that a labor curia be created, consisting of twenty-seven chambers which would elect nine deputies. Qualifications for voting in the new curia, which was to be added to the four already in existence, were to be Austrian citizenship, knowledge of reading and writing, a two-year domicile, membership in a sickness fund, and the attainment of the age of twenty-four. Two years later, his plan was expanded by Dr. Josef Baernreither and introduced in parliament under the auspices of the United German Left; the labor curia, under this plan, was to control twenty seats. Plener's name thereafter was linked with the concept of a separate labor curia, and in December, 1905, he again referred to his scheme. He agreed that he was not opposed to a considerable extension of the franchise, as long at it did not threaten the German position in Austria. Industrial laborers, he was sure, were responsible for most of the agitation which had conquered Gautsch; might it not be well to create a professional organization of these laborers and grant them the franchise on the basis of membership in sickness funds? Plural suffrage, to his mind, hardly seemed a more fortunate solution.[91] Plener's renewed interest in a labor curia aroused sharp criticism in the Lower House. Had Baron Plener, once noted for his active political sense, been overwhelmed by the mustiness of decay in the Upper House, asked Šuklje. It would seem so, when one considered how unpopular the idea of a labor curia was among laborers.[92] Plener's halfhearted suggestion received no more attention, nor did Plener make any effort to revive it.

91 *S. P. H.*, p. 11133, Dec. 2, 1905.

92 *S. P. A.*, XXXVI, 32556-7, Dec. 4, 1905.

Partial utilization of the vocational scheme for selecting members of parliament was recommended in October, 1905, by the Pan-German Stein who desired that half of the mandates in the new parliament go to the Germans. The other half would be selected by vocational or professional bodies. The Pan-Germans, he declared, fully favored universal suffrage, but they were insistent that the German position in Austria be safeguarded at the same time.[93] For entirely different reasons, Count Dzieduszycki suggested a partial acceptance of vocational representation. Let half of the members of the new house be elected by the fifth curia, he said; the other half could be elected by the diets from four professional corporations representing agriculture, industry, commerce, and labor. The Polish leader, of course, desired a return to indirect elections by the diets and was willing to compromise his ambitions by a reference to professional representation. He did not mention the latter part of his plan again in the debates.[94] Both Stein and Dzieduszycki were masking their real objectives with a tongue-in-cheek advocacy of vocational representation.

Count Sylva-Tarouca, representative of the Bohemian landowners, made the most cogent and sincere plea for a trial of vocational representation in the Lower House on March 9, 1906, in an address which was one of the most profound delivered by an avowed opponent of universal equal suffrage. Recalling Hohenwart's recommendations of the year 1895, Sylva-Tarouca declared that the Conservatives of Austria still maintained that the only just plan for Austria was representation of interests on the basis of universal suffrage, and he reminded the Christian Socialists that they repeatedly had joined with the Conservatives in calling for professional representation. There existed in the empire several professional corporations which could be utilized in such a plan-lawyers, doctors, notaries, men in trade and commerce. Agricultural associations

93 S. P. A., XXXV, 32249, Oct. 6, 1905.

94 S. P. A., XXXVI, 32573-4, Dec. 4, 1905.

had representatives in the diets, and industrial associations would undoubtedly prosper under such a system, once their bureaucratic officials were eased out of office. As for organized labor, it had developed independently in answer to the organization of large industry and trade in cartels, syndicates, and trusts, all of which were harmful to the common weal. The state should take the greatest interest in guaranteeing freedom, stability, and security to the productive classes, primarily, the laboring classes. The worker should not be abandoned to hunger and suffering but should be bound more and more by enlightened state action to an interest in the state. A strong state, depending on a strong army and navy, is responsible for industrial prosperity; the welfare of the worker depends on industrial prosperity. If the laborer is protected by the state and guaranteed a decent living, he will soon see the need for a strong army and navy. Gautsch's plan stressed the need for respecting nationalistic impulses in Austria; it would be far better to realize that the people are also differentiated economically. Gautsch had said that a good electoral reform would result in a system of representation that might be compared to a photograph of the state and its peoples. Sylva-Tarouca, looking at Gautsch's version of reform, remarked that the latter seemed to be a rather unfortunate amateur photographer. As a fly-by-night craftsman, his plans had the advantage of cheapness but lacked beauty and an approximation of reality. For the Bohemian count, reality was representation of interests through professional groups; Gautsch's plans were cheap because they flattered the nationalistic impulses which had wellnigh wrecked the empire. In the future, parliament should concern itself with the great economic and social questions of the day. The question of a Gymnasium or of the lingual abilities of a subordinate official should no longer be permitted to create a state crisis.[95]

Gautsch replied to Sylva-Tarouca's challenge in debate a few days later with the statement that all classes and vocations

95 S. P. A., XXXVIII, 34979-84, Mar. 9, 1906.

were not organized and that many individuals could not be embraced in such a plan. Law-makers would be at a loss to decide the organization of the empire in such a scheme. The parliamentary order of the day would be filled with continual complaints and motions for new regulations. Gautsch agreed that professional representation would be excellent in urban representative bodies, but not in the imperial legislature.[96] Sylva-Tarouca's speech received high praise from several deputies who did not agree at all with his reasoning but who expressed admiration for a conservative opponent who had the courage to offer a constructive alternate plan. Dr. Lecher tempered his praise with the dry remark that Sylva-Tarouca had practically admitted the absence of professional organizations in Austria; consequently, the conservative landowners would be compelled to accept universal suffrage, *faute de mieux*. The Bohemian count, continued Lecher, had blamed the government and the bureaucracy for this situation, whereas in reality the institution of capitalism was the cause. Even a high-born aristocrat was an industrialist or a member of a cartel, dependent on stocks and bonds and owing his wealth to the labor of the masses. The " professional " aristocrat of the old days would continue to be pushed into the background by the new " capitalistic " aristocrats.[97] Another objection to Sylva-Tarouca's plan came from Dr. Ebenhoch, who was in the tradition of Vogelsang and Catholic Socialism.[98] For practical reasons, explained Ebenhoch, he could not support a franchise based on professional representation. In Upper Austria the existing associations were exclusively professional and nonpartisan; they would be ruined if drawn into political activity.

96 *S. P. A.*, XXXVIII, 35141-2, Mar. 14, 1906.

97 *S. P. A.*, XXXVIII, 35272, Mar. 15, 1906.

98 For Vogelsang, see Joseph Schwalber, *Vogelsang und die moderne christlich-soziale Politik* (Munich, 1927) and Karl Huemmer, *Der ständische Gedanke in der katholisch-sozialen Literatur des 19. Jahrhunderts* (Würzburg, 1927), pp. 84-105.

The connection of the chambers of commerce in Austria with politics, for example, had not worked out to the advantage of the chambers.[99]

In the sessions of the electoral committee of the Lower House, Gessmann reiterated Ebenhoch's belief that professional representation had much in its favor but that practical requirements made other decisions imperative.[100] The Pan-Germans again moved the adoption of their scheme for a parliament partially elected by vocational bodies, but the " conservatives " on the committee made no effort to implement Sylva-Tarouca's suggestions. The latter expressed his regret at the committee's failure to respect the economic structure of Austria during the second reading of the committee's report, but his brief reference eloquently bespoke the general lack of interest in vocational representation.[101] The Upper House had practically ignored the issue, the ministry had rejected it, and even Sylva-Tarouca finally abandoned it in favor of a demand for far-reaching provincial autonomy.

PROPORTIONAL SUFFRAGE

Opponents of universal equal suffrage attempted to modify Gautsch's project by means of plural suffrage, residence requirements, and, to a certain extent, by recommendations of vocational representation. At the same time, deputies who desired no restrictions whatsoever on universal equal suffrage were advocating proportional suffrage, woman suffrage, a reduction in the age of qualification, and a modification of the rules which disfranchised persons who were dependent upon public charity.

Proportional suffrage would have meant that representation in the Lower House was to be based upon the grand totals of votes received by every party in Austria. Such a device theo-

99 *S. P. A.*, XXXIX, 35590-1, Mar. 22, 1906.

100 *Beilagen*, p. 195, Mar. 29, 1906.

101 *S. P. A.*, XLIII, 39561-2, Nov. 7, 1906.

retically would have ensured a definite Slav control of the Lower House, yet the Slavic deputies in the debates ignored the entire issue. On November 28, 1905, Gautsch had promised that plural and proportional franchise would be given careful consideration, but warned that the latter was successful in other countries only as a result of safeguards that were incompatible with Austrian complexities. Moreover, a proportional system entailed so many technical difficulties that it was justly termed a good device for mathematicians, a poor one for political leaders. The Minister-President was of the opinion that electoral reform should guarantee every man an uncomplicated, intelligible franchise which could be exercised with the minimum of administrative interference. Therefore, the ministry rejected the *principle* of proportional suffrage but promised to protect wherever possible minorities who had a just claim for greater representation.[102] Viktor Adler warmly greeted Gautsch's promise to look into the matter of proportional suffrage; in Lower Austria, said Adler, the Social Democrats controlled about 40 per cent of all of the votes and, under a proportional system, would increase their mandates appreciably. Adler then admitted that the system would hardly work everywhere in Austria, since it was a contradiction of the idea of small, nationally compact districts advanced by Gautsch.[103] Noske, the Progressive deputy from Vienna, shared Adler's enthusiasm for proportional suffrage in nationally compact areas; he felt that the device would protect minority parties from electoral terrorism, which had been used by the Christian Socialists, for instance, against the middle-class Liberals and the Social Democrats in Vienna. Proportional suffrage undoubtedly was the electoral system of the future, but even the Social Democrats should give the ministry adequate time to study the impact of such a system on all of Austria.[104]

102 *S. P. A.*, XXXV, 32320.

103 *S. P. A.*, XXXV, 32456, Nov. 30, 1905.

104 *S. P. A.*, XXXV, 32518-20, Dec. 1, 1905.

Gautsch's plan of February, 1906 ignored proportional suffrage as such, and the omission excited no comment pro or con in the debates which followed. The reason for this singular lack of interest may be gleaned from the discussions of plural suffrage carried on in the electoral committee of the Lower House seven months later. Committee members who fought plural suffrage reminded Tollinger and his allies that the highly touted Belgian system of plural suffrage was modified by proportional suffrage, which gave all classes representation. Plural suffrage without proportional suffrage would be well-nigh impossible in Austria. Tavčar, who readily confessed his desire to scuttle reform on any pretense, declared that he would vote for plural suffrage because he knew it would hasten the coming of proportional suffrage! [105] German and Slav moderates had rallied behind Gautsch in February, 1906, when the latter implicitly rejected plural suffrage. In return for Gautsch's refusal to recommend pluralism, the moderates had fulfilled their part of what might be called an informal bargain by ceasing to refer to proportional suffrage. Once Tollinger's pluralistic schemes had been rejected, the issue of proportional suffrage again was discarded.

Woman Suffrage

Woman suffrage received a minimum of attention in the general discussions of the nature of electoral reform in 1906. During the first reading of Gautsch's proposals in March, 1906, the Czech National Socialist Klofáč announced that his party would move that women be given the right to vote, if only for theoretical reasons,[106] and his party colleague Choc made the necessary motion in the electoral committee on September 12, 1906. The party felt that women were just as important as men in modern life, said Choc, and Czech women especially protested being placed in the same category as

105 *Beilagen*, p. 584, Oct. 3, 1906.

106 S. P. A., XXXVIII, 35183-4, Mar. 14, 1906.

criminals and paupers.[107] A Young Czech member of the committee, Hrubý, had no hope of securing suffrage for women, but he did protest that the new proposals had failed to consider the fact that some women had voted under the old system.[108] To remedy this injustice, he moved that women who had an income of 1000 kronen or who independently carried on a business or ran a farm be given a vote.[109]

Both motions aroused little approbation. Kaiser saw no good in dragging politics into family life; the further participation of women in all non-family pursuits should be limited as much as possible, not encouraged. He would be willing to safeguard the rights of women who had voted under the old system, but he would not accept the 1000 kronen proposal. The reform simply made no provision for such a census of incomes.[110] Speaking for the ministry, Bienerth was of the opinion that universal equal suffrage did not necessarily mean female suffrage. Hrubý's plan did have a certain justification, but it would be wrong to create financial stipulations for women when none existed for men under the new reform.[111] Adler, on the other hand, was willing to vote for Choc's motion, which he was sure would not pass, but rejected Hrubý's plan, which he asserted would favor rich women at the expense of thousands of working women.[112]

When Choc continued to press for woman suffrage, which he was careful to distinguish from the emancipation of women, Bienerth impatiently refused to review all of the arguments against Choc's plan. Some supporters of female suffrage, warned Bienerth, should realize that active voting rights for

107 *Beilagen*, p. 431.

108 In some cases women landowners had been permitted to vote for deputies representing the large landowners' curia in Austria.

109 *Beilagen*, p. 433, Sept. 13, 1906.

110 *Beilagen*, p. 434, Sept. 13, 1906.

111 *Beilagen*, pp. 435-6, Sept. 13, 1906.

112 *Beilagen*, p. 436, Sept. 13, 1906.

women would also mean their eligibility for public office.[113] On September 13 both of the motions in behalf of woman suffrage were defeated. In the second reading of the committee's recommendations in the Lower House, Adler promised that his party would continue to fight for women's rights, though he knew that the time for granting such rights had not yet come in Austria.[114]

AGE REQUIREMENTS

Viktor Adler carried on a single-handed fight to reduce the age required of male voters from twenty-four to twenty or twenty-one. The fifth curia reform had specified that voters be at least twenty-four years old, and the deputies in the Lower House evidently saw no reason to change the age qualification. Adler maintained that laborers " came of age " at seventeen or eighteen and often died early in life; as far as efficiency and wage-earning capacity were concerned, they were often "dead" at thirty-five. The average laborer was liable for military duty when he reached the age of twenty-one; at that age he knew more of the problems of earthly existence than members of the well-to-do class ever knew.[115] In the committee meeting of September 13, 1906, Adler repeated his view that twenty-one should be the minimum age for voters but refused to fight any longer what was obviously a hopeless battle.[116]

DISFRANCHISEMENT OF PERSONS DEPENDENT ON CHARITY OR WITH POLICE RECORDS

Article 8 of the new Election Law of the Reichsrat provided for the disfranchisement of persons who had been condemned

113 *Beilagen*, p. 438, Sept. 13, 1906.

114 *S. P. A.*, XLIII, 39598, Nov. 8, 1906. Earlier, Adler had argued that women were subject to a "blood tax" which really cost them more pain than men's services in war, namely, the pangs of giving birth to offspring. Viktor Adler, *Das allgemeine, gleiche und direkte Wahlrecht und das Wahlunrecht in Österreich* (Vienna, 1893), p. 35.

115 *S. P. A.*, XXXVIII, 34985, Mar. 9, 1906. Adler used precisely the same arguments in behalf of young workers and peasants a decade earlier, *op. cit.*, pp. 33-34.

116 *Beilagen*, p. 436.

for criminal offenses, who had been bankrupt, who enjoyed public charity, etc. Several deputies moved that the restrictions recommended by the ministry be modified. Choc, the Czech National Socialist, wanted to reduce the period of disfranchisement of men who had served in prison or who had been under police surveillance, while Adler argued that the law was too general in its terms and would deprive disabled and infirm workers of the right to vote. In a sense, both deputies were seeking a liberal formula to protect political offenders and unfortunate laborers, who normally would vote for "radical" parties, but their efforts were defeated by the committee.[117] Moreover, the Lower House, in considering Article 8 during the final debates on reform, also disfranchised habitual drunkards; this amendment might be considered another check, admittedly trifling, on the laboring class, which usually felt the brunt of legislation aimed at alcoholics.

Every single modification of the ministerial program of reform recommended by various "radical" deputies failed to pass. It should be emphasized, of course, that the advocates of these modifications fully realized the hopelessness of their position and that they devoted a far greater amount of time in fighting plural suffrage and other plans submitted by "conservative" deputies. Very sensibly, the "radicals" were determined to sacrifice many of their own cherished projects for the sake of a reasonable facsimile of universal manhood suffrage in Austria, and in this endeavor Adler and his colleagues were generally successful.

THE EFFECT OF UNIVERSAL MANHOOD SUFFRAGE UPON NATIONALISTIC STRIFE IN AUSTRIA

The establishment of dualism in the Habsburg monarchy in 1867 had been a violent blow to the hopes of many Slavs and some Germans who desired a federal constitution for the em-

---

117 For the committee's discussion of Article 8, *Beilagen*, pp. 478-80, Sept. 19, 1906.

pire. In effect, dualism surrendered to the Hungarian magnates all of the non-Magyar nationalities in Hungary and left the Germans in strategic possession of the Austrian half of the monarchy. Prior to the year 1905, there had been ministries which had attempted federalistic schemes in Austria, with no concrete results, and there had been ministers like Taaffe, who blunted the edge of Slavic discontent by concessions which never really threatened the centralization of power in Vienna. It is noteworthy that Taaffe's fall from power in 1893 was caused to a large extent by his electoral reform bill, which a majority of the Germans deemed to be an opening wedge for a reconstitution of the empire along federalistic lines. In 1905-06, the struggle between federalists and centralists was renewed, though its manifestations were sometimes curiously blurred.

The key to a clarification of this confused struggle is found in the obvious statement that the federalists were not united in desiring a greater degree of democracy for Austria nor were the centralists united in opposing an electoral reform which some of them considered the beginning of the end of the Habsburg monarchy. Practically all of the Polish and Czech representatives of the great landowners were convinced federalists, but they had little good to say for universal manhood suffrage. On the other hand, no party had profited more in the past from centralization than the German Liberals, whose successors generally were willing to accept universal manhood suffrage. The Social Democrats, who labored mightily to secure reform, might talk and plan of cultural autonomy for all nationalities and plead for the creation of a " people's state " in Austria; essentially they were centralists, depending upon a strong administration in Vienna to bring to life their dreams of a socialist state, and their efforts in behalf of universal suffrage are to be interpreted as hopes for a strong central government democratically controlled. No group was more conscious of the necessity for federalism than the Young Czechs under Kramář; no group was more intent on preserving the loyalties and the

institutions of the venerable empire than the Christian Socialists. Yet both groups joined forces to support Gautsch's plans
for electoral reform for the same reason, namely, the hope that
reform would be a basis for intelligent understanding among
all of the nationalities of Austria. The first great problem facing the political leaders of Austria in 1905-06 had been the
definition of universal equal suffrage; the second great problem was the search for a compromise of nationalistic differences
by means of electoral reform.

Many earnest leaders in Austria were not at all convinced
that electoral reform would smooth the way for a settlement
of the acrimonious bickering of the nationalities. Gautsch himself, in September, 1905, had tried to avoid demands for electoral reform by asserting that far-reaching changes in suffrage
requirements could only come after the historical rights of all
nationalities had been effectively safeguarded.[118] Replying to
critics in the debate which followed, he refused to change his
stand as long as he received from his critics no satisfactory
explanation of the effect which universal suffrage would have
on national minorities. Some deputies might say that national
frictions would disappear once universal suffrage had been put
into operation, but Gautsch declared that he had no confidence
in such optimistic beliefs. It was up to tne ministry to see to it
that the historical importance of the Austrian nationalities
was not subjected to the mechanical dictatorship of mere
numbers.[119]

Only a few deputies in these early debates agreed completely
with Gautsch that a settlement of nationalistic problems was a
prerequisite of electoral reform. Many of the German deputies
warned that any reform would have to protect all of the nationalities of Austria and expressed little hope that reform
would secure good relations among the nationalities. Lecher,
for instance, was pessimistic about the chances of achieving

118 S. P. A., XXXV, 31422, Sept. 26, 1905.
119 S. P. A., XXXV, 32239-40, Oct. 6, 1905.

peace among the nationalities, which he considered to be a utopian dream which ignored the sinful nature of mankind. Though national peace was impossible, argued Lecher, it was absurd to say that electoral reform *ipso facto* was impossible or undesirable.[120]

Gautsch's reversal of policy in November, 1905, was accomplished with a minimum of respect for his previous demand for an honest settlement of nationalistic strife. The Minister-President emphasized the ministry's complete unwillingness to accept population figures as the sole basis of representation, of course, as he had done in the previous month, and promised that justice would be done all of the nationalities. Significantly, he did not attempt to predict that the proposed reform would necessarily ameliorate the antagonisms among the nationalities. A few deputies did make such a prediction, but the Young Czech Herold [121] and Ofner asked [122] that no one expect electoral reform to accomplish a lasting settlement of nationalistic issues. Electoral reform was not made for such a use, said Herold, while Ofner warned that the real problem of securing a greater degree of democracy for all would only be weakened by attaching nationalistic programs to it. Nevertheless, some Czech National Socialist deputies took advantage of the discussions of reform to campaign for a federalization of Austria. They were alarmed by the thought of a topheavy centralized parliament without constitutional decentralization. One of them, Baxa, demanded that dualism be replaced by trialism; the new empire would include the provinces of the throne of Hungary and Croatia, the kingdom and dependent provinces of Bohemia, and the so-called patrimony of the Habsburgs, including Galicia, which would have special status.[123]

120 *S. P. A.*, XXXV, 32255, Oct. 6, 1905.
121 *S. P. A.*, XXXV, 32502, Dec. 1, 1905.
122 *S. P. A.*, XXXVI, 32619, Dec. 5, 1905.
123 *S. P. A.*, XXXIX, 35579, Mar. 22, 1906.

Extension of the Competence of the Provincial Diets

No major figure among the autonomists and federalists, however, advanced concrete proposals which would have upset the Ausgleich of 1867 as such. Nevertheless, the autonomists did make a determined effort to extend the competence of the provincial diets, with moderate success. The Polish Club took the lead in demanding a rephrasing of Article 12 of the Fundamental Law on Imperial Representation, which listed the powers of the provincial diets, and its activity was aided in somewhat lukewarm fashion by the Young Czechs, German Clericals, and South Slav groups. These half-hearted allies of the Polish Club had a well-founded fear that some of the members of the Polish Club would deliberately raise the issue of the competence of diets merely to delay reform. In the light of these fears, one can comprehend Ebenhoch's approval " in principle " of an extension of the competence of diets [124] and Šusteršič's reassurance that a truly popularly elected Lower House would turn over to the diets their proper spheres of competence.[125]

Article 12 of the Fundamental Law on Imperial Representation provided that: " All matters of legislation, other than those expressly reserved to the Reichsrat by the present law, belong within the power of the Provincial Diets of the kingdoms and countries represented in the Reichsrat and are constitutionally regulated by such Diets." [126] The matters of legislation expressly reserved to the Reichsrat left little to the competence of the diets; the competence of the Reichsrat extended to commercial treaties, certain types of political treaties, the regulation and financing of military affairs, the budget, the granting of taxes and the imposition of customs duties, the regulation of the monetary system, banks of issue, telegraphs,

---

124 *S. P. A.*, XXXIX, 35590, Mar. 22, 1906.

125 *S. P. A.*, XXXIX, 35428, Mar. 20, 1906.

126 Dodd, *op. cit.*, I, 80.

posts, railways, and navigation, legislation concerning banks, credit, patents, weights and measures, public health, citizenship, passports, census, confessional relations, the rights of assembly, association, and of the press, the educational system, etc.[127] The non-German nationalities had consistently fought for a modification of the Reichsrat's power over provincial schools, in determining the languages to be used in judicial and administrative work, and in controlling the universities, finances, and taxation. Most of the obstruction of the years before 1905 could be traced to disputes of this nature, particularly in the fields of education and administrative languages.

In the second meeting of the electoral committee of the Lower House, Dr. Stanislaus Starzyński, of the Polish Club, announced that his group would vote against electoral reform unless diets were given a clear-cut definition of their competence and unless Galicia were given " the representation due her " in the apportionment of mandates.[128] The first demand was put aside until the autumn sessions of the committee, when Starzyński moved that a subcommittee of nine be appointed to study and report on changes in Articles 11 and 12 which would secure once and for all the proper amount of competence due the diets. The spokesman for the Polish Club argued that provincial autonomy had been violated in the past by the central parliament or by decrees issued by various ministries, thanks to the indefinite wording of Articles 11 and 12. Moreover, matters which aroused nationalistic passions could be settled much more calmly in the diets, which also should be entrusted with the many problems arising from the new social and industrial developments in Austria.[129] Baron Beck immediately agreed with Starzyński that conflicts over the interpreta-

127 For the text of Article 11 of the Fundamental Law on Imperial Representation, which lists the powers of the Reichsrat, Dodd, *op. cit.*, I, pp. 78-79.

128 *Beilagen*, pp. 192-3, Mar. 29, 1906.

129 *Beilagen*, pp. 446-7, Sept. 14, 1906.

tions of Articles 11 and 12 should be eliminated. He acutely remembered applications of "centralist" laws which simply provoked a degree of agitation that rendered impotent all laws, imperial and provincial. Beck hinted that the proposed subcommittee would do well to confine its activities to a search for clarity, however, and not attempt any destruction of valid imperial rights.[130]

Starzyński's motion excited a controversy which took up the entire session of September 14, 1906. Kramář was of the opinion that provincial autonomy was not to be secured by the labors proposed for the subcommittee, as long as officials in the provinces were not responsible to the diets. However, he suggested that the subcommittee be formed and given fourteen days' leave of absence to study the problem. The German deputies, save for Stürgkh, were uniformly opposed to the motion; they argued that the electoral committee had no competence to deal with a constitutional question and implied that their colleague Stürgkh favored the motion only to delay the reform. Stein openly accused Beck of supporting Starzyński and the Poles in payment of the Polish consent of electoral reform. Beck vigorously denied Stein's accusation and claimed that he simply believed that some clarification of Articles 11 and 12 should be attempted. The Christian Socialists refrained from comment until Starzyński bluntly stated that the Poles wanted an extension of the power of the diets in such matters as school regulations, language requirements in the lower and middle strata of the bureaucracy, and provincial finances. Gessmann, speaking for the Christian Socialists, quickly expressed opposition to these frankly autonomist views and moved that the subcommittee's jurisdiction be limited to a discussion of ironing out conflicts between the Reichsrat and the diets in provincial cultural affairs. Even Stürgkh refused to approve in any way Starzyński's new tack, while the Ruthene representative Wassilkó declared that his people preferred to limit the compe-

130 *Beilagen*, pp. 448-9, Sept. 14, 1906.

tence of the Galician diet as long as they were not guaranteed fair treatment at the hands of the Poles. Several German deputies intemperately accused Kramář of conniving with the Poles, but the astute Young Czech firmly denied any intention of attempting a full-scale discussion of autonomy.

By a roll-call vote, Starzyński's plan for a nine-man subcommittee to clarify Articles 11 and 12 were accepted, twenty-one to nineteen. In opposition were eighteen German deputies and one Ruthene deputy. The motion was carried by the votes of some five German deputies representing the landowners' curia or rural communes in the " Princely County " of Tyrol, an area which had often exhibited autonomist tendencies. Tollinger, who was to rely heavily on Polish votes for his scheme of plural suffrage, was one of the Tyrolese deputies voting for Starzyński's motion. The Czechs, Italians, and the Rumanian representative also supported the Poles, but the Southern Slavs did not vote either way.[131]

The subcommittee held two meetings later in September, 1906, and from these meetings emerged, as the somewhat bemused reporter, Grabmayr, put it, no less than five proposed solutions to the problem. The Conservative deputy of the Bohemian landowners' curia, Sajfert, recommended sweeping changes which would give the diets the right to pass laws on agricultural and forestry affairs, the right to control primary and secondary school systems, and the right to approve the organization and personnel of the provincial administration. In addition, Sajfert planned to turn over to the diets the power of making all necessary language regulations for the administrative and court systems.[132] The second solution, proposed by Starzyński, called for additional paragraphs in Article 12 which would stand as an authentic interpretation of the competence granted the diets on one hand and the competence granted

131 The discussion of Starzyński's motion and the vote which followed is found in the *Beilagen*, pp. 449-62, Sept. 14, 1906.

132 Text of Sajfert's motion, *Beilagen*, pp. 517-18, Sept. 24, 1906.

the central parliament on the other hand.[133] Tollinger supplied the third solution. He suggested that the executive committees of the provinces be asked to supply necessary data on conflicts of competence and that the ministry, on the basis of the information supplied, introduce bills in the Reichsrat to eliminate the confusion.[134] The last two solutions were derived principally from discussion within the subcommittee. Grabmayr dutifully reported that there was a fourth opinion to the effect that the committee should only issue a general resolution clarifying the doubts aroused by questions of competence. The fifth solution was almost wholly negative. Its supporters felt that no decisions of any sort should be made by the committee, lest the chances of a real extension of autonomy be impaired.

Grabmayr added his own personal views to his report. He said that he believed that Sajfert's motion was merely *pour l'honneur du drapeau;* he dreaded the results of a discussion of this plan for far-reaching autonomy in the already overheated committee. Starzyński's plan seemed to be far more moderate, since it did not change any of the powers expressly granted the Reichsrat in Article 11.[135] Dr. Otto Mettal vigorously denied that his colleague, Sajfert, had intended his motion to be an empty gesture; for decades, the conservative landowners had tried to endure the endless confusion in provincial finances, caused by the erroneous grant of competence to the Reichsrat. His group's continuing aim would be an administration free of pressure in every province.[136]

Speaking for the ministry, Bienerth, as was anticipated, expressed approval of Starzyński's plan, which had been modified somewhat when presented to the full committee. With no more ado, the committee accepted Starzyński's additional paragraphs for Article 12 by a vote of twenty-two to sixteen. Once again,

133 Text of Starzyński's original motion, *Beilagen*, p. 517, Sept. 24, 1906.

134 *Beilagen*, p. 557, Sept. 26, 1906.

135 Grabmayr's report, *Beilagen*, pp. 703-6, Oct. 26, 1906.

136 *Beilagen*, p. 709, Oct. 26, 1906.

the opposition consisted of Germans assisted by one Ruthene, while the victors included representatives of the Poles, Czechs, Italians, Rumanians, and South Slavs, plus a scattering of Germans.[137]

Starzyński's amendments, which were finally accepted as part of the reform by both houses, specified: (1) that provinces, in regulating affairs clearly within their own competence, could adopt necessary measures in the fields of criminal justice, police justice, and civil law; and (2) that provinces could regulate the organization of public administrative offices which had been created in accordance with the provincial power to organize autonomous administrative departments, even though the activities of such offices were based upon the principles reserved to the Reichsrat by Article 11. The amendments were a slight improvement over the sometimes laconic, sometimes involved phraseology of Article 11; in no sense could they be considered a smashing victory for the autonomists. Provincial control of schools, finances, and less weighty matters was still a dream.

Universal Equal Suffrage in Diet Elections

Autonomists of all shades of opinion were very much interested in the effect which the introduction of universal equal suffrage in parliamentary elections would have upon the methods employed in elections for the provincial diets. The provinces were in no sense bound to follow the example of the central parliament, but conservative and liberal autonomists realized quite well that the example set in Vienna would influence provincial decisions appreciably. Indeed, the diet sessions in all parts of Austria which followed the failure of the motions of urgency in October, 1905, were directly influenced by the discussions held in Vienna. In Salzburg, Carniola, Gorizia, and Dalmatia, the diets voted approval of universal, equal, and direct suffrage. The Silesian diet agreed to the

137 The roll-call vote, *Beilagen*, p. 724, Oct. 29, 1906.

creation of a curia which would embrace all adult males, lowered the tax qualifications in other curias, and instituted secret and direct voting. In Moravia, a similar curia was created for adult males, as part of the great compromise between Czechs and Germans. An extensive electoral reform for Upper Austria was to be prepared by the *Landesausschuss* there, the diet decided, while the Styrian diet voted support, " in principle," of universal suffrage. However, nothing concrete was accomplished by the diets of Galicia, Bohemia, Tyrol, and the Bukovina in their deliberations.[138] With the resumption of the Reichsrat's sessions and Gautsch's decision to sponsor a reform, the question of possible changes in diet elections took on greater significance. In the Lower House, several Czech deputies hopefully predicted that privileged groups in the diets would soon be discarded in favor of universally elected members; reform could not be stopped at the doors of the diet, where the Bohemian people eventually would triumph.

Almost simultaneously, conservative members of the Upper House also were canvassing the possible effects of imperial reform upon the composition of provincial diets. Count Franz Thun, in his caustic comment on Gautsch's change in opinion on electoral reform, declared that the government could not possibly restrain agitation for universal suffrage in all of the provincial capitals. The regime had already revealed its lack of strength in dealing with mobs; how could it push the people away from the doors of the diets?[139] Dr. Mattus, the former Old Czech, was willing to admit the necessity of opening the portals of the diets to those who called themselves the disinherited of the earth, but with the presumption that all important elements of the provincial population were given their due representation in the diets. Persons who had an important place in the province, because of their possessions,

138 Gustav Strakosch-Grassmann, *Das allgemeine Wahlrecht in Österreich seit 1848* (Leipzig and Vienna, 1906), pp. 80-82.

139 *S. P. H.*, p. 1120, Dec. 2, 1905.

their productive activity, their intellectual endeavors, or their contributions to the empire or to their own people, should not be denied an influential position in the diets. Mattus implied, of course, a system of diet election similar to that prescribed by the electoral reform of 1896.[140]

The continuation of the debates in both houses and in the respective electoral committee and special commission during the year 1906 revealed similar expressions of sentiment. Dr. Karl von Grabmayr, in the Lower House, attacked the idea that equal suffrage could be kept from the diets. Simple political logic, aided by the agitation of the Social Democrats, would force its adoption; after the conquest of the diets, the concept of equal suffrage would invade communal elections. Some might agree, continued Grabmayr, that this process of equalization would improve the relations among the nationalities; of less childlike faith, he was of the opinion that the deeper one dug into the strata, the more chauvinism one would extract.[141] In the electoral committee, Stein was equally apprehensive; he refused to assume that universal suffrage would not go into effect for diet and communal elections, with disastrous results for many " communities." [142] During the final debates on electoral reform in the Upper House late in 1906, there were more pessimistic predictions of the fate of the electoral arrangements of the diets.[143] Since neither house of parliament could do anything to freeze or modify the provincial arrangements, the remarks were only of academic interest in

---

140 S. P. H., pp. 1129-30, Dec. 2, 1905.

141 S. P. A., XXXVIII, 34837-9, Mar. 7, 1906. For an appraisal of Grabmayr's attitude toward the reform, see Edmund Benedikt, "Karl von Grabmayr," Neue österreichische Biographie (Vienna, 1923-1935), VI, 95-96.

142 Beilagen, p. 199, Apr. 24, 1906.

143 The predictions were generally unfulfilled. For a description of the methods of voting for the diets of the various crownlands in the years immediately following 1907, see Josef M. Baernreither, Zur böhmischen Frage (Vienna, 1910), pp. 65-66.

that they helped to make up some of the verbal ammunition utilized by the opponents of universal equal suffrage. They also revealed the cleavage existing among the autonomists, some of whom were more interested in the social and economic implications of electoral reform than they were in securing more seats for their particular nationalities.

ELECTORAL REFORM AS A MEANS OF PROTECTING MINORITIES

The protection of minorities in Austria by means of electoral reform was accomplished in a generally satisfactory manner by the electoral committee of the Lower House in its apportionment of mandates and creation of electoral districts. Gautsch originally had recommended the creation of electoral districts as nationally homogeneous as possible, and the modifications of his plan at the hands of his successors and the members of the committee did not violate his principle. Some electoral districts, of course, had larger populations than did others, so that the complaints from various deputies that their own nationalities were cheated of their due representation were valid.

Galicia, however, provided a special problem. Gautsch and his successors could never hope to secure an electoral reform without the support of the powerful Polish Club in the Lower House. For decades, the Ruthenes in Galicia had been the step-children of the Habsburgs; backward and relatively free of the self-esteem developed by full-blown nationalism, they had been easy victims of the Poles, who knew how to bargain effectively with the Habsburgs.[144] In eastern Galicia, predominantly inhabited by Ruthenes, there was a sizeable Polish minority which economically and socially was superior to the Ruthenes. The Polish Club made no attempt to hide its determination to secure favorable treatment of this minority, and the various cabinets readily acceded to the Polish demands.

---

144 See Friedrich F. G. Kleinwaechter, *Der Untergang der oesterreichischungarischen Monarchie* (Leipzig, 1920), pp. 113-15, 176-8, and Paul Samassa, *Der Völkerstreit im Habsburgerstaat* (Leipzig, 1910), pp. 33-34.

Thanks to electoral geometry, Ruthene votes were few in the Lower House and Polish votes were many. Practical politics dictated the results which followed.

According to Gautsch's plan of February, 1906, certain districts in eastern Galicia were to elect two deputies, in contrast to the general rule that every electoral district should choose one deputy. Candidates in these districts were to be considered elected if they received more than one-third of all of the votes cast.[145] With the exception of the Polish Socialist Breiter, the Polish deputies in the Lower House ignored Gautsch's obvious favor and belabored the Minister-President for his failure to grant Galicia a larger number of mandates. The Ruthene spokesman, Romanczuk, was less tendentious in his remarks, but he clearly disapproved of electoral districts which were not ethnically homogeneous. He declared that the system of proportional elections recommended by Gautsch should be practised only in districts which had a minority definitely numbering one-third of the total population of the district, implying that such was not the case in all instances proposed by the ministry.[146] In the electoral committee, another Ruthene deputy, Wassilkó, openly denounced the plan as robbery of Ruthene rights, asserting that it took 65,000 Polish votes to elect a deputy in Galicia, while 114,000 Ruthene votes were necessary to accomplish the same thing.[147] A few weeks prior to Wassilkó's outburst, Gautsch had been forced to resign because of Polish dissatisfaction with the number of mandates assigned to Galicia. The new Minister-President, Hohenlohe, then attempted to appease the Poles by increasing the number of seats falling to Galicia and by modifying the plan for elections in eastern Galicia. The new plan provided that, in districts which elected two deputies, the first mandate would go to the candidate who received an absolute majority of all votes cast;

145 *S. P. A.*, XXXVIII, 34657, Feb. 23, 1906.

146 *S. P. A.*, XXXIX, 35441, Mar. 20, 1906.

147 *Beilagen*, p. 221, May 18, 1906.

the second mandate would fall to the candidate who received more than one-fourth of all of the votes cast.[148] Despite Wassilkó's energetic protests that Hohenlohe's scheme was even more unfair to the Ruthenes than Gautsch's had been, the committee adopted the Hohenlohe plan after lengthy Polish-Ruthene quarreling.[149] A relatively unbiassed critique of this final decision was offered by Dr. Viktor Adler during the second reading of the committee's proposals in November, 1906. The electoral reform as a whole, said Adler, was a liberation of all nationalities in Austria; in details, however, it was not free of violent injustices, particularly those done the Ruthenes. Ruthene party leaders were grieved by these blemishes, but they were not silly or stupid enough to fail to see that the reform was at least a point of departure for a regeneration and political development of their people. At least, the introduction of direct secret voting would eliminate some of the abuses of the heretofore infamous Galician elections.[150]

Undoubtedly the most vulnerable minority in Austria in the first decade of the twentieth century was the Jewish minority. Anti-Semitism of the rankest type had flourished since the disastrous financial panic of 1873, thanks chiefly to the Christian Socialists and some of the Pan-Germans. The Jews, of course, could hardly be called a nationality, for the Zionist movement had not made great progress. Consequently, the various ministries made no conscious effort to treat Austrian Jews as a nationality entitled to a certain number of mandates. Nevertheless, several Jewish deputies emulated their colleagues in proclaiming the number of seats which should be given their co-religionists, while Poles were careful to disclaim as their share of parliamentary power any seats which they expected to fall to Jewish candidates. Dr. Straucher, the avowed Jewish Nationalist deputy from Czernowitz, claimed for the Jews the

148 *Beilagen*, p. 226, May 25, 1906.
149 See below, p. 159.
150 *S. P. A.*, XLIII, 39599-600, Nov. 8, 1906.

rights of a single individual nationality. He declared that the Jews, like the Irish, might use another nationality's language; even so, they formed a distinct people whose rights should not be neglected by the government in planning electoral reform. They realizea their powerlessness and comparative insignificance, but relied on the inscription on the gate of the Kaiserburg: *"Justitia regnorum fundamentum."* [151] After Gautsch's plan for apportionment of mandates was submitted to the Lower House, Straucher again asked that the Jews be treated as a definite national group, not as a religious community. He submitted statistics to the effect that Jews comprised 4.69 per cent of the total Austrian population, urging that special attention be paid to the large number of Jews in Bukovina (13 per cent of the population) and in Galicia (11 per cent of the population). According to the ministerial demarcation of districts, the Jews would control only six or seven seats, where a just system would guarantee them sixteen seats. Straucher asserted that the Jews wished to be recognized as a nationality and represented by men who admitted publicly and manfully their membership in the Jewish community. Such men could be expected to stand up for their persecuted " co-nationals." [152] Another Jewish deputy, Emil Byk, who represented a Galician urban district, maintained that the proportional system of elections in eastern Galicia should be used in all Galician cities so that the Jewish minority could receive representation and protection,[153] but nothing was done to satisfy the wishes of either deputy. The most prominent Jewish deputies in the Lower House, Viktor Adler and Julius Ofner, did not make any mention of the Jewish community; as practising economic radicals,

151 *S. P. A.*, XXXVI, 32568-9, Dec. 4, 1905.

152 *S. P. A.*, XXXVIII, 35108-14, Mar. 13, 1906. Straucher's campaign for a recognition of a Jewish nationality met with ready response from influential Viennese Jews who, though not Zionists, were increasingly fearful of anti-Semitism. Sigmund Mayer, *Die Wiener Juden 1700-1900* (Vienna and Berlin, 1918), p. 482.

153 *Beilagen*, p. 204, Apr. 24, 1906.

they were interested in justice for all laborers, regardless of nationality or religious confession. Despite the lack of concrete proposals in behalf of the Jews, the general debates on the entire subject of reform were conspicuously free of virulent anti-Semitic remarks which were a commonplace a decade earlier. It should be remembered, of course, that the Christian Socialists had become ultra-respectable and that the Pan-Germans were almost entirely consumed by fear of Pan-Slavism.

The common German fear of being swamped by a flood of Slavic deputies has already been touched upon in the discussion of German claims to cultural, and, therefore, political supremacy in Austria.[154] The Pan-Germans were undoubtedly the most frantic prophets of the approaching annihilation of Germanism as a result of electoral reform, but there were many thoughtful and reasonable Germans who shared the same concern for the German position in Austria. Briefly, these deputies reasoned that Gautsch's electoral reform and its modifications, which did nothing really to improve the German position, would reduce the Germans to a minority status in Austria. With such a premise in mind, all were alarmed; some were insistent that Germans be granted full protection of their "rights" before being relegated to a subordinate place in Austrian affairs.

Only the Pan-Germans, however, advanced a definite scheme which theoretically would ensure a continued German predominance in Austria. One of them, Franz Schalk, indicated his party's line of attack during the first reading of Gautsch's proposals, which, he asserted, were a declaration of war upon the Germans. Thanks to Gautsch, continued Schalk, a war to the death between Germans and Slavs had been proclaimed. Austrian foreign policy and the alliance with the German Empire

154 The Czech-German rivalry was the chief cause of German fear. For an admirable survey of the development of this rivalry at the beginning of the twentieth century, see Elizabeth Wiskemann, *Czechs and Germans* (London, New York, and Toronto, 1938), pp. 51-69.

would be nullified by the vengeful Slavs, while Slavic bureau-crats would swarm into areas inhabited by the Germans and lord it over them. Quite probably, a Slavic language would become the required speech in parliament, and the Slavic par-liamentary majority would continually whittle away at the re-maining German mandates. Faced with such tactics, the Ger-mans would be forced to leave the House of Parliament—and the House of Austria. The only hope of retaining German predominance in Austria lay in the granting of special status to Galicia, a step which had nothing to do with federalism, said Schalk, since Austrian Poland had never really belonged to the empire. Influential Polish deputies would be glad to co-operate with the Germans in attaining an objective pleasing to both nationalities: comparative self-government for Galicia and the consequent removal of a large number of Galician deputies from the central parliament. Unless special status were granted, the Pan-Germans would refuse to accept reform.[155]

Just as the Lower House prepared to choose its electoral committee in March, 1906, the two Pan-German fractions, led by Schönerer and Wolf, introduced motions of urgency which aimed at special status for Galicia. The former merely quoted a motion which had been introduced in 1871 by Polish depu-ties, demanding special status for the province; the ministry was expected to follow this old program, in conjunction with the preparation of electoral reform.[156] Wolf's motion, however, was more explicit, listing at length the powers which the Galician diet was to have as a result of special status, and it was signed by several of the leading German Populists.[157] In accordance with parliamentary procedure, debate got under way at once. Gautsch pointed out that Galician deputies had not raised the issue and accused the Pan-Germans of petty party politics. The ministry resolutely refused to surrender the

155 S. P. A., XXXIX, 35430-40, Mar. 20, 1906.
156 S. P. A., XXXIX, 35660-1, Mar. 27, 1906.
157 S. P. A., XXXIX, 35661-2, Mar. 27, 1906.

slightest amount of state unity, continued Gautsch, though he implied that demands for greater autonomy would not be considered as dangerous as demands for special status.[158] The deputies of the Polish Club declared their willingness to vote for the motions of urgency, but their action was undoubtedly inspired by a general hostility to Gautsch's program of reform and by a desire to use all possible means of delay and obstruction.[159] After two days of debate, the motions were voted upon, on March 28, 1906; in favor were 153 deputies, opposed were 147.[160] A two-thirds vote was required for the passage of motions of urgency; consequently, the Pan-German campaign failed for the time being. The results of the vote had little bearing upon the issue of special status for Galicia; no more than thirty deputies sincerely desired the administrative separation of the province from the rest of Austria. Many deputies merely used the motions as a means of expressing their distaste for Gautsch and his version of electoral reform.[161] Nevertheless, at least one sincere friend of reform, the Social Democratic writer Karl Renner was gladdened by the peculiar political configurations caused by the issue. He was doing his best in Austria in 1906 to deflate talk of future Slavic and anti-Slavic blocs in the Lower House, and, in his opinion, the balloting of March 28, 1906, was ample proof of the futility of such talk. No other question was more likely to force Slav against German than the Galician question, thought Renner, yet " Germans voted against Germans, Slavs against Slavs, Galicians against Galicians, even the Poles did not vote uniformly." [162]

158 *S. P. A.*, XXXIX, 35711-12, Mar. 27, 1906.

159 Beaumont, *op. cit.*, p. 623.

160 The roll-call vote, *S. P. A.*, XXXIX, 35787.

161 Beaumont, *op. cit.*, p. 624. For general discussions of the question of special status for Galicia, see Kleinwaechter, *op. cit.*, pp. 116-7, Geoffrey Drage, *Austria-Hungary* (New York, 1909), p. 540, and André Chéradame, *L'Europe et la Question d'Autriche au Seuil du XXe Siècle* (Paris, 1906), pp. 150-3, 286-7.

162 *Grundlagen und Entwicklungsziele der österreichisch-ungarischen Monarchie* (Vienna and Leipzig,, 1906), p. 132, footnote. In an earlier

The Pan-Germans refused to consider their cause lost. In the sessions of the electoral committee, they moved that Galicia, Bukovina, and Dalmatia all be accorded special status,[163] but their motion was decisively defeated. Thus ended the most impractical German attempt to avoid minority status in the new Lower House. Save for futile demands that Germans be guaranteed an absolute majority of seats in the new Lower House, the other German deputies advanced no plan comparable to that proposed by the Pan-Germans. Two of the most influential German deputies in the Lower House, Anton Pergelt and Josef Baernreither, earnestly cited reasons for a continuance of German predominance in parliament, but their efforts were nullified by most of the Christian Socialists and a majority of the German Populists, who preferred half a loaf to none. Pergelt pointed out that the percentage of German strength in the Lower House had dropped from 62 per cent to 48 per cent between the years 1873 and 1905 and warned that a further decrease in strength would be ruinous for the empire.[164] Baernreither declared that the Germans of Austria had reached a decisive turning-point in their history. The secession of dissident nationalities would inevitably come about unless the Germans settled the problem of the nationalities while they still had a strong position. Baernreither quoted numerous deputies who had, at one time or another, recommended a simultaneous passage of autonomy for all nationalities and universal equal suffrage; obviously, there was a clear connection between electoral rights and constitutional reform which the Germans could ignore only at their peril.[165] Baernreither's insistence on gradualness in taking steps caused non-

---

volume, *Der Kampf der österreichischen Nationen um den Staat (erster Theil,* Vienna, 1902), p. 227, Renner dismissed the Pan-Slav threat to Austria as a mere phantom.

163 Motion of Stein, *Beilagen*, p. 200, Apr. 24, 1906.

164 *S. P. A.*, XXXVIII, 35085-7, Mar. 13, 1906.

165 *S. P. A.*, XXXIX, 35487-8, Mar. 21, 1906.

German deputies to distrust his motives, while his broad hints in favor of autonomy alarmed those Germans who still hoped to attain their objectives in a centralized parliament, where technically they might be a minority. To the very end of the debates, various German deputies painted frightening pictures of the fate Germanism would suffer as a result of reform. Only one deputy, Otto Lecher, was careless enough to imply that the Germans had fared quite well in the apportionment of mandates, as he fought the proposal for plural suffrage.[166] The realization by most Germans that they had salvaged a great deal of their power from the wreckage created by universal manhood suffrage accounted for their willingness to talk of discrimination while failing to act cohesively to block the entire reform.

CHAPTER IV
THE MACHINERY OF REFORM

THE major constitutional revision effected by the electoral reform of 1907 was the enfranchisement of virtually every male Austrian citizen. The implications of this great step encouraged friends and enemies of universal manhood suffrage to seek further constitutional revisions which would expand or limit, respectively, the original concept of suffrage for all men. The changes effected in Article 12 of the Fundamental Law on Imperial Representation have already been cited as an example of the desire of conservative autonomists to clarify constitutional issues while they still had a modicum of influence in the Lower House. There had been outright demands for a complete renovation of the constitution along federalistic lines, as well as schemes for vocational representation, suggestions of a return to the choice of parliamentary deputies by diets, and so forth. Autonomists and centralists were united in agreement that nationalistic problems were chiefly to blame for the years of parliamentary anarchy, and here, too, there were suggestions which aimed at decreasing the unholy effect nationalism had on orderly procedure in parliament. Of course, the motives behind these suggestions were federalistic; for instance, the Young Czech Josef Herold argued that the new Lower House should limit itself to the conduct of international affairs, the codification of laws, the security of the empire, and the overall economic and social problems of the empire, while the provinces of Austria would handle the other problems.[1] His Czech colleague, the Conservative Count Sylva-Tarouca, blandly declared that parliament should be relieved of some of its excessive burdens, namely, the settlement of nationalistic quarrels; anything which might offend national sensibilities should be kept out of the sphere of parliamentary competence. In return,

1 S. P. A., XXXV, 32502, Dec. 1, 1905.

parliament should receive greater power to deal with foreign affairs, the army, and the navy; such changes would be the tonic necessary to revive Austrian patriotism.[2] More modest was the suggestion made by the Rumanian deputy Onciul; he felt that special " peoples' days " should be set aside for discussion of nationalistic problems in parliament.[3] Aside from the paragraphs added to Article 12 of the Fundamental Law on Imperial Representation, however, nothing was done to limit or expand the competence of the central parliament.

THE ATTACK ON THE UPPER HOUSE

The fate of the Upper House of the Austrian parliament in the event of the passage of universal manhood suffrage was a constitutional question which received notable attention in the debates on reform. According to the Fundamental Law on Imperial Representation, all laws had to receive the approval of both houses of parliament and the sanction of the Emperor. This proviso opened up all sorts of possibilities for the supporters and the opponents of a popularly elected Lower House. The former wished to abolish the Upper House or pass regulations which would ensure its compliance with the desires of the Lower House; the latter wished to limit the right of the crown to appoint new members to the Upper House and to reconstitute the Upper House in such a way as to permit the representation of interests which would be abolished by electoral reform. Deputies of various nationalities and divergent political views agreed that a reconstitution of the Lower House would mean little without corresponding changes in the Upper House, but the conflict over the nature of the changes to be made prevented any sweeping modifications of the composition of the Upper House.

A few members of the Lower House demanded a reform of the Upper House prior to Gautsch's decision to sponsor a re-

2 *S. P. A.*, XXXVIII, 34984-5, Mar. 9, 1906.
3 *S. P. A.*, XXXV, 32396, Nov. 28, 1905.

form bill. Ivan Šuteršič alleged that the Upper House's lack of contact with the people and its lack of a sense of responsibility outweighed the immense sum of knowledge and experience represented by its members. He suggested that in the future the various historic provinces of the empire be represented in the Upper House, as was the case in the German Empire.[4] Count Dzieduszycki quoted John Stuart Mill to the effect that provision must be made to send to parliament worthy men who consciously avoid the rough and tumble of a democratic election. Should electoral reform be accepted, the Upper House should of necessity be recreated in order to take care of such men.[5] The Czech National Socialist Fresl impatiently dismissed such schemes; nothing less than the complete abolition of the Upper House would suffice. The deputies who were to be popularly elected should have the sole right to minister to the necessities of the people.[6]

In November, 1905 Gautsch cautiously admitted that the ministry, in preparing an electoral reform, was considering the possibility of changes in the Upper House which would afford a retention of the traditional representation of interests, about to be abolished in the Lower House. The extent of the changes would depend entirely upon practical considerations; the ministry was convinced, however, that it was quite necessary to safeguard the representation of interests which were significant in the life of the empire.[7] The Minister-President's elusive reference to the Upper House evoked a variety of comments. Count Sternberg's was the most novel; he suggested the creation of a third parliamentary body, which would be elected by the diets and which would relieve the Emperor of odious tasks by mediating the differences between the existing two

4 S. P. A., XXXV, 32117-18, Oct. 5, 1905.

5 S. P. A., XXXV, 32241, Oct. 6, 1905.

6 S. P. A., XXXV, 32266-7, Oct. 6, 1905.

7 S. P. A., XXXV, 32322, Nov. 28, 1905.

houses.[8] Artur Skedl, the German Progressive, welcomed Gautsch's intimations of a change in the Upper House. In his opinion, the latter should be freshened by the election of some of its members in place of imperial appointment; the hereditary members should not be disturbed, but it would be well to provide for the election to the Upper House of those representatives of the chambers of commerce who were about to be expelled from the Lower House.[9] His party colleague Konstantin Noske enthusiastically seconded the idea of securing representation of trade and industry in the Upper House; in addition, he recommended the adoption of regulations which would permit the government to appoint enough new members to control the majority in the Upper House.[10]

On December 1, 1905 Gautsch informed the Upper House of his plans for universal manhood suffrage and expressed his hopes that his listeners would cooperate with the ministry. In the past, he noted, the Upper House had been free of partisan influences and of popular pressure in examining proposed legislation, unlike the Lower House. His one desire was the enhancement of the strength of the Upper House, so that it might be of even greater importance to the state. Then, in very vague terms, Gautsch implied a reconstitution of the Upper House, which he hoped would accomplish two objectives: (1) a restraint of the reinvigorated impulses of the Lower House, and (2) the protection of interests which would lose their representation in the Lower House.[11] Count Franz Thun castigated Gautsch for his nebulous terminology; if there was to be a reform of the Upper House, the ministry's announcement of the event should be first made in the Upper House.[12] Baron Plener saw no need for a reform of the Upper House; as for

8 *S. P. A.*, XXXV, 32394, Nov. 28, 1905.

9 *S. P. A.*, XXXV, 32445, Nov. 30, 1905.

10 *S. P. A.*, XXXV, 32523-4, Dec. 1, 1905.

11 *S. P. H.*, pp. 1111-12, Dec. 1, 1905.

12 *S. P. H.*, p. 1121, Dec. 2, 1905.

the idea that landowners would transfer their representation from the Lower House to the Upper House, Plener felt that the Upper House would be strengthened thereby but that the proposal would have no real political consequences.[13] Count Piniński was critical, like Thun, of Gautsch's failure to clarify his intentions; a political leader who introduces such a fundamental issue should be willing to explain it. Otherwise, persons might support the idea without any comprehension of its true ramifications.[14] One of Gautsch's few sympathizers in these unpleasant debates on reform, Count Friedrich Schönborn, refused to believe that the Minister-President intended to throw open the Upper House to those deputies who no longer could expect to win seats in elections to the Lower House. Even so, he warned, many "lame ducks" would get into the Upper House and in no time would allege that they were the only persons entitled to sit there.[15] After four hours of rather steady berating at the hands of the members of the Upper House, Gautsch attempted to explain his remarks on the proposed reform of the body. He refused to submit a concrete formula until the entire reform was ready for discussion. Somewhat testily, he denied that the Upper House had always been a model of cooperation; its refusal to act on some 200 ministerial proposals and on its own resolutions helped to explain his desire to effect changes in its personnel.[16]

The Upper House's hostile reception of Gautsch's endeavors to gain support for universal manhood suffrage was closely scrutinized by deputies in the Lower House. The Slovene Clerical Šuklje declared that he was convinced by the tirades in the Upper House that the latter was in extraordinary need of reform. Apparently, the peers no longer understood the soul of the people or the emotions of their spirit and were,

13 *S. P. H.*, pp. 1135-6, Dec. 2, 1905.
14 *S. P. H.*, p. 1140, Dec. 2, 1905.
15 *S. P. H.*, p. 1147, Dec. 2, 1905.
16 *S. P. H.*, p. 1151, Dec. 2, 1905.

therefore, dangerous to the state. Undoubtedly, the Upper House should function as a brake upon the popular passions aroused in the Lower House. However, now that the Upper House had reached the point of stopping every progressive move, it was time to throw open its windows to let in some fresh air.[17] Straucher likewise was of the opinion that the Upper House's inimical attitude toward reform revealed a need for its own reform; its members seemed to forget that any ministry could appoint enough peers to obtain support for ministerial measures.[18]

Gautsch, however, decided to avoid any comprehensive tampering with the composition and selection of the Upper House, contenting himself in his definite program of February, 1906 with the proviso that no person could simultaneously hold seats in both houses. The leaders of the parties in the Upper House, volunteered Gautsch, were disinclined to accept any other changes.[19] Only a few deputies in the Lower House seemed to be concerned over the ministry's abandonment of a reform of the Upper House. Dr. Karl Beuerle repeated the suggestion made by his party, the German Progressive, that at least part of the non-hereditary members be elected rather than appointed,[20] while the Pan-German Wolf was keenly disappointed that Gautsch had failed to change the Upper House into a body of estates resting on a professional and vocational basis.[21] Šušteršič reiterated his suggestion that the members of the Upper House be elected to represent the provinces of Austria, as a counterweight to the centralizing tendency of the Lower House.[22]

17 S. P. A., XXXVI, 32555-6, Dec. 4, 1905.

18 S. P. A., XXXVI, 32564-5, Dec. 4, 1905.

19 S. P. A., XXXVIII, 34660, Feb. 23, 1906.

20 S. P. A., XXXVIII, 35166, Mar. 14, 1906.

21 S. P. A., XXXIX, 35562, Mar. 22, 1906.

22 S. P. A., XXXIX, 35425, Mar. 20, 1906.

The unpredictable Otto Lecher also regretted that Gautsch's good intentions fell short of a reform of the Upper House, whose members he pilloried in devastating fashion. According to Lecher, the membership of the Upper House consisted of three elements, the genuine aristocrats, the former members of ministries, and the scholars and artists. The aristocrats had done a great deal that was worthwhile in the development of the empire, but one had the impression that their remoteness from active public life rendered their ideals useless. The former members of ministries were the men who cleverly opposed reform. They were the gentlemen who had a beautiful future behind them, who never wearied of proclaiming the great deeds they had performed for Austria, and who looked upon every one of Gautsch's successes as a personal insult. The last group, the scholars and artists, were the most pitiable of the lot. Any scholar who avoided the taint of socialism and any artist who eschewed unorthodoxy inevitably would be named to the Upper House, willingly or not, when he reached the suitable age. For such men, appointment to the august body was merely another sign of old age, like bad teeth or a sluggish digestion. Thus, one might look at men who were accustomed to the free flights of imagination, sitting dumbly in the Upper House, shoulders bowed and eyes melancholy, like the caged eagles at Schönbrunn. Only a few of the many members of these three groups were cognizant of the realities of life; they stood out in the confusion like grease spots floating in water. The Upper House needed more practical men, said Lecher, and he urged the ministry to take the necessary steps to bring in new blood.[23]

Gautsch continued to ignore demands for a reform of the Upper House, as did his successors, Hohenlohe and Beck. The entire issue was reopened in the winter of 1906, however, with the Upper House's demand that a limit be placed on the number of men whom the Emperor could appoint to the Upper House

23 *S. P. A.*, XXXVIII, 35268, Mar. 15, 1906.

—the famous *numerus clausus*. As previously recounted,[24] the ministry finally agreed to *numerus clausus,* which was to limit the number of appointees to a maximum of 170, a minimum of 150. In the words of the reporter of the special commission of the Upper House, the independence of that body had to be protected from the manipulations of future ministries dependent upon the favor of the Lower House. On December 21, 1906 the Upper House agreed in effect to accept the electoral reform approved by the Lower House, if the latter would accept *numerus clausus.*

Few members of the Lower House were pleased by the Upper House's price for reform. Most of the opponents of *numerus clausus* bewailed loss of the ministry's complete initiative in naming new members in order to force a favorable decision in the Upper House; how could the Upper House ever be forced to recognize the needs of the people and the exigencies of modern life? Kramář discerned, on the other hand, a certain improvement in constitutionalism in the device. Naturally, he preferred that the Upper House be a true " senate of the provinces," but he was unwilling to hinder the passage of universal manhood suffrage by proposing his preferred plan. Kramář, of course, was well aware that the Upper House could not be expected to retreat an inch on *numerus clausus,* and he was compelled to vote for it in order to save the reform. The Christian Socialists adopted the same policy of criticism and acquiescence.[25] Starzyński, of the Polish Club, heartily welcomed the peers' demand as a necessary part of a constitutional system; the possibility of an unrestricted number of members in a representative body would undermine the true significance of parliamentary government. Baron Beck also stressed the necessity of offering the Upper House enough

---

24 See above, p. 63.

25 Richard Kralik, the historian most sympathetic to the Christian Socialists, probably mirrored the party's real point of view on *numerus clausus* by declaring that the device was praiseworthy as a guarantee of " conservatism." *Oesterreichische Geschichte* (Vienna, 1914), p. 612.

security to fend off needs of the moment, and on January 10, 1907 the Lower House accepted the required additions to Article 5 of the Fundamental Law on Imperial Representation.[26] The Upper House had been unable to prevent universal manhood suffrage, but at least it had repulsed all attempts to change its composition and had, in addition, gained a powerful weapon for self-defense in the adoption of *numerus clausus*.

THE QUESTION OF COMPULSORY VOTING

A controversy second only to the one aroused by plural suffrage developed over the question of including a provision for compulsory voting in the electoral reform. Whereas the German Clericals and the peers of the Upper House led the campaign for plural suffrage, the Christian Socialists were most insistent upon compulsory voting. Karl Lueger first introduced the issue into the general discussion on October 3, 1905, when he predicated his support of reform upon a universal duty to vote.[27] Ebenhoch contested the efficacy of such a regulation during secret balloting; empty ballots would be the answer of voters who were compelled to exercise the franchise.[28] In turn, his objections were derided by Schöpfer, who argued that the object of compulsory voting was not necessarily the filling in of a ballot; on the contrary, the device simply would force citizens to take a step which otherwise they might avoid. The apathy in public life had to be ended, and compulsory voting would be an effective agent in the process. One could predict that of a hundred voters forced to go to the polls, probably only one would fail to fill out his ballot.[29]

Gautsch avoided the issue of compulsory voting in his speech recommending electoral reform in November, 1905, but sev-

---

26 For a summary of the debate in the Lower House on *numerus clausus,* Czedik, *op. cit.,* III, 414-16. The complete debate is given, *S. P. A.,* XLV, 41352-87, Jan. 10, 1907.

27 *S. P. A.,* XXXV, 31783.

28 *S. P. A.,* XXXV, 32237, Oct. 6, 1905.

29 *S. P. A.,* XXXV, 32263-4, Oct. 6, 1905.

eral deputies took time to argue the merits of such a system in the debate which ensued. On the eve of the resumption of parliamentary activity, the Christian Socialists had held a mass meeting in Vienna to elaborate their program for electoral reform, and, under the leadership of Lueger, they had continued to press for compulsory voting.[30] This program was supported in the Lower House by a few deputies of other factions; the Ruthene Romanczuk seemed to agree that the plan would aid the political schooling of citizens, but avoided demanding compulsory voting as a *sine qua non* of his support.[31] Socialists and German Progressives were quite suspicious of the Christian Socialist clamor. Adler argued that men who did not understand politics should not be forcibly pitted against those who did; he also felt that compulsory voting would seriously impair the chances of clean elections, since it would give undue influence to superintendents of polling places who would be called upon for advice by inexperienced voters.[32] Ofner declared that the right to vote carried with it only a moral duty to vote. Pressure exerted through regulations and the decisions of judges should be eschewed, or else the natural desire to vote would never permeate the masses. He pointed out that alleged failures to vote could be proved only by tedious depositions and attestations that would arouse further distaste for the entire procedure of voting.[33]

The Minister-President and his advisors were seemingly impressed by the arguments advanced by the foes of compulsory voting, for the concrete proposals of February, 1906 shunned the matter. According to Gautsch, the device would have been incompatible with the will of the people and would have created many administrative difficulties.[34] The Christian

30 *Neue Freie Presse, Abendblatt,* Nov. 27, 1906, p. 8.

31 *S. P. A.,* XXXV, 32510, Dec. 1, 1905.

32 *S. P. A.,* XXXV, 32456-7, Nov. 30, 1905.

33 *S. P. A.,* XXXVI, 32619, Dec. 5, 1905.

34 *S. P. A.,* XXXVIII, 34659, Feb. 23, 1906.

Socialists, though generally pleased by Gautsch's plan of reform, steadfastly refused to surrender their advocacy of compulsory voting and the issue was turned over to the deliberations of the electoral committee. Despite Ebenhoch's skepticism of the previous year, it was one of his German Clerical associates, Schlegel, who asked for a rediscussion of Article 4 of the Election Law of the Reichsrat, in order to move the adoption of a final paragraph which would compel enfranchised males to vote. According to his motion, the provinces would be empowered to pass the laws necessary to implement the general concept of compulsory voting; any other regulatory system, said Schlegel, would fail to pass the Lower House.[35]

German Liberals of various fractions immediately denounced Schlegel's maneuver, which they felt was inspired by the Christian Socialists. Grabmayr, the Constitutionalist deputy of the landed curia, refused to believe that the interests of the state were of sufficient magnitude to enforce such a limitation of an individual's freedom of action. Entrusting the diets with the enforcement of the law was equally reprehensible, in that it opened up the chances of new assaults upon the powers of the central parliament. The Christian Socialists had once said they could not accept a reform which did not include a five-year domiciliation provision; nevertheless, they had agreed to a great modification of that particular demand, and one could assume a similar strategic withdrawal as far as compulsory voting was concerned.[36] Lecher also defended abstention from voting as a right of political demonstration. He was of the opinion that the enforcement of the law by partisan electoral commissions would lead to unjust fines or negligible fines, depending upon the political views or national background of the offender. Consequently, it would be wrong to allow each province to have its own schedule of penalties.[37] Other Lib-

---

35 *Beilagen*, pp. 559-60.

36 *Beilagen*, pp. 560-1, Oct. 1, 1906.

37 *Beilagen*, pp. 564-5, Oct. 1, 1906.

eral deputies professed to find an autonomist plot concealed in the motion, or else they called attention to the costs of enforcing the proposed ruling.

Adler repeated his criticism of a law which would force persons who had no political convictions to vote. In close elections, such disinterested citizens, who would come chiefly from the middle classes or who would be *déclassé,* such as servants, would be forced to decide great issues which they had no ability or will to comprehend. Adler accused Schlegel of letting the issue simmer for a long time, then combining it with overtones of autonomy as bait; the resultant debate would only delay the general work of the committee. Anyone familiar with the technique of elections should realize the futility of the scheme; its chief weakness was its sheer impracticality.[38] Gessmann, the Christian Socialist, turned on Adler with the remark that compulsory voting was absolutely essential to combat the electoral terrorism of the Social Democrats. Bourgeois parties generally had failed to build up the requisite organization to fight the Social Democrats; now, willing or not, the indolent middle classes and even Viennese servants would be forced to defend their position.[39]

Bienerth, the Minister of the Interior, informed the committee that its members would be forced to make their own conclusions on the subject. He could hardly agree that electoral duty should be enforced by the power of the state; on the other hand, he could see the justice of linking duty with right. He reminded the committee that election officials already had tremendous tasks to fulfill, but he agreed that real equality stemming from the participation of all enfranchised males in elections might be worth the cost. Possibly the committee might effect a compromise, which would create imperial legislation to establish the principles and general rules of enforcing compulsory voting, while leaving the enforcement of the rules

38 *Beilagen,* pp. 562-4, Oct. 1, 1906.
39 *Beilagen,* pp. 566-7, Oct. 1, 1906.

to provincial legislation.[40] Following Bienerth's remarks, a motion was made to refer the entire subject to a subcommittee of ten, which was chosen on October 2 and which made its report on October 5.

Within the subcommittee, Schlegel and the Young Czech Hrubý combined plans which their colleagues accepted. The new motions left the entire issue of compulsory voting in the hands of the provinces. The diets were to decide whether or not enfranchised males were to be compelled to vote in parliamentary elections, and they also were to have sole control of enforcing such rulings, if made.[41] The German Populist Kaiser wanted to insert a general schedule of penalties which would obtain in every part of the empire, though his own party rejected any accommodation with the principle of compulsory voting.[42] The Italian deputy Malfatti also suggested an amendment to the effect that diets could not pass rules on compulsory voting unless three-quarters of the members of the diet were present and unless two-thirds of those present approved.[43] Both suggested amendments were rejected, and the plan elaborated by Schlegel and Hrubý was accepted by a vote of twenty-one to thirteen. With trifling changes in terminology, the addition to Article 4 was later accepted by both houses of parliament. As a result, some Austrian citizens were fined when they failed to avail themselves of the privileges bestowed upon them by the reform of 1907, while others had full right to ignore the complexities of Austrian elections.

In February, March, and April of 1907, no less than six provinces passed laws which forced their enfranchised citizens to vote at parliamentary elections, namely, Lower Austria, Silesia, Voralberg, Moravia, Upper Austria, and Salzburg. In general, failure to vote was punishable by fines ranging from

40 *Beilagen*, pp. 567-8, Oct. 1, 1906.

41 *Beilagen*, p. 611, Oct. 4, 1906.

42 *Beilagen*, p. 613, Oct. 5, 1906.

43 *Beilagen*, p. 614, Oct. 5, 1906.

one to fifty kronen. A certain number of excuses were permitted: sickness of the voter or of members of his family, imperial professional duties, urgent family matters, lack of means of transportation. In Moravia and Silesia, persons who were seventy years old also might be excused. In Upper Austria, all excuses were evaluated by judges.[44]

THE COMPETENCE OF THE NEW PARLIAMENT: FOREIGN AFFAIRS AND DEFENSE

Properly speaking, the discussions of electoral reform in Austria in 1905-06 did not go beyond the sphere of activity outlined by Gautsch's original proposals. The ministry made no recommendations for constitutional changes in regard to the competence of parliament over foreign affairs and defense measures and undoubtedly would have utterly condemned any efforts made by deputies to go into these matters. Nevertheless, the fate of the Triple Alliance and of the Austrian armed forces was constantly intruding itself into the debates, for no one could be sure what a universally elected Lower House might attempt in the future.

The most casual student of the system of alliances developed in Europe after 1871 realizes that parliamentary bodies rarely, if ever, were consulted or advised of the terms of the treaties or agreements which bound their countries to other great powers. The Austrian parliament was no worse informed in this respect than the French Chamber of Deputies or even the British parliament (at least, in the case of the Grey-Cambon correspondence). Moreover, the Austrian Fundamental Law on Imperial Representation explicitly stated that the competence of parliament extended to " the examination and approval of commercial treaties and of those political treaties which place a financial burden upon the empire or upon any part thereof, which place obligations upon individual citizens, or which have as a consequence a change of the territory of the

44 Beaumont, *op. cit.*, p. 638, footnote 1.

kingdoms and countries represented in the Reichsrat." [45] Had the precise terms of the latest renewal of the Triple Alliance been available to the members of parliament, the terms still might have been interpreted as above and beyond the proper competence of parliamentary inquiry. However, the danger of a possible denunciation of the alliance with Germany and Italy was not entirely remote, and the Pan-Germans were fond of attacking the entire reform from this angle.

The Czechs and Poles in Austria were the most consistent opponents of the Triple Alliance, but only the former group indirectly implied a hope that the new parliament would weaken or end the tie with Germany. Czech deputies were of the opinion that the new Lower House should busy itself with international affairs and with the security of the empire and leave less pressing matters to the provincial diets.[46] The Germans did not deign to respond to these transparent overtures, but Gautsch felt compelled to make an effort to quiet growing concern in some German quarters with respect to the future of the alliance with Germany.[47] During the first reading of his proposals, the Minister-President declared that a few persons had been alarmed by talk that the alliance would not be renewed by a Lower House containing a Slavic majority. In the first place, argued Gautsch, such a majority could be reached only by improbable party alliances. In the second place, there was a big question as to whether or not the new parliament would presume to tamper with the imperial alliance system and thereby move against imperial interests. No other parliament had behaved in such a reckless fashion, and, according to Gautsch, past history revealed that groups which fought im-

45 Part (a) of Article II, Dodd, *op. cit.*, I, 78.

46 See above, pp. 126-27.

47 Robert W. Seton-Watson pointed out that the reform would strengthen groups which Berlin regarded with the greatest suspicion, and, as a good Englishman with Southern Slav sympathies, expressed hope that the reform would weaken the Triple Alliance. *The Future of Austria-Hungary and the Attitude of the Great Powers* (London, 1907), pp. 10-11.

perial interests ended by weakening their own position. It was not to be expected that the new house would disregard past experiences.[48]

Gautsch's veiled warning brought an immediate response from Kramář. The Young Czech definitely stated that the new house would discuss Austrian foreign policy, the Minister-President notwithstanding. The people who paid for the policy had the right to discuss it. As for talk of a non-renewal or modification of the Triple Alliance, had not the German chancellor declared that an "extra dance" could be permitted a member of the Triple Alliance without prejudicing the continuance of the alliance?[49] Kramář, however, ended his remarks with the reassuring comment that at the present nothing could be said against the alliance, though Italian loyalty to its provisions was dubious.[50] The reaction of the German deputies to Kramář's somewhat impish remarks was mixed. The Pan-German Schalk alleged that the Slavs hated the German alliance, which had done so much to restore Austrian prestige and to protect the empire during the difficult period of industrialization. As evidence of the Slavic hatred, he claimed that their representatives in the Delegations did everything possible to nullify the good effects of the alliance, thereby giving comfort to the empire's enemies.[51] Ebenhoch took up Schalk's fears and interpreted them in a light favorable to reform. In his opinion, it was ridiculous to fear that anti-alliance elements would wreck the tie with Germany in a new house, when they could achieve the same objective much more easily in the Delegations by refusing to vote the necessary military funds. The fact they had not done so seemed to indicate that foreign policy was dictated by necessity rather than sympathy.[52]

48 S. P. A., XXXVIII, 35144, Mar. 14, 1906.

49 A reference to Bülow's famous speech before the Reichstag on Jan. 8, 1902. See Sidney B. Fay, *The Origins of the World War* (New York, 1929), I, 146.

50 S. P. A., XXXVIII, 35249, Mar. 15, 1906.

51 S. P. A., XXXIX, 35433-4, Mar. 20, 1906.

52 S. P. A., XXXIX, 35588, Mar. 22, 1906.

Closely allied with the problem of possible parliamentary decisions on foreign affairs was the problem of parliamentary acquiescence in voting military credits. According to the Fundamental Law on Imperial Representation, the Reichsrat had competence over " all matters which relate to the form as well as to the regulation and term of military service; particularly the annual grant of military forces, and the general provision regarding the furnishing of relays, and the maintenance and quartering of troops." [53] Several German deputies feared that a universally elected Lower House would fail to grant adequate funds for Austria's great-power position, but the problem received only perfunctory notice in the general debates. The most sensible reply to the German fears was voiced by the Slovene Šuteršič who asserted that an empire blessed by reform always would patriotically rally to its own defense.[54] More explicitly, in the same year, Popovici was informing the Austrian public that federalism would remove all threats to Austria's position as a great power.[55] In the German camp, Stürgkh predicted that reform would threaten the use of German as the army's language of command, but his remarks did not evoke any response in parliament or in the Hofburg, whose master was notoriously sensitive about the appearance of unity in his army.[56]

In summary, it can be said that future parliamentary interference in foreign affairs and in military activities was not a complete phantom of the imagination; nevertheless, the raising of the issue did nothing to affect the eventual passage of the reform. The opponents of the alliance with Germany and the opponents of increasing military expenditures were too realistic to expect relief from a mere electoral reform. Significantly, amid all of the talk of a greater degree of democracy

53 Part (b) of Article II, Dodd, *op. cit.*, I, 78.

54 *S. P. A.*, XXXIX, 35426, Mar. 20, 1906.

55 *Die vereinigten Staaten von Gross-Österreich* (Leipzig, 1906), p. 345.

56 *S. P. A.*, XXXIX, 35641, Mar. 23, 1906.

for Austria, no mention was made of changing the essentially
German nature of the army's officialdom. The great families no
longer monopolized the chief posts, to be sure, but the aristocratic spirit which nearly all of the officers assumed was in no
danger of being broken. Admirers of a genteel *esprit de corps*
still could single out the Austrian army as a model.[57]

THE APPORTIONMENT OF MANDATES AND THE DIVISION OF ELECTORAL DISTRICTS

The general debate which opened the proceedings of the
electoral committee of the Lower House [58] was filled with the
usual cries for "justice" in the apportionment of mandates
and in the division of electoral districts. Even the men most
interested in the final passage of the reform (excluding Viktor
Adler) were careful to point out that their final consent was
predicated on satisfaction of their nationality's proper claims.
Adler, however, criticized men who would wreck the entire
reform for the sake of a few seats more or less,[59] and Karel
Kramář, the spokesman of Czech aspirations, was quick to
admit that many "nationalists" were merely using these
means to harass the sincere adherents of reform.[60]

Gautsch had submitted a new apportionment of seats and
division of districts within the various provinces when he discussed his plan for reform on February 23, 1906.[61] His fall from
power and the accession of Hohenlohe as Minister-President
resulted in another apportionment of mandates. On May 18,
1906 Hohenlohe had informed the committee that he was
hard at work trying to effect a new compromise. As soon as

---

57 For an example of the admiration aroused by such gentility, see
Archibald R. Colquhoun, *The Whirlpool of Europe* (London and New York,
1907), pp. 225-34.

58 The entire proceedings of the electoral committee are published in
the *Beilagen*, p. 189 ff.

59 *Beilagen*, p. 217

60 *Beilagen*, p. 205.

61 Gautsch's entire plan, *Beilagen*, p. 15 ff.

this was reached, he would submit it to the committee. However, if no compromise could be reached, he promised to submit his own plan. The committee voted to proceed with the consideration of this program as soon as it was ready.[62]

The members reassembled on May 25. Several deputies demanded that Article 7, which set forth the basis on which the franchise was to be exercised, be settled first. Some opponents of equal, direct, and universal suffrage, as well as its warm supporter, Adler, desired that this concept be accepted or rejected before tempers were further frayed by the problem of apportionment. Hohenlohe refused to commit himself on the matter, and finally the chairman's suggestion that Article 6, dealing with the apportionment of mandates and demarcation of districts, be discussed first was accepted.

Hohenlohe first said that no complete compromise had been attained; nevertheless, the need for speedy action forced him to offer a new plan which at least might be a basis for agreement. Under the revised plan, forty seats in addition to those proposed by Gautsch were to be granted as follows: fourteen for Galicia, nine for Lower Austria, four for Bohemia, three for Bukovina, two each for Moravia, Silesia, Upper Austria, and Tyrol, and one each for Salzburg and Trieste. In Bohemia, Moravia, and Silesia the seats were to be divided equally between Czechs and Germans. In Galicia, the fourteen new seats were to go to urban districts; the seventy already promised for rural districts there were to be retained. The principle of proportional elections in part of Galicia was kept, and Hohenlohe promised that the Galician rural mandates would still elect the old ratio of forty-three Poles to twenty-seven Ruthenes.

In Bukovina, Ruthenes, Germans, and Rumanians each were to receive a new seat. In Lower Austria, five were to go to Vienna, four to new town and market districts. In Upper Austria, one was to be rural, the other urban, the latter to center

62 *Beilagen,* pp. 219-24.

around Linz. In Salzburg, the capital was to be favored with the increase. In Tyrol, one mandate was to go to the Germans, the other to the Italians; the latter also would benefit by the new seat for Trieste.[63]

The new division of mandates would break down by provinces as follows: Bohemia, 122; Dalmatia, 11; Galicia, 102; Lower Austria, 64; Upper Austria, 22; Salzburg, 7; Styria, 28; Carinthia, 10; Carniola, 11; Bukovina, 14; Moravia, 46; Silesia, 15; Tyrol, 23; Voralberg, 4; Istria, 5; Gorizia and Gradisca, 5; Trieste, 6.

The tentative demarcation of electoral districts was still in the hands of the ministry's advisors. Kramář argued that this delay was no real hindrance to a vote on the larger issue of the number of seats to accrue to each province, but this view was hotly contested by members who wished to study the entire plan before voting for individual parts of it. Gessmann's motion that a subcommittee be appointed to decide on the actual formation of the districts was withdrawn in the face of disillusioned comments on the efficacy of committees.[64]

The next meeting, held on June 7, found the situation changed in some respects. Hohenlohe had been replaced by Beck as Minister-President; the new Minister of the Interior was Bienerth, who was to be one of the leading figures in the negotiations which followed. Moreover, several members of the committee had been called into the ministry, including the chairman, Dr. Marchet.[65] Since the plan initiated by Hohenlohe was still unavailable, the committee had to postpone discussion once again.

Beck's declaration of policy on the following day stressed the great need for settlement of the reform issue. He had no intention of impeding progress by taking time to work out an-

---

63 *Beilagen*, pp. 226-7.

64 *Beilagen*, p. 230.

65 Dr. Ploj became acting chairman; on June 12, he was elected permanent chairman.

other ministerial plan; previous solutions would have to be used as groundwork. He promised full cooperation with the committee and said that the cabinet would accept any changes which would facilitate final agreement. In short, he wisely put full responsibility on the shoulders of the members, without prejudicing the cabinet's position by taking a stand on all of the issues presented.[66]

In spite of grumbling on the part of some Germans, most of the men admitted that the committee itself was chiefly to blame for delay. Dr. Löcker, the German Populist, moved that Article 6 be accepted as planned, plus an extra seat to go to the Germans in Carniola. Needless to say, he took the precaution of refusing to identify himself with every aspect of the apportionment.[67] Discussion as to whether or not apportionment by provinces should be combined with the corresponding creation of districts within the provinces was finally resolved by the passage of a motion that they be so combined.

The stage was finally set for action. The committee really began to work on June 12, when Dalmatia was brought up for discussion, in lieu of Bohemia.[68] The ostensible reason was lack of data on Bohemia; one might suspect that the committee was not unhappy to concentrate first on a relatively simple problem.

Dr. Matteo Bartoli, Italian Liberal representative of the chamber of commerce in Rovigno, Istria, reproached the regime for failure to respect the rights of the Italian minority in Dalmatia. He moved that the tax-districts of Zara and Borgoerizzo be combined, an arrangement which meant a new seat for Dalmatia. If this should be rejected, at least Zara and Pago

---

66 *Beilagen,* pp. 233-4.

67 *Beilagen,* p. 235.

68 In 1910 the Serbs and Croats accounted for 96.17 per cent of the total population of Dalmatia, the Italians, 2.84 per cent. See Bertrand Auerbach, *Les Races et les Nationalités en Autriche Hongrie* (2me. éd.; Paris, 1917), pp. 307-8.

should be united to form a district so that Italians might have a chance to capture a seat.

Dr. Vincenz Ivčevič, the Croatian Party's representative, resolutely opposed Bartoli's demand on the grounds of an insufficient number of Italians and because Dalmatian Italians had gone unrepresented for a long time already. Evidently considering the whole matter a bagatelle, he turned to the more pressing problem of the Croat-Serb balance of power. According to population figures, the Croats should receive nine seats, the Serbs two; yet the government's planning of districts might assure the Serbs three seats or no seats. He submitted a plan for district divisions which would assure the Serbs their rightful quota, two seats.

At this point, Bienerth, Minister of the Interior, interrupted in behalf of the ministry. He pointed out that Dalmatia had received full recognition, if not more, in being granted eleven mandates. In answer to Bartoli's reproach, he declared it was most impractical to " protect " a minority of 3 per cent of the total population. Nor would the creation of the districts proposed by Bartoli guarantee an Italian mandate. Ivčevič's new division of districts did not seem to be any improvement over the ministry's plan, he declared, since it tended to produce districts either too large or too small. It would be best to rely on the government's program.

Ivan Plantan, speaking for the Serbs of Dalmatia (though himself a Slovene), expressed amazement that Bienerth should reject a compromise accepted by both Serbs and Croats. Such a move definitely contradicted Beck's remarks.

The committee evidently was impressed by the pleas of Ivčevič and Plantan, for it voted down Bartoli's request for another Dalmatian mandate while scrapping the government's division of districts in favor of the compromise by Ivčevič.[69]

The following discussion on Upper Austria resolved itself chiefly into a debate between Dr. Josef Schlegel and Dr. Julius

[69] Debate on Dalmatia, *Beilagen*, pp. 239-42.

Löcker, deputies of the fifth curia and the city curia, respectively. Here there was no national problem to solve, save for a motion made by the Czech National Socialist Václav Choc, which, if it had passed, would have cut the number of Upper Austrian mandates from twenty-two to sixteen. But there very definitely was present a contest between urban and rural interests, which Löcker chose to express as a struggle between liberals and conservatives.

Schlegel contended that the ministry's division of districts marked off rural and urban districts in direct contradiction to the true principle of universal, equal, direct, and secret suffrage. Population factors and geographical considerations had been ruthlessly sacrificed to party claims. He moved that districts be created as nearly equal in population as possible, with no differentiation between country and town.

Löcker countered with the argument that the higher levels of intelligence and the greater tax-incidence among urban inhabitants had to be respected. After all, was community of interests a negation of true universal and equal suffrage? To further the cause of justice, he moved that eight rather than seven of the districts be allotted to urban groups and submitted a plan mirroring this modification.

Bienerth rejected both proposals. He defended the separation of rural and urban areas as the best possible scheme for protection of varying interests; moreover, a certain regard for tax-incidence could not be ignored. He did not believe that districts could be created merely to confirm them in the possession of individual parties; nor could they be planned without due consideration of the political forces active there.

Bienerth's arguments carried great weight, for, on the recommendation of Gessmann, the committee sustained the government in every respect.[70]

A decision on Salzburg was easily reached. Without debate, the committee voted to accept the government's recommenda-

70 Debate on Upper Austria, *Beilagen*, pp. 243-8.

tion for seven seats, along with its scheme of electoral districts.[71]

The casual foreign observer of Austrian affairs in 1906 probably would have been surprised by the nationalistic bickering over Lower Austria. Indeed, there is even some humor to be gleaned from the remarks of Leopold Steiner, the Viennese Christian Socialist, who somewhat plaintively declared that he had expected no national battle over Lower Austria. He could only regret that the calm life hitherto enjoyed by the province was being disturbed by such issues. But the resentments fostered by radical nationalists in every camp gave no quarter even when Vienna was considered.

The first clashes over Lower Austria were to be expected. Dr. Otto Lecher took up the cudgels for Viennese Liberalism by proposing readjustment of some Viennese wards. Gessmann, the Christian Socialist, whose party had long fought Liberalism in Vienna, judiciously hinted that the government's plan was the result of a spirit of compromise which should not be pushed too far. Dr. Adler (who, incidently, represented a Bohemian fifth curia district), declared it was obvious that the proletariat was being choked by the undue regard vouchsafed propertied interest by the present plan. But, to set a good example for others to follow, he was prepared to vote for it in spite of the sacrifices thereby entailed.

This felicitous coordination of Christian Socialist compromise and Social Democratic abnegation was upset momentarily by the Young Czech Josef Čípera. Recalling the government's promise to protect national minorities, he declared the Lower Austrian division of mandates was ludicrous, for the Czechs living there had been totally ignored. According to his computations, they should be granted four mandates in Vienna, where the majority of them lived. Choc heartily supported this view; if Germans in Prague were to have mandates, why not the same treatment for Czechs in Vienna?

71 *Beilagen*, p. 248.

The German Progressives Gustav Gross and Anton Pergelt were outraged by the comparison of the well-established position of Germanism in Prague with the new Czech settlements dispersed throughout Lower Austria. After further recriminations on such a point as the motive of Charles IV in founding the University of Prague, a vote closed the issue by defeating every project save the one recommended by the ministry.[72]

The first lengthy discussion and vote on Styria lasted from June 15 through part of the meeting of June 22, 1906.[73] During these four sessions, the Slovene-German rivalry in Styria, Carinthia, and Carniola gave ample warning that no separate decision for each province could possibly be expected. The settlement was confused even more by *entr' acte* debates on Bukovinan and Galician affairs; for the sake of clarity, the dispositions accorded each of these three provinces will be treated as a whole.

Franz Hagenhofer, German Clerical deputy from a rural curia, was aroused by the government's seeming negligence in incorporating twenty-three decidedly industrial areas within rural districts. He introduced a new scheme of electoral districts which would better correspond to actual conditions as he saw them and likewise moved that Styria as a unit receive thirty-one rather than twenty-eight mandates. One was to go to a town and market district, a second to a German rural district, the third to a Slovene rural district.[74]

This modest olive branch extended to the Slovenes was bitterly denounced as treason to Germanism by Dr. Josef Pommer, a teacher representing the storm center of Cilli, and by

72 Debate on Lower Austria, *Beilagen*, pp. 248-51.

73 First debate on Styria, *Beilagen*, pp. 252-75.

74 In 1910, 70.5 per cent of the population of Styria gave German as their language, 29.4 per cent spoke Slovene. In Carinthia, German accounted for 78.6 per cent, Slovene for 21.2 per cent. In Carniola, 94.36 per cent spoke Slovene, 5.36 per cent spoke German. Auerbach, *op. cit.*, pp. 88-90.

Heinrich Wastian, a German Populist, who was a deputy of the slightly less stormy town of Marburg.[75] Pommer ridiculed the pretensions of Slovenes and illiterate peasants; such persons had no right to control other men better favored than themselves. Experience clearly revealed, he said, that every progressive modification of electoral requirements resulted in a loss of quality among voters. Springing at once to the attack on Carniola, he declared he would never vote for reform as long as the Germans there went unrepresented. Wastian blamed the growing tension between the two peoples on the " unchristian " politicking carried on by the Slovene clergy. In closing, he moved that several changes be made in the electoral districts so that Germans might be guaranteed certain seats intended for them.

Dr. Friedrich Ploj, Marchet's successor as chairman of the committee, stepped down to argue the Slovene case. He contended that it was obvious that the government planned to favor the German *Volkspartei* at the expense of Slovene and agrarian interests. To remedy the situation, he moved that eight seats be allotted to Lower Styrian rural districts and expressed approval of Hagenhofer's demand for three additional Styrian mandates. He likewise asked that the Cilli district be enlarged by incorporation of all Lower Styrian market towns, Marburg excepted. While denying any personal ambition to run for office in such a district, he slyly admitted Pommer might have trouble being reelected there. As for compromise, a new German seat in Graz might be traded for a new Lower Styrian mandate. Nothing whatsoever could be discussed on the subject of German claims in Carniola.

In the face of an apparent deadlock between the Slovenes and the members of the German *Volkspartei*, Bienerth arose to say that the government would agree to Hagenhofer's compro-

---

75 In 1888 Taaffe had promised Slovene parallel classes in the German Gymnasia in Cilli and Marburg. The failure to redeem the promise in Cilli led to continual friction and obstruction until 1895, when the classes finally were authorized. Kolmer, *op. cit.*, V, 511-15.

mise on division of rural and urban districts, if all other interested parties would also agree. He likewise admitted that some of Wastian's modifications were worthy of further study. But he rejected all plans for an increase in the total representation.

Hagenhofer changed his motion so that now only fourteen industrial centers were to be removed from rural areas. The acceptance of this modification, in addition to a favorable vote for some of Wastian's proposals, revised the government's division of districts somewhat.

Less pleasing to Pommer and Ploj was the rejection of their motions, both of which called for another seat which would benefit their own nationality. The latter's motion was voted on by roll-call, the first so to be treated. As might be expected, the Germans, with an Italian and a Social Democrat, were opposed by a Slavic bloc.

For a time, at least, Styria was settled.

Following an abortive attempt to resolve the Galician problem and the more successful treatment of Bukovina and Voralberg, the committee voted to consider Carinthia and Carniola (July 3).

The arguments over Carinthia touched upon practically the same grievances which had obtained in Styria. Ploj declared that the adoption of the ministerial plan would mean national annihilation to the 90,000 Slovenes in Carinthia, who had been divided among eight districts. He submitted a new plan of apportionment which would guarantee the Slovenes one seat and give them a fair chance at another. Dr. Artur Lemisch, a Carinthian *Volkspartei* deputy, replied that compromise was not to be had at such a late date. Should two districts be vouchsafed the Slovenes, the inhabitants still would elect Germans. He maintained that the conflicts in Carinthia were economic rather than national.

Kramář was quick to seize upon this argument as the best one made for Ploj's motion. If the Germans were so sure Slovenes would vote for Germans, why any opposition? Bienerth tried to calm both sides by a declaration that the government had been actuated by a desire to stave off too great a demarcation of national and urban-rural lines in Carinthia. Ploj's plan would create districts unequal in population.

Adler dropped some of his vaunted objectivity by inveighing against Ploj's plan; he feared the Socialist strength would be weakened under this new scheme. The final vote defeated Ploj's chief motion decisively, but his substitute motion (calling for less thoroughgoing changes), was defeated by only one vote. He was supported by three German Clericals; in time, he might count on some concessions. In Carinthia, however, the ministerial plan was victorious.[76]

German agitation for an extra seat in Carniola, to center about the Gottschee district,[77] was not the only strife unleashed by the speeches made. The Slovenes themselves, that is, the Liberal Plantan and the Clerical Šusteršič, were at swords' points over the division of districts.

It will be recalled that Dr. Löcker had recommended the passage of Hohenlohe's allotment of seats, plus an extra mandate for the Germans of Carniola. In accordance with this plan, he also moved that the district boundaries be changed. Other German deputies recited the usual figures on taxation and the usual proofs of culture in backing up Löcker's move. Their disgust over the voluntary denationalisation of Germans in Carniola was exceeded only by their desire to reclaim the erring ones.

Šusteršič denied the validity of the German claims to Gottschee, but he announced his willingness to compromise in return for justice to the Slovenes of Styria and Carinthia. Beck unexpectedly praised the spirit of Šusteršič's offer, while refusing to commit the cabinet to any compromise per se. Adler and Gessmann expressed hope that a real settlement

---

76 Debate on Carinthia, *Beilagen*, pp. 314-22.

77 Auerbach's discussion of Gottschee, *op. cit.*, pp. 91-93, is most useful as a guide to other literature on the subject, less useful as an objective judgment.

could be arranged, much to the alarm of less conciliatory Germans. Choc complicated matters by renewing his demand for Czech seats in Lower Austria; in some respects, his logic was correct.

Löcker's motion to increase Carniola's mandates from eleven to twelve passed by a vote of twenty-three to seventeen. The opposition included Adler, the Italian, and the Slavic members of the committee. His new composition of the Gottschee district also was accepted, with some minor changes. The attempts made by Plantan to modify the districts in favor of the urban middle class were defeated.[78]

Šusteršič at once moved that Carinthia and Styria be reconsidered with the object of guaranteeing two Slovene mandates in Carinthia together with a new seat for a Slovene rural district in Styria. According to the order of business, such reconsideration had to be approved by the same number of votes which previously had defeated Ploj's motion. In the case of Carinthia, the vote was insufficient; in the case of Styria, the twenty-six votes necessary were forthcoming, thanks to the Christian Socialists and the German Clericals.[79]

The most bitter tirades of the sessions held so far greeted this result. Open accusations of governmental bargaining with Šusteršič were voiced by the Germans and by the Slovene Liberal Plantan. Nor were the Christian Socialists and German Clericals spared; Hagenhofer, the Styrian who had voted in "Slovene interests," was finally forced to declare he would not vote for another Styrian seat.

Adler chided the more violent speakers for their belief that the people really were aroused by such a petty issue. His own party had been mistreated worst of all, but he did not create such scenes. Beck loyally stuck by his convictions that Slovenes were entitled to some concessions in return for the German victory over Gottschee. Kramář was of the opinion that the

78 Debate on Carniola, *Beilagen*, pp. 323-5, 331-4, 336-8, and 341-3.
79 *Beilagen*, p. 343.

Germans would forget the whole issue completely in ten years; for the moment, they had best pursue a middle course if they hoped for any future.

By a vote of twenty-three to nineteen, Styria's mandates were increased from twenty-eight to twenty-nine. This time Adler and three Christian Socialists supported the Slovene wishes. Ploj reintroduced his motion on the composition of the new district in a revised form which Wastian approved. Thus it was adopted.[80]

The last action of the committee before adjourning for the summer was a further reconsideration of Styria called for by Löcker's "great compromise." The Slovenes did not contest the new seat allotted the Germans; the final total for Styria was thirty mandates.[81]

While the final decisions were being made for Styria, Carinthia, and Carniola, some progress was forthcoming in the case of other provinces. Voralberg's number of mandates (four) and division of districts had been adopted as the government desired without debate on July 3.[82] On July 2, the debate on Bukovina began; a final settlement was made on the next day.

In view of the complicated relationships among nationalities in Bukovina,[83] the various claims were unusually mild. Hohenlohe had proposed an increase of three seats, one each for the Germans, Rumanians, and Ruthenes. Choc, the Czech National Socialist, first demanded that the new seat planned for the Germans be rejected, but he received small support.

Stanislaus Gląbinski, Polish National Democrat, also wanted to tamper with the arrangement by creating a fifteenth seat. This mandate would include a variety of nationalities, among whom the dispersed Polish groups would possibly be dominant. Bienerth's veiled disapproval of any increase in the total man-

---

80 Rediscussion of Styria, *Beilagen*, pp. 344-59.

81 *Beilagen*, p. 428.

82 *Beilagen*, p. 313.

83 See Auerbach, *op. cit.*, pp. 261-75.

dates was repaid by defeat of the Polish maneuver. Wassilkó, the Ruthene National Democrat, was not pleased with the treatment meted out to his people, but he acquiesced for the sake of harmony.

Motions made by Onciul, the Rumanian Liberal, and by Gustav Gross, German Progressive, calling for readjustments of several district limits, were passed with the ministry's approval. The grand total of mandates remained at fourteen.[84]

When discussion of Galicia was begun on June 22, the Pan-German Franz Stein, who represented Eger in Bohemia, formally moved that the ministry prepare a law recognizing special status for Galicia and Bukovina, a rallying cry of nationalistic German parties ever since the Linz Program of 1882.[85] Parliamentary rules, however, forced Stein to ask merely that discussion cease on Galicia, a motion favored by only eleven members.

In the meantime, Dr. Gląbinski's motion to consider total apportionment separately from division of districts had been accepted. Following up this success, he first asked that Galicia receive 140 seats, which was only its due according to his figures on population and tax-incidence. Should this be defeated, he demanded at least 110 seats, eight more than Hohenlohe had condescended to grant. Then Ruthenes and Poles both would be satisfied, and their strife would cease.

The Ruthene champion, Wassilkó, poured scorn on this new solicitude revealed by the Polish Club. Certainly he could not deny that Galicia did need more mandates, but he refused to believe an increase would benefit Ruthenes. Gautsch's plan had guaranteed twenty-seven seats to Ruthenes; by adroit maneuvers, the Poles had persuaded Hohenlohe to create a new system which would deprive Ruthenes of eight of these mandates.

Gląbinski denied that Hohenlohe's plan injured the Ruthenes; on the contrary, it created districts where Poles were

84 Debate on Bukovina, *Beilagen*, pp. 309-13.

85 A good résumé of the Linz Program can be found in Kolmer, *op. cit.*, III, 211-14. Dalmatia also was to receive special status, in the orthodox view.

reduced to a minority of 8-9 per cent where it had been 25 per cent. However, if Ruthene peasants preferred to vote for their Polish landlords, no system of districts could prevent such a result.

The open German fear of increased Slavic power found expression in a motion sponsored by Kaiser, German Populist, and Demel, German Progressive, specifying the grant of one extra seat for the town and environs of Biala. The men admitted the total German population there was disproportionate to the general average for Galicia. But their justification was the non-representation of over 250,000 Germans scattered throughout Galicia. A German deputy from Biala could speak for all of these Germans.[86]

Bienerth opposed any increase of seats, Polish or German. In the first place, Galicia had been given full credit for its population as modified by its taxation. In Biala, there were only 15,000 Germans; in all of Galicia, there were but 212,000 Germans, of whom 140,000 or 150,000 were Jews. All who favored reform should vote for the ministry's plan.

On June 28 the motions of Głąbinski and Kaiser were defeated in favor of the government's total of 102 seats. Kaiser's motion was supported by Wassilkó, who declared he was motivated by the Ruthene sense of justice for all. It was opposed by the Christian Socialists.

Galicia, it will be remembered, was to enjoy a system of proportional elections in the eastern portion of the province. Gautsch had submitted a plan which declared that any two candidates in districts which were to elect two deputies were to be considered elected if each received one-third of the votes cast. But Hohenlohe had recommended a change; now one candidate would have to receive at least one-half of the votes, the second at least one-fourth.[87]

---

86 A very fair analysis of Germans in Galicia during these years is given by Auerbach, *op. cit.*, pp. 252-257.

87 *Beilagen*, pp. 227-8.

Wassilkó was bitterly displeased by this revision. Nine of the eastern districts were to elect two Ruthene deputies, nine more were to elect one Ruthene deputy. He maintained the former situation would never obtain unless the Ruthenes were allowed to garner only one-third of the votes each. If one should have to capture at least one-half and the other at least one-fourth, the Polish minority would combine with other elements to defeat one of the Ruthenes. In spite of reassurances from Bienerth, he demanded a return to the Gautsch provisions. Otherwise, Polish terrorism would see to it that Ruthenes were rejected at elections by threatening recalcitrant Ruthene peasants with starvation. He called upon Kramář and Šusteršič to repeat their private remarks along the same lines.

Kramář, obviously embarrassed by this disclosure, first took pains to compliment the Polish Club for its conciliatory attitude. He said that he believed the nine districts intended for eighteen Ruthenes probably would elect eighteen Ruthenes. Nevertheless, to quiet Wassilkó's fears, he asked that a vote be postponed until some rectifications could be made in six of the districts. Abrahamowicz, the Polish Conservative, expressed agreement, and the chairman suspended the entire Galician discussion, on July 2.[88]

On July 6, Głąbinski announced that the Polish Club was ready to propose several changes in the districts mentioned by Kramář. These modifications reduced the Polish minorities in each district to 10-22 per cent; this respect for Ruthene desires, however, brought in its train unwieldy districts and destruction of many urban-rural lines of demarcation. On no account could the Polish Club ever permit abolition of proportional voting where it had already been planned.

Wassilkó recognized the improved intentions of the Poles, but he insisted that either proportional voting be abolished or else applied to the whole province. In case any proportional districts were retained, he would prefer the Gautsch formula.

88 First debate on Galicia, *Beilagen,* pp. 275-309.

Bienerth took such an opinion to be a sign of conditional compromise. Therefore, the ministry would be glad to recommend the adoption of Głąbinski's changes. The vote sustained his request; Löcker's motion to accept Hohenlohe's phraseology of Articles 34 and 35 of the new law on elections to the Reichsrat was adopted along with an additional phrase contributed by Starzyński.[89]

The committee's inability to reach a decision on Tyrol and Bohemia reopened the whole Galician question as well. On July 21, Löcker suggested a compromise, which, among other things, increased Galicia's mandates by four, all of which were to be "Slavic."

Starzyński soon pointed out that the previous Polish plea for 110 mandates was predicated on a house of 455 members. If Löcker's plan for a 516-member house should pass, Galicia would be forced to ask for at least 114 of the seats. Unfortunately for Starzyński, the committee evidently felt itself forced to vote otherwise, for Löcker's figure was accepted.

Głąbinski had worked out a new system of districts, which Bienerth recommended. Two seats were divided between Lemberg and Krakov; the other two were to go to a new rural district in eastern Galicia. Only one of the latter two was to be Ruthene. Wassilkó denounced this ministerial " partisanship " to no avail; Głąbinski's plan was triumphant. The representatives of Galicia had come a long way since Gautsch first promised them eighty-eight seats.[90]

On July 13 the Littoral territories (Istria, Gorizia and Gradisca, and Trieste) were considered as a whole. It was obvious that a compromise already had been reached between the Italian Bartoli and the Croat Ivčević in the face of lively opposition from the Slovene representative from the rural commune of Gorizia, Oskar Gabrščik.

89 Further debate on Galicia, *Beilagen*, pp. 327-31.
90 Final debate on Galicia, *Beilagen*, pp. 421-6.

The ministerial plan called for five Istrian seats, three Slovene and two Italian. The compromise added one Italian seat to make a total of six. In Gorizia and Gradisca, an extra Italian seat was to be centered in the city of Gorizia. In return for these favors, the Italians surrendered the extra mandate in Trieste which Hohenlohe had promised them.

Adler lost no time in asserting that Bartoli's new grouping of districts purposely split up the workers' votes in Trieste. He asked that the old Gautsch delimitation be followed. Bienerth seemed nonplussed by the compromise but limited his disapproval, if any, to the warning that Italians still would be limited to a grand total of eighteen seats. The Slovene Šušteršič at once declared that his people accepted the compromise only with this stipulation. Seven Germans and the isolated Gabrščik failed to defeat Bartoli's new plan; even Adler voted in its favor.[91]

The morning of July 16 was devoted to a shortlived discussion of Tyrol. Hohenlohe had planned two new seats for Tyrol, one German, one Italian, bringing the total to twenty-three. After the compromise on the Littoral, however, Germans and Slovenes seemed intent on denying Italians a new mandate in Tyrol. Malfatti, Bartoli's Italian Liberal colleague, reminded the anti-Italian bloc that he had refused to surrender Italian claims in Tyrol for those in the Littoral.

The issue was further complicated by a series of changes in electoral districts which Eduard Erler, German Populist, sponsored in the interests of urban centers. The Christian Socialist Josef Schraffl repudiated all such schemes; but both were in perfect harmony in favoring a mandate for the obscure "Ladine nationality," at Italian expense. Faced with such contradictory currents, the committee decided to postpone the whole discussion.[92]

91 Debate on the Littoral, *Beilagen*, pp. 360-4.

92 First debate on Tyrol, *Beilagen*, pp. 366-70.

Löcker's "great compromise," offered on July 21, reopened the Tyrolean problem by recommending twenty-five mandates for the province—two new German seats in return for the Italian seat imperilled by the Littoral compromise. It was evident that practically all factions involved had come to an agreement. Erler and Schraffl composed their differences in a joint motion on composition of districts, which passed, and the Italian Dr. Enrico Conci grudgingly declared he would vote for Löcker's plan.[93]

In great contrast to the fiasco attending the first discussion of Tyrol on the morning of July 16, the afternoon session on Silesia proceeded with a great show of calm and conciliatory gestures.

The fifteen seats planned by Hohenlohe were to be divided as follows: nine for the Germans, three for the Czechs, and three for the Poles. A Czech-Polish combination moved that a sixteenth seat be given to the Poles, but Bienerth firmly refused assent. At the same time, he justified as well as he could the varying bases followed by the government in setting up districts. As for changes suggested by the Poles and Czechs, he did not believe they would injure or improve the situation.

In the decisive vote, a German-Italian-Social Democratic alliance defeated the proposed sixteenth seat; on the other hand, some rectifications desired by the Czechs and Poles were granted.[94]

A combination of expedients kept Bohemia from the order of business until July 17. No other crownland offered difficulties as great as those offered by the two extremely well-developed national groups existing there. In Galicia, the ministry could always turn to the Ruthenes as a counter-weight to the Polish Club. So it went in nearly every province where national rivalries predominated. In Bohemia, no settlement could possibly please both Czechs and Germans, nor did any cabinet

93 Final debate on Tyrol, *Beilagen*, pp. 426-7.
94 Debate on Silesia, *Beilagen*, pp. 371-6.

dare try to resolve the problem by a clear recognition of either Czech or German supremacy. In the light of these circumstances, the ministry's makeshift compromise was nothing short of a minor triumph.

The 122 mandates promised Bohemia by Hohenlohe were to be divided as 72 for the Czechs, 50 for the Germans. The Young Czech Čípera opened the arguments with a lesson in mathematics purportedly proving Bohemia's right to 125 mandates. He moved that this increase be accepted, with the proviso that Czechs be given 75 of the deputies. Choc raised the price to 128 seats, of which 80 were to be Czech.

The Germans of Bohemia were not to be outdone in proclaiming the need for greater provincial representation. Pergelt wanted 130 seats, 58 of which were to be German. As he pointed out, Hohenlohe regrettably had already promised the Czechs 72 seats, which now they would never relinquish. Whatever the final decision might be, the ratio should remain 72:58.

Kramář had exhibited great reserve throughout the previous debates, but Pergelt's plan stirred him to a burst of oratory which put to shame the usual petty verbosity of most of the committeemen. Who were these German Bohemians, he asked, before the great industrial expansion of the 1870's? How did they amass their wealth and consolidate their position if not by selling their goods, amply protected by tariffs, to Czech consumers? As a confirmed believer in reform, he had manifested the greatest amount of accommodation possible. Czechs could not be stampeded into accepting a mockery of justice. As a final thrust, he informed the Germans that constant repetition of the glories of Goethe would scarcely induce the Czechs to deprecate their own cultural heritage.

The rest of the debate was a series of accusations and counter-claims involving such matters as the accuracy of the last census, the proportion of taxes borne by Czechs or Germans, German responsibility for the Czech literary revival, opportunities open to Germans in the provincial bureaucracy, etc. It was all too clear that a decade of open hostility combined with the heat of a Viennese summer actually threatened collapse of the whole reform.

On July 21 Löcker announced his compromise plan. With obvious government backing, he made the pill easier for other Slavic groups to swallow by tempting them with more mandates. Bohemia was now to have eight new seats, five German and three Czech, making a total of 130. Kramář complimented Löcker on his personal honesty of purpose and self-sacrifice but rejected the plan. Pergelt likewise insisted on his own solution.

The vote which followed offered an interesting sight. Voting against the compromise were such men as Kramář, Čípera, and Choc, the Pan-Germans Malik and Stein, and fourteen other Czech and German deputies of slightly less chauvinistic tinge. Christian Socialists, Poles, South Slavs, and Italians, with some support from Löcker's party, carried the day for the compromise. The new ratio was to be 75:55, and the districts were to be *preponderantly* German or Czech. The task of working out district lines was left to a future date.[95]

When the committee reassembled after the summer recess, Pergelt and Kramář announced that each nationality had elaborated a plan for the composition of the districts allotted to it, but they both asked for more time to consider petitions from their constituents (September 12).[96]

On October 10, 11, and 12 the plans were finally submitted and discussed. Kramář reiterated the determination of the Czechs to fight the apportionment ration in the coming parliamentary readings and moved that the Budweis district be counted as a German rather than Czech district. This last ditch maneuver was decisively defeated, and the plan for the fifty-five German seats was accepted with a few changes. The Czech plan for their seventy-five seats suffered even fewer revisions.[97]

95 Debate on the total mandates for Bohemia, *Beilagen*, pp. 377-418.

96 *Beilagen*, p. 430.

97 Debate on Bohemian districts, *Beilagen*, pp. 624-48.

On the afternoon of July 21, the last day before the recess, Löcker's compromise proposal for Moravia was accepted after limited discussion. The Czechs resented the ministry's plan because it followed the recent compromise on diet elections in Moravia. They averred that they had accepted this compromise only to gain a minimum of justice; they were not prepared to accept the same "stepchild" treatment in imperial representation. Choc condemned the whole Moravian compromise as the source of an unnatural tendency, differentiation of Bohemian and Moravian aspirations.

Nevertheless, Löcker's plan was victorious. Moravia was to have forty-nine mandates, thirty Czech and nineteen German. Actual demarcation of districts was left to conferences to be held during the summer.[98]

On October 9 the German and Czech plans for division of their respective mandates were accepted, after a violent tirade from Choc failed to reopen the entire series of decisions on Bohemia, Moravia, and Silesia.[99]

At last the chief task of the committee was finished. The lengthy parliamentary review to follow did not upset the committee's decisions on apportionment, in spite of vigorous efforts on the part of various deputies.

The nationalities were to receive the following mandates: German, 233; Czech, 107; Polish, 82; Ruthene, 33; Slovene, 24; Serbo-Croat, 13; Italian, 19; Rumanian, 5.[100]

What of the heartless disregard of the Ladines, the peers of all the historic nationalities in Austria?

Such a question, or less absurd variations on a like theme, tempted some writers into compiling long tables of statistics proving the inequalities and injustices of this particular "balance of power." Full recognition of the value of such inquests is not to be denied for a moment.

98 Debate on total mandates for Moravia, *Beilagen*, pp. 418-21.

99 Debate on division of Moravian mandates, *Beilagen*, pp. 617-23.

100 As given in the committee's report, *Beilagen*, p. 5.

Hindsight, admittedly an ambiguous ally, hints that such external proof of inequality was but one manifestation of a mistaken policy of centralism; as such a manifestation, it is best left subordinate to the judgment pronounced upon the whole reform.

THE RETENTION OF THE RURAL-URBAN DIVISION OF ELECTORAL DISTRICTS

The electoral reform of 1907 would indubitably have met with the fate suffered by Taaffe's reform of 1893 had not the demarcation of electoral districts met with the grudging approval of the majority of the nationalities of Austria. The greatest single achievement of the Lower House's electoral committee was its work in arranging successive compromises among the nationalities in the creation of electoral districts. In addition to effecting these compromises, the committee had to deal with the clash of rural and urban interests; aside from different economic desires, city and country often manifested different attitudes toward the position of the Roman Catholic Church. Many exceptions could be found to this generalization in 1907, for the Christian Socialists, avowedly devout, had effective support in rural and urban areas. Nevertheless, religious issues were secondary only to economic conflicts between town and country, and the committee was saddled with the task of lessening such conflicts wherever possible.

Under the curial system, rural communes had been separated from urban areas in the construction of electoral districts. However, the districts created in 1896 for the voters in the fifth curia were admittedly too large, so that in effect they tended to modify the earlier separation of rural and urban voters. Consequently, Gautsch was confronted with the problem of retaining a strict division of voters along rural and urban lines or of scrapping the old procedure in favor of amalgamated districts. In November, 1905 he was content to say that electoral districts would be as nationally homogeneous as possible; his lack of reference to a continuing separation of rural and urban interests caused several deputies to urge no break with the past. Skedl, the German Progressive deputy of urban centers in Bukovina, asked the Minister-President to emphasize the separation of provincial towns from rural districts in his elaboration of electoral districts, because of their completely disparate interests.[101] The German Populist Herzmansky declared that German farmers would not support a reform without a separation; they were already prepared to leave industrial districts and markets in the hands of the Social Democrats.[102] The Czech Agrarian spokesman, Zázvorka, declared that agrarian representatives of every nationality would stand united in achieving a strict division of rural and urban areas.[103]

No opposition to these demands was made in the Lower House, and Gautsch's specific delimitation of districts, introduced in February, 1906, clearly continued the practice of a rural-urban separation. The Minister of the Interior, Bylandt, defended his handiwork with the statement that separation seemed to be the best means of protecting the interests of all voters in Austria.[104] For the most part, the ministry's attitude was praised in the first reading which followed. Schlegel spoke of petitions from market-places which previously had voted in urban districts and whose inhabitants resented their proposed incorporation in rural districts,[105] and other deputies raised similarly minor points. However, Kramář expressed distinct disapproval of Gautsch's plan. A reform based on such a principle would be socially unjust, in his opinion, for the larger tax receipts of the cities would have to be considered in the apportionment of mandates.[106] Kramář's public objections

101 *S. P. A.*, XXXV, 32444, Nov. 30, 1905.

102 *S. P. A.*, XXXVI, 32601, Dec. 5, 1905.

103 *S. P. A.*, XXXVI, 32614, Dec. 5, 1905.

104 *S. P. A.*, XXXVIII, 34827, Mar. 7, 1906.

105 *S. P. A.*, XXXVIII, 34843, Mar. 7, 1906.

106 *S. P. A.*, XXXVIII, 35250-1, Mar. 15, 1906.

were not above suspicion; as the leader of a party which depended more and more on bourgeois Czech support, he obviously was fearful of a rigid demarcation which would solidify the power of his rivals, the Czech Agrarians. The Young Czechs could continue to keep their influence in rural areas only if the rivalry of town and country was de-emphasized in the electoral arrangements. For similar partisan reasons, the Slovene Clerical Šusteršič opposed the division of country and city; he reasoned that a town had more in common with the country surrounding it than it did with other towns 20 to 50 kilometers distant.[107] Privately, the able Slovene leader might have been accused of desiring to submerge the relatively few Slovene urban voters in a sea of devout rural voters. His Liberal Slovene colleague Ferjančič openly alleged that Gautsch had delivered the Liberal city-dwellers to the power of the rural Clericals.[108] Perhaps no better tribute could be paid the ministry's labors than this simultaneous criticism from Liberal and Clerical Slovenes. Despite considerable Young Czech pressure, the concept of a division of rural and urban areas was maintained in the final demarcation of districts, for nearly every party seemed to feel that such a division would enhance its own chances of victory in the future.

PROVISIONS FOR CHANGES IN THE ELECTION LAW OF THE REICHSRAT AND IN THE APPORTIONMENT OF ELECTORAL DISTRICTS

On October 9, 1906 the electoral committee finished its herculean task of apportioning mandates. Any individual armed with population figures could point out numerous examples of inequality among the nationalities and could prove very easily that the Germans controlled mandates to which they were not entitled on the basis of population. No Slavic leader would deny for a minute that the Germans had done very well for

107 *S. P. A.*, XXXIX, 35425, Mar. 20, 1906.
108 *S. P. A.*, XXXIX, 35459, Mar. 20, 1906.

themselves; the Slavs, it was agreed, had accepted the German price for the sake of universal equal suffrage. The capital question of the day, however, revolved about possible revisions of the Election Law and of the apportionment of mandates in the future. In the new Lower House, the Slavs would theoretically control 259 mandates as against 233 theoretical German mandates, with Italians and Rumanians making up the remaining 24 seats. If changes were to be made by a simple majority, it was obvious that even a combined German-Italian-Rumanian bloc would be unable to withstand Slavic desires. On the other hand, if a certain percentage of all members of the Lower House had to be present for changes in the law or in the electoral districts, the Germans might well be able to block any modifications forever, simply by absenting themselves from the Lower House.

The problem of creating machinery for modifications of the electoral reform was put off as long as possible. Hohenlohe, when Minister-President, had recommended that the vital articles of the new Election Law and the delimitation of electoral districts be modified only if one-half of the members of the Lower House were present to vote on suggested changes and only if two-thirds of these members agreed to the changes. Technically, the Slavic deputies would be able to make modifications, if they were the only deputies present; in reality, the two-thirds rule was a permanent assurance that the Germans never would be coerced by Slavs, Italians, or Rumanians. The Czechs had been particularly incensed by Hohenlohe's proposal, and their rage, according to one observer, was the real reason for Hohenlohe's abrupt departure from Vienna.[109] On October 17, 1906 the burning issue between Germans and Slavs could be postponed no longer; discussion of a proposed Article 42 of the Election Law of the Reichsrat, which would specify the procedure for modifying particular parts of the Election Law and the demarcation of electoral districts, was begun in the electoral committee.

109 Beaumont, *op. cit.*, pp. 627-8.

The German Populist Chiari leaped to the defense of Hohenlohe's proposal with the blunt assertion that Germans would
accept reform on no other basis. The proposed article guaranteed no more than a minimum of protection for the Germans,
and it was a just price that the cabinet had to pay.[110] Kramář,
in rebuttal, warned his listeners that it was erroneous to believe that the Czechs would accept anything, just to secure
electoral reform. If a just reform had been forthcoming, the
Czechs would have been glad to accept the two-thirds rule. But
apportionment had not been just, and the Czech people refused
to accept another evidence of political inferiority. In Kramář's
opinion, it was stupid to fear either a Slavic or a German bloc
in the Lower House; internal conflicts within each nationality
were too great. Were the Germans honestly afraid of a two-
vote Slavic majority? The Czechs had already surrendered a
great deal in accepting the 75:55 ratio of mandates for
Bohemia; they absolutely refused to undergo another
Canossa.[111]

The German Progressive Gross refused to take Kramář too
seriously. After all, the Germans had told every cabinet that
the two-thirds rule was absolutely necessary, for they could not
hope to oppose unjust changes forever by obstruction alone.
In a chiding manner, Gross asked Kramář to reflect a little on
the two-thirds rule. It was not really so frightful, when one
considered that the hard-won decisions on electoral reform
should have some immunity from sudden momentary attacks.
Would Kramář, a true friend of reform, like to see plural suffrage introduced by a simple majority, for instance? [112] Instead
of placating the Czechs, Gross seemed to arouse them further.
Zázvorka, the Czech Agrarian, pledged his party's support of
Kramář's refusal to compromise and announced that those per-

110 *Beilagen*, pp. 650-1, Oct. 17, 1906.
111 *Beilagen*, pp. 651-4, Oct. 17, 1906.
112 *Beilagen*, p. 654, Oct. 17, 1906.

sons who feared that Czechs could be seduced by an electoral reform into an acceptance of a centralized empire could now relax; the German insistence on a two-thirds rule proved to Czechs that they could expect nothing from reform.[113]

The first day's discussion had gone very badly. Kramář had won an enviable place in the esteem of his colleagues, thanks to his ability and unquestioned devotion to the cause of electoral reform; the very tone of the remarks made by Gross was evidence of the German desire to conciliate the Young Czech leader. Into the vacuum stepped the Italian deputy Malfatti with a compromise proposal. For eighteen years, Hohenlohe's formula would obtain; thereafter, changes might be made by the affirmative vote of 60 per cent of all of the deputies of the Lower House.[114]

The resumption of discussion on the following day widened the breach between Germans and Czechs. The Young Czech Stránský said that the controversy was a matter of sheer survival as well as of national honor with his people. An individual without honor would vegetate and be useless; the same was true of a nationality, the sum of all of its individual members.[115] For the rest of the day's session, the violent Czech nationalist Choc led the Czech offensive. His remarks revealed a certain disagreement with Kramář's attitude, but the disparity was of no consolation to the Germans. Choc asserted that the Young Czech leader had no right to say that the Czechs would have agreed to the two-thirds rule in return for full justice in apportionment of mandates; Kramář, according to this critic, was treacherously demanding less than what was due the Czechs.[116] The next two sessions were marred by continuing recriminations between Czechs and Germans. Löcker begged Kramář to realize that every ministry was duty-bound to see to it that

113 *Beilagen*, pp. 654-5, Oct. 17, 1906.

114 *Beilagen*, p. 657, Oct. 17, 1906.

115 *Beilagen*, p. 659, Oct. 18, 1906.

116 *Beilagen*, p. 669, Oct. 18, 1906.

a great reform, which would create enough confusion as it was, be protected from rash new assaults. State interest, not narrow interests, demanded the retention of the rule.[117] The Czechs were not convinced, and the battle continued.

By October 23 the seriousness of the situation was causing grave concern in the highest circles. Abrahamowicz, the spokesman of the Polish Club in the committee, was summoned by the Emperor, who informed him that every effort was to be made to prevent the holding of the general election of 1907 on the old basis of curial representation; in other words, every effort was to be made to save the electoral reform.[118] In the committee meeting of the same day, Abrahamowicz declared that the Polish Club would vote for any plan that would substantially guarantee permanence to the decisions already made.[119] Other deputies seemed equally desirous of ending the dangerous developments. Šušteršič expressed profound dislike for the two-thirds rule, but agreed that some formula had to be found to escape the dilemma.[120] Adler optimistically asserted that reform could not be wrecked by violent nationalists, whose utterances fortunately merely aroused the curiosity of the masses. The masses, according to Adler, would decide when the reform was obsolete; they were the decisive two-thirds. Consequently, the Social Democrats scorned the essentially useless " means of protecting " the new system which were being discussed.[121] Towards the close of discussion, Stránský offered a surprise motion which would permit changes in the Election Law by a two-thirds vote of at least one-half of the membership of the Lower House (Hohenlohe's formula), while al-

117 *Beilagen*, p. 674, Oct. 22, 1906.
118 Steinitz, ed., *op. cit.*, p. 212.
119 *Beilagen*, p. 685.
120 *Beilagen*, pp. 680-1.
121 *Beilagen*, pp. 681-2.

lowing changes in the division of districts by a simple majority.[122] The deadlock was beginning to dissolve.

On October 24 the Emperor applied more pressure by summoning the five members of Beck's cabinet who had been deputies in the Lower House. To these representatives of the Germans, Czechs, and Poles, Francis Joseph repeated the admonition given Abrahamowicz on the previous day.[123] Beck and his ministers vigorously pursued negotiations with Czechs and Germans, and on the following day, Gessmann introduced a compromise which had the consent of practically all concerned.[124] No changes could be made in certain articles of the Electoral Law [125] or in the demarcation of electoral districts unless 343 members of the future Lower House of 516 were present. Not to be reckoned in this total were deputies who at the time of voting were members of the cabinet or of the presidium of the Lower House, or who had been chosen to act as reporters in recording the balloting. In cases involving changes in the law which applied to a district which elected more than one deputy or in case of a proposed change in the demarcation of such a district, at least half of the deputies representing the province in which such districts were located had to be presented when balloting took place. Should any proposed change fail to attract the necessary number of deputies, it was to be considered defeated. Finally, the regular order of business of the Lower House was not to be used as a means of getting around the new ruling.

Gessmann's compromise still assured the Germans control over modifications of the law and of electoral districts, if the Germans maintained complete control of the 233 mandates theoretically guaranteed them. Should the Germans fail to

122 *Beilagen*, p. 684.

123 Sieghart, *op. cit.*, p. 97.

124 *Beilagen*, p. 691, Oct. 25, 1906.

125 Specifically, Articles 1, 4, 5, 33, 34, 35, 36, 37, 42.

maintain internal unity or lose a large number of seats to German Social Democrats who might favor revision, then the Slavs might have a chance to change the decisions made in 1906. The compromise was accepted by a vote of thirty-two to twelve. In the opposition were the Pan-Germans, several German Progressives and Populists, a few Czechs (no Young Czechs), a Ruthene, and a Slovene. The Ruthene representative could hardly be expected to endorse a plan which meant a continuing Polish vise on Galicia; the ministry once again had paid the Polish Club a handsome commission.

THE ATTEMPT TO REVISE PARLIAMENTARY PROCEDURE

The Lower House of the Austrian Reichsrat enjoyed an unparalleled notoriety for its inability to discipline its own members. Obstruction was the order of the day from 1898 to 1904; by the year 1905, many deputies were convinced that electoral reform was a prime necessity, but that electoral reform would be of little consequence without a new order of parliamentary procedure. Parliamentary anarchy was indeed a great compulsion for reform, but reform could not hope to succeed without adequate checks on the multitude of nationalistic and party views which would be found in the universally elected new Lower House. Gautsch was clearly worried by the latter possibility; in announcing his support of an electoral reform in November, 1905, he declared that a new order of business had to be evolved, as a preventative measure. Otherwise, great expectations of improvement would be deceived by a recurrence of parliamentary paralysis.[126]

The Minister-President did not advance any specific recommendations, and his reference to a new procedure did not excite a great deal of comment. The German Progressive Artur Skedl warned Gautsch not to insist on a new order of business in connection with electoral reform, lest the latter suf-

126 *S. P. A.*, XXXV, 32322, Nov. 28, 1905.

fer;[127] Adler ridiculed "practitioners of procedure" who were fanatically particular in setting up rules and regulations. The worst type of procedure, he said, would function famously in a good house, and vice versa.[128] Other deputies who mentioned the issue of procedure were not disposed to welcome Gautsch's remarks with enthusiasm. The Italian deputy Lenassi pointed out that the small number of Italian deputies forced them to be very wary of considering procedural changes; in his opinion, it would be better to turn the problem over to the new Lower House.[129] The Polish Socialist Breiter emphatically denounced the proposal as a senseless shackling of the new house by the old house.[130]

Undeterred by the few voices of dissent, Gautsch included in his definite program of February, 1906 a request for a modification of the law of May 12, 1873,[131] which regulated the Reichsrat's order of business. The new regulation would enforce a greater degree of discipline in parliamentary sessions, and it also would limit the right of deputies to attack verbally persons not in parliament, a right, which, Gautsch felt, had been abused. It would be difficult to discern any party or national alignments in the discussions which followed. The Czech National Socialists, it is true, bitterly attacked the proposed provision which required thirty signatures for the introduction of an interpellation of the ministry; such a requirement, they said, would isolate and make impotent the small parties. They also protested the modification of the immunity of deputies, arguing that the bureaucrats would soon have no respect what-

127 *S. P. A.*, XXXV, 32445, Nov. 30, 1905.

128 *S. P. A.*, XXXV, 32455, Nov. 30, 1905.

129 *S. P. A.*, XXXVI, 32562, Dec. 4, 1905.

130 *S. P. A.*, XXXVI, 32595, Dec. 5, 1905.

131 For the text of the law, Leo Geller, *Oesterreichische Verfassungs-Gesetze* (Vienna, 1896), pp. 94-101.

soever for the members of the Lower House.[132] Dr. Otto Lecher was similarly opposed to the new procedure. All parties, he pointed out, were moving toward an uncertain future, and he was of the opinion that it would be stupid to surrender without a fight the trusty weapon of obstruction. Obstruction was indeed a sign of fever and illness, but could one expect other remedies for the fever in the future? Nationalistic strife would not disappear in the new house, and vices and failings such as lust for power, egoism, even violent action would be pardoned when exercised in the interest of a particular nationality. The Germans unquestionably would be forced into a minority status if they relinquished the right of obstruction; the procedure of business should be modernized, but not in connection with electoral reform.[133] The German Agrarian Seidel was even more pessimistic about the effect a new procedure would have upon the German people; in his estimate, the adoption of Gautsch's plans would mark the grave of Germanism.[134] Adler continued to discount the effect of new procedure on obstruction, which was only the symptoms of a sickness which procedure could not remedy. As for the new checks on freedom of speech in parliament, Adler supported them on the condition that they be used to guarantee the absolute freedom and honor of persons outside of the Lower House.[135] A German deputy of the landowners curia, Count Trauttmansdorff, had his own interpretation of Gautsch's recommendation of a new order of

132 Speeches of Karel Baxa, *S. P. A.*, XXXIX, 35579, Mar. 22, 1906, and of Václav Klofáč, *S. P. A.*, XXXVIII, 35190-3, Mar. 14, 1906.

133 *S. P. A.*, XXXVIII, 35264, Mar. 15, 1906. Lecher was franker in his general insistence upon obstruction than other "Liberals" of German sympathies. Friedrich von Wieser, for instance, simply implied in his writings that a revised procedure inspired in him no confidence in improved parliamentary conditions. *Über Vergangenheit und Zukunft der österreichischen Verfassung* (Vienna, 1905), p. 114.

134 *S. P. A.*, XXXIX, 35517, Mar. 21, 1906.

135 *S. P. A.*, XXXVIII, 34987-8, Mar. 9, 1906.

business; the Minister-President felt insecure, for he realized that those who did not need a more stringent procedure had been slated to leave the Lower House.[136]

A few deputies welcomed the project of a new procedure for parliament. Dr. Josef Baernreither, though skeptical of the entire reform, felt that some means of discipline should be made available to the presiding officers of the Lower House, providing a settlement of the irritating problems of translation of deputies' speeches into German was made simultaneously.[137] Another German deputy, Haueis, predicted no decrease of obstruction unless a strict new order of business was introduced as part of the general reform,[138] and his views were echoed by Olszewski, of the Polish Populists.[139] At the close of debate, it was fairly obvious that the Lower House was disinclined to tamper with its existing order of procedure, at least in connection with the introduction of universal manhood suffrage. The electoral committee ignored the issue, and Gautsch's successors did not press the matter. Consequently, the committee submitted a report to the Lower House which did not mention a modification of the law of May 12, 1873. The Conservative autonomists, Sylva-Tarouca and Abrahamowicz, resolutely condemned the committee for its failure to attempt a change in procedure,[140] while Piniński, in the Upper House, was so much alarmed by the lack of a new procedure that he refused to vote for any part of electoral reform.[141] These objections were of no consequence; the fate of a new procedure was left to the disposition of the new parliament. Obstruction still could be the order of the day.

136 *S. P. A.*, XXXVIII, 35332, Mar. 16, 1906.

137 *S. P. A.*, XXXIX, 35489, Mar. 21, 1906.

138 *S. P. A.*, XXXIX, 35448, Mar. 20, 1906.

139 *S. P. A.*, XXXIX, 35494, Mar. 21, 1906.

140 Speech of Sylva-Tarouca, *S. P. A.*, XLIII, 39562, Nov. 7, 1906; of Abrahamowicz, *S. P. A.*, XLIII, 39683, Nov. 9, 1906.

141 *S. P. H.*, p. 1425, Dec. 21, 1906.

CHAPTER V
THE ELECTIONS OF 1907 [1]

In accordance with the revised Electoral Law of the Reichsrat, general elections to the Lower House of the Austrian parliament were held in May, 1907. For the first time in history, European political scientists who alternately feared and hoped for the collapse of the Habsburgs had an opportunity to study the expressed will of Francis Joseph's Austrian subjects, many of whom had never before exercised the right to vote. Simultaneously, Austrians had a chance to grope for an answer to many of the questions which seemed to perturb the members of the last privileged Lower House. Would the agrarian masses, as the liberals of all nationalities feared, troop to the polls to vote in accordance with the real or presumed instructions of their priests and thereby pave the way for a renaissance of clerical influence in affairs of state? Or, would the previously disfranchised masses vote emphatically for the Social Democrats, whose social and economic program appeared to many to be an unparalleled threat to stability, even decency? Would the necessary sums for the defense of the empire be forthcoming, or would a group of anti-militarists in the new Lower House expose the empire to shame and defeat by questioning the recruiting laws and the alliance system? Worst of all, would the disappearance of the relatively non-partisan privileged groups result in a general increase of nationalistic bickering within the Lower House? In more optimistic vein, would the new Lower House eschew the arid disputes which had disfigured parliamentary life since 1893 and turn its attention to the pressing social and economic problems of Austria?

1 For an excellent survey of the results of the elections of 1907, see Gabriel-Louis Jaray, " L'Autriche Nouvelle: Sentiments Nationaux et Préoccupations Sociales," *Annales des Sciences Politiques*, XXIII (1908), 293-310, 664-683. For a comparison of the results of these elections with previous Austrian elections, see Table I, Appendix.

The actual process of voting gave cause for considerable optimism, for the campaign was relatively calm despite a vast array of candidates and parties. There were the usual disturbances in Galicia, though quite mild, and sporadic outbursts in Trieste and Czernowitz. General economic prosperity blunted the edge of possible proletarian resentment, for the business " crisis " of 1907 had not yet appreciably affected Austria; the agrarian classes were particularly pleased by the rising price of meat. The government studiously avoided any attempt to influence the voters, though its distaste for the Social Democrats and Pan-Germans was an open secret. Nevertheless, Italian irredentists alleged that Beck used governmental pressure to promote Social Democratic victories in Trieste; one may well doubt that Italian Social Democrats were preferable to irredentists in the eyes of the cabinet. As a matter of fact, only one member of the cabinet who was a candidate for the Lower House, Prade, was elected on the first ballot; his German Populist colleague Derschatta was only able to triumph at a second election, thanks to the Social Democrats, who preferred him to a Christian Socialist. Marchet, the able and influential German Progressive, who had done much to further reform, was decisively defeated. In Galicia, the Ruthenes found that even secret balloting did not eliminate manipulation, but their complaints could not be justly laid at the cabinet's doorstep; the Polish political machine, operating through electoral commissioners, was too effective to disintegrate overnight. The elections attracted considerable interest, and the number of voters participating was encouraging.[2]

In brief, what were the significant results of the elections of 1907? In the first place, the guardians of privilege virtually disappeared, as expected. In the second place, the parties which

2 Some 4,617, 360 persons voted (roughly 82 per cent of the total estimated electorate.) See Table II, Appendix. In 1897 in Dalmatia, only 4 per cent of those entitled to vote in the fifth curia did vote; in 1907, 48 per cent of the electorate participated. In the same elections of 1897 and 1907, participation in Galicia increased from 33 to 85 per cent, in Bukovina, from 13 to 69 per cent. Gayda, *op. cit.*, pp. 52-53.

were generally representative of the middle class suffered losses. The German Progressives elected nineteen deputies, in contrast to thirty-nine elected in 1901; the Young Czechs dropped from fifty-three elected in 1901 to twenty-one. The German Populists, who vied with the Christian Socialists for the support of the lower German bourgeoisie, succeeded in capturing only twenty-nine of the fifty-one mandates they had secured in 1901. The chief beneficiaries were the Christian Socialists, who jumped from twenty-two to sixty-eight, and the Social Democrats, who astounded themselves by increasing their overall strength from ten to eighty-seven. Equally significant were the victories of the Agrarian and Clerical parties in all parts of the empire; the avowed anticlerical Richard Charmatz gloomily counted 187 friends of the Church among the 516 deputies. Finally, it might be said that the most violent nationalists of every nationality were rejected by the electorate; this generalization is a relative one, for the elections of 1901 had returned the most intransigent nationalists yet seen in Austria. Schönerer's Pan-Germans in 1907 obtained only three seats, though the milder Pan-German fraction led by Wolf won fourteen. This modification of Pan-German strength is more significant, as are all of the results, when one remembers that the new Lower House had 516 members instead of 425. Of the 516 members, over 300 had not belonged to the previous Lower House.

THE GERMAN DEPUTIES

Theoretically, the Germans of Austria, who formed 35.8 per cent of the total population, had been guaranteed 233 mandates (45 per cent of the total of 516). Actually, 232 deputies of German nationality or cultural background were elected, but fifty of them were Social Democrats, pledged to combat assertive Germanism in favor of the brotherhood of all nationalities. The popular vote was distributed as follows among the various German parties: 720,000 for the Christian Socialists, 146,000 for the Agrarians, of both Catholic and Liberal persuasion, 146,000 for the Populists, 116,000 for the Progressives, 71,000 for Wolf's Pan-Germans (who soon adopted the name of German Radicals), and 20,000 for Schönerer's Pan-Germans. The German Social Democrats garnered 514,-000 popular votes. A sort of poetic justice had delivered to the avowed German parties a percentage of the mandates (35.27 per cent) almost identical with the percentage of Germans in Austria. Even so, these parties had room for misgivings, for, on the basis of popular votes, the Social Democrats should have taken sixty-seven of the mandates assigned to the Germans.

A striking development in the German electoral districts was the almost complete repudiation of the erstwhile deputies of the curia of the great landowners. Of the thirty deputies who called themselves " loyal to the constitution " in the previous Lower House and the dozen or so who were generally known as German Catholic Conservatives, some fifteen had the temerity to enter the lists as candidates on the basis of universal suffrage. It will be remembered that the proponents of reform had urged these men to run for the new Lower House and thereby avail Austria of an opportunity to make use of their talents and experience. Only three of the candidates were successful, despite the fact that practically all of them ran in their own home districts. Among the unsuccessful candidates were Count Bylandt, Dr. Baernreither, Count Stürgkh, and Dr. von Grabmayr. Count Bylandt ran as a Christian Socialist, while the other three mentioned campaigned as Liberal Agrarians, with the tacit support of the German Progressives. The German Clericals contrived Stürgkh's defeat, while the Christian Socialists ended Grabmayr's hopes. In September, 1906 a professor had publicly wondered if it would not be advisable to absorb as many deputies of the landed curia as possible into the traditional German parties, to lessen their effectiveness as critics of the new parliamentary era,[3] but only the Christian

3 Friedrich von Wieser, *Neue Freie Presse*, Sept. 19, 1906, quoted by Jaray, *op. cit.*, p. 663.

Socialists openly welcomed two aspirants, both of whom were defeated. Judging from the almost complete lack of success which attended the former representatives of " privilege," one cannot wonder at the lack of enthusiasm shown by the parties. The German electorate evidently was not impressed by the experience and skill of a Baernreither; lesser figures were well advised to shun an appeal to the masses. The blow of popular disfavor was dissipated somewhat in June, 1907, when Baernreither, Grabmayr, Stürgkh, Sylva-Tarouca, and five other former deputies of the landed curia were appointed to the Upper House for life, along with Marchet. The fresh breeze needed to clear the stuffy atmosphere of the abode of the peers was evidently not available.

The defeats suffered by the German Progressives and the German Populists were not unexpected. The former group was quite generally considered as the heir of the discredited German Liberals, despite its apparent willingness to cooperate in achieving electoral reform and its lip-service to the cause of labor. Under the curial system, it was able to dominate the chambers of commerce, which were usually in the hands of German businessmen, and it also profited from the tax requirements in urban districts. With the inundation of the well-to-do German middle class and intelligentsia by mass voting, the German Progressives were bound to lose ground. Their conquerors were not rabid nationalists, but men who represented social and economic points of view which the German Progressives could not possibly endorse. The German Populists suffered from the same handicap, aggravated by the unending strife within the party. The lower middle class in the provincial towns and cities once had admired the appropriate mixture of watered-down radicalism and nationalism offered by the Populists; in 1907, Christian Socialism and Social Democracy were more potent lures. Moreover, the Populists were subjected to an effective campaign of rumors in regard to their attitude toward the protection of Germanism. On one hand, they were condemned for compromising with the Slavs on electoral reform and in settling the composition of the Moravian diet; on the other hand, the activities of some Populist candidates caused them to be suspected of sympathy with the Pan-Germans. Internal disunity and lack of glamor comparable to that exuded by Lueger and his lieutenants cost the Populists much of their strength among the lower bourgeoisie. In many cases, Progressive and Populist candidates were eliminated on the first ballot, leaving the field open to Christian Socialists and Social Democrats. Middle class voters were bewildered by the distasteful choice offered them, despite the advice of one Progressive who declared that every Liberal, when confronted by a choice of " Black " or " Red," should vote " Red." [4] To many, subdued anti-Semitism and clericalism must have been preferable to Social Democracy, whose revisionist and wellnigh pro-Habsburg tendencies were obscured by popular visions of " red revolution."

Despite the nationalist bitterness which marred the debates on electoral reform, the elections of 1907 were far freer of nationalistic turmoil than had been the election of 1901, which had climaxed the agitation aroused by Badeni's language regulations. In 1901 the Pan-Germans under Schönerer and Wolf took full advantage of German resentment at Slavs and Jews alike in a campaign which spared neither dynasty nor Church. The result of their intemperate harangues was a sad commentary on the Germans of Austria. In 1897 the Pan-Germans had won only five seats; in 1901 they secured control of twenty-one, six of which were in the fifth curia. By 1907 the rupture between Schönerer and Wolf was complete; in September, 1906 the former had even denounced the Linz Program as part of a general renunciation of all things Austrian.[5] Wolf's group had moderated its tone somewhat and at least remained theoretically true to the Linz Program. Indeed, Wolf made an

4 Dr. Josef Unger, *Neue Freie Presse*, May 19, 1907, quoted by Jaray, *op. cit.*, p. 668.

5 For a recent appraisal of the Linz Program, see A. J. P. Taylor, *The Habsburg Monarchy 1815-1918* (London, 1941), pp. 201-3.

astounding electoral pact with the Christian Socialists; his candidates refrained from attacks upon the dynasty and the Church, merely stressing the defense of Germanism in Austria and a continuing fight against the Jews. In return, the Christian Socialists were able to boast among their lower middle class supporters of an anti-Semitic coalition which had Austria's interests at heart. Wolf's followers secured only two seats at the regular elections; their grand total was boosted to fourteen only by alliances with bourgeois elements who preferred rabid German nationalism to the Social Democrats. Schönerer himself was defeated; only three candidates of his persuasion eventually obtained mandates.

The sensational development among the Germans was the smashing victory achieved by the Christian Socialists. This party, for twenty years, had labored to capture both rural and urban districts; prior to 1907, its strength still resided chiefly in Vienna and the provincial German towns. Its early campaigns had excited the distrust of Catholic aristocrats and higher clergy, and the Emperor was only gradually convinced that Lueger's followers were constructive rather than disruptive. The traditionally conservative Catholic bloc of the Alpine provinces had suffered a secession of influential members who desired a rapprochement with the inelegant Christian Socialists in the late 1890's; thereafter, the seceders under Ebenhoch, calling themselves the Catholic People's Party, had worked in close cooperation with the Christian Socialists. The remnants of the original Catholic bloc fought vigorously to withstand the continuing pressure of Lueger's men, and the Tyrol was the focal point of the rivalry between 1901 and 1907. During these years, the parliamentary deputies Schraffl and Schöpfer created an efficient Christian Socialist party organization in the Tyrol which eventually enlisted the support of practically all of the lower clergy. During the actual electoral campaign, numerous meetings were held, stressing the grievances of the peasants and full of promises of Christian Socialist relief. Despite the open hostility of the higher clergy, particularly the bishop of Bozen, the peasants voted overwhelmingly in favor of the Christian Socialists.[6] The conservative Catholic bloc in the Tyrol was destroyed.

Elsewhere, there was compromise between the bloc and the Christian Socialists, thanks chiefly to Ebenhoch. In Styria, twelve seats sure to go to Catholic Agrarians of one group or the other were divided by party chieftains, before the campaign; four went to the Christian Socialists, eight to the Catholic Conservatives. In Salzburg, as well as in Upper Austria, the latter's potential mandates were not contested by the Christian Socialists; the party, thanks to Ebenhoch's efforts, made an effective appeal to the populace, and the final results of all of the elections gave Ebenhoch's group and the old Catholic Conservative group combined twenty-eight mandates, somewhat less than their strength in the previous Lower House. As a matter of fact, Ebenhoch's fraction clearly dominated the activities of all of the German Clericals during the elections; after the elections, those who were left of the old conservative wing accepted membership in the Catholic People's Party. This fusion was short-lived, for in the autumn of 1907, it was merged with the Christian Socialists, a step which Ebenhoch had desired for years.

Lueger's party now included ninety-six members, the largest single party in the Lower House. Since the stormy 1880's, the group had refined its techniques considerably. The new tone was evident in Gessmann's speech in the general party congress held in Vienna in March, 1907. The upper clergy were still suspect to a certain extent, and emphasis was placed on the "Christian" rather than on the "clerical" nature of the party. Anti-Semitism was practically neglected in face of the Marxist menace. Further moderation came with the absorption of Ebenhoch's men. Great stress was placed on duty to dynasty

6 The Christian Socialist electoral manifesto called for obligatory social insurance for the peasants, cheap credit for rural workers, and "sensible" prices for farm products, i. e., necessary tariff protection. Jaray, *op. cit.*, p. 680.

and empire, the defense of Germanism was no longer ignored as an embarrassing issue, and the party clearly attempted to appeal to middle class, artisans, and peasants alike. Austrian minister-presidents soon discovered that the Christian Socialists were quite close to the heir to the throne and that Christian Socialism, in its chastened form, had become a trusty weapon in the struggle to keep the empire alive.

Electoral reform had meant that almost 62 per cent of all seats were allotted to rural areas, with the result that the peasant masses of Austria were adequately represented for the first time. Mention has already been made of the Christian Socialist success in winning peasant votes and Ebenhoch's ability to retain rural mandates for his fraction. The deputies so elected might well be considered as Catholic Agrarians, despite their membership in the enlarged Christian Socialist group, for they certainly were compelled to work for agrarian aims. Not all of the German peasants were willing to vote for the announced friends of the Church. To satisfy their desire for an agrarian program prudently free of clerical entanglements, a " Liberal " Agrarian Party had been in existence since the turn of the century. In truth, its members simply were a branch of the German Populists, under the leadership of Peschka, with special organizations in the Alpine Provinces, Bohemia, Moravia, and Silesia. Thanks to a cleverly planned program in 1907, the party won nineteen mandates. Its electoral manifesto stressed centralism and the use of German as the state language, special status for Galicia and the Bukovina, economic separation from Hungary and her bothersome (to agrarians) grain fields, a customs union of Central Europe (excluding the Balkans, another source of cheap farm products), reduction of military service to two years, and social insurance for the agrarian classes. Though this party bitterly fought Catholic Conservative and Christian Socialist candidates in Upper Austria, Salzburg, Styria, and the Alpine lands, it steadfastly refused to condemn the Church and rejected all suggestions of anticlericalism. In Bohemia, it had to contend with the Social Democrats, who were powerful among the artisans of the villages; consequently, it formed an alliance with the Populists and Progressives there which ensured the election of fifteen "Liberal" candidates. The German Agrarian Party was seldom to suffer from the clashes of rural and urban interests which weakened the Christian Socialists after 1907, but there was some jockeying for power on the part of the great landowners and small farmers within the group. These struggles merely added to the appalling heterogeneity of the Austrian scene.

The Social Democrats were expected to win large segments of the urban vote, but their surprising strength in the rural areas was a shock to both Liberal and Catholic Agrarians. In 1897 the Social Democrats had entered the Lower House for the first time with fourteen members; as a result of bourgeois alliances against them and the general swing toward ultra-nationalism in 1901, they had been reduced to ten. In 1907 German cities and rural areas elected fifty Social Democrats, a number which did not fairly indicate the impressive total of popular votes for Adler's colleagues. In Vienna, 125,000 voters of a total of 335,000 voted Socialist; the fatal duel between Christian Socialism and Social Democracy had begun, for the former rolled up 80 per cent of all votes cast in the province of Lower Austria. Indeed, the motto of the Social Democrats had been " War on the Clericals! ", and the verbal exchanges between the two groups were correspondingly bitter. Even in the Tyrol, the scene of a major Christian Socialist triumph, the towns furnished sizeable Socialist returns. In German Bohemia, the Social Democrats actually won eight rural mandates, to the consternation of both Agrarian groups and the Pan-Germans; indeed, only four urban seats in German Bohemia fell to a party which primarily would have appealed to the urban proletariat. The existence of a strong rural proletariat among the Germans in Bohemia and the lack of a truly radical German Agrarian party partly explain the Socialist successes. However, the German wing of the Social Democrats continued to be representative of the urban rather than of the rural masses, and its success in the cities unveiled another chapter in the progressive disintegration of the middle-class Liberals and increased the inevitable friction with the Christian Socialists. The latter, in time, would fail to keep the allegiance of many of their urban supporters and would take on much more of a conservative and agrarian cast.

THE CZECH DEPUTIES

The Czech electorate displayed many of the same tendencies revealed by the Germans, though the conflict between the two nationalities continued to be the most powerful disruptive force in Austria. One can honestly say that the general coincidence of results among both nationalities indicated the futility of German claims of political and cultural superiority, for the Czechs clearly desired representatives who would fight primarily for social and economic amelioration and generally rejected the more violent Czech nationalists. Masaryk's election in itself was evidence of a Czech renaissance which the Germans could continue to deny only at the cost of wrecking the empire. But the election results could not be taken at their face value once the Germans and the Czechs met again in the Lower House; the men who had promised to fight for economic or class interests inevitably entangled themselves in the vexing Bohemian problem. The last act of the drama of collapse of empire had received its settings and properties.

The general retreat of Pan-Germanism was matched in Czech districts by the failure of radical Czech nationalists to increase their power. In 1901 these radicals, termed Czech National Socialists for the sake of convenience, had obtained five of the fifteen seats allotted to the fifth curia voters of Czech nationality, and they had played a disproportionately large part in the debates on electoral reform, which they had roundly abused as a swindle of Czech rights. In 1907 Klofáč, Choc, and Fresl appeared as leaders of the Czech National Socialists in the electoral compaign, abetted by Baxa, leader of a " Radical State's Rights Party " and by Hajn, leader of

a " Progressive State's Rights Party." To complete the confusion of party labels, this radically nationalistic coalition
called itself the " Young Czech Parties " and preached revenge
on the real Young Czechs, who had " sacrificed " Czech historic rights and the unity of Bohemia and its dependent lands.
On the first ballot, only one candidate was elected. In supplementary elections, the threat of Social Democratic victories
forced bourgeois Czech elements to support the coalition,
which was then able to secure eight more mandates. One more
Czech might be considered as part of the radical nationalist
group, the unpredictable Count Sternberg, who continued his
independent war upon the empire and the dynasty. Even so,
only 10 per cent of the Czech deputies could be considered intransigent nationalists; the friends of Austria abroad were
quietly hopeful of compromise after all.[7]

The solid success achieved by the Czech wing of international Socialism likewise gave rise to false hopes. Before the
turn of the century, the central organization of Social Democracy in Vienna had somewhat unwillingly given Czech Social
Democrats virtual autonomy in their own political affairs, and
this first break in the united Socialist front was widened during the elections of 1907. On the first ballot, Czech Social
Democrats captured ten rural mandates and seven urban mandates; as in the German areas of Bohemia, the lack of a radical
agrarian party accounted for the somewhat surprising rural
results.[8] Emboldened by success and desirous of greater suc-

7 Robert W. Seton-Watson, no convinced friend of the Dual Monarchy,
pointed out during the course of the first World War what seemed obvious
to most friends of the Monarchy, namely, that the German-Czech bitterness
had been intensified by the rise of the middle class within each nationality,
in his *German, Slav, and Magyar* (London, 1916), p. 163. Unfortunately,
the political emergence of the masses witnessed no appreciable decrease
in bitterness.

8 Election statistics for Bohemia, Moravia, and Silesia underline the
surprising Social Democratic successes. Of 1,103,629 votes cast in Bohemia,
451,252 went to Social Democrats. In Moravia the Social Democrats secured
144,832 of 457,648 votes cast; in Silesia, 55,129 of 105,727 votes cast.
Wilhelm Kosch, *Die Deutschen in Österreich und ihr Ausgleich mit den
Tschechen* (Leipzig, 1909), p. 64.

cesses in the by-elections, the Czech Social Democrats published a new electoral manifesto after the first elections. The manifesto warmly demanded all sorts of schools for Czechs, a second Czech university in Moravia, and a federation of free nations within the imperial framework. These objectives were to be secured by alliances with Social Democrats of other nationalities, promised the manifesto, in accordance with the accepted Social Democratic thesis of autonomous development for all nationalities. This program was effective, for seven more Czech Social Democrats were victorious in the by-elections.

The Young Czechs, who expected some losses as a result of universal manhood suffrage, were unprepared for the crushing defeat which overtook them. In 1901, despite the effective jibes of the ultra-nationalists, Kramář's men had won fifty-three seats in the Lower House; in 1907 they were reduced to twenty-one.[9] Their situation was paralleled by the unhappy position of the German bourgeois parties; the masses of Austria, both rural and urban, seemed to prefer candidates of the Marxist, Agrarian, or Clerical parties. The days of the uneasy compromise between feudal elements and the rising bourgeoisie had ended in parliamentary affairs, for the masses generally rejected the candidates of both groups. The Czech middle class did find some comfort in the election of Masaryk, who, with another professor, campaigned as a Czech Realist. Masaryk had already overshadowed Kramář as a leader of intelligent Czech endeavor, and his conciliatory electoral program seemed to point to a new orientation for the well-to-do bourgeoisie and intelligentsia. His program stressed the need of an intelligent settlement with the Germans, a good neighbor policy with the Social Democrats, and a continuing development of Czech in-

9 During the electoral campaign, Young Czech rallies were often interrupted by married women who had been told that the party planned to work for a liberal divorce law. The women presumably desired no law which might pave the way for "younger and fairer substitutes." V. Hussey Walsh, "Through the Austrian General Election," *The Fortnightly Review*, LXXXI, new series (1907), 985.

tellectual capacities unhindered by clerical influences.[10] The passage of time, however, revealed that Masaryk's prestige meant, somewhat paradoxically, relative weakness for the Czech Realist Party. The Young Czechs continued to represent the great majority of the well-to-do Czech bourgeoisie.

Despite the growth of the Czech middle class, Bohemia and Moravia remained predominantly rural, so that the electoral victories of Clericals and Agrarians were no surprise. The former Czech deputies of the landed curia made little effort to remain in parliamentary life; a mere two or three were elected as Independent Agrarians or Clericals. The Bohemian aristocracy had never developed a Liberal group comparable to the German Constitutionalists, and practically all of its influence went to Clericals and Agrarians (of a non-Liberal persuasion). The chief opponents of the Catholic Agrarians (for it is well-nigh impossible to separate Czech Clericals from Czech Catholic Agrarians) were the Czech Liberal Agrarians, who had a half-dozen representatives in the old Lower House. During the campaign of 1907 these Liberal Agrarians violently attacked the Catholic Agrarians, with whom they vied for the rural vote, and the Young Czechs, whose influence they wished to eliminate in the rural areas. The party insisted that it was simply independent of any religious control and denied the Clerical assertions that it would become part of an anti-clerical bloc. Its candidates, twenty-eight of whom were elected, were nearly all modest farmers; the leader of the party, Karel Prášek, a simple dairyman, was the first man ever to become a cabinet member without benefit of a title of nobility or a university degree. His colleagues in the Lower House were essentially conservative in economic and social questions and proved to be good Czech nationalists. The Czech Catholic Agrarians were more active than Prášek's group in the electoral campaign, putting up fifty-one candidates, of whom seven-

10 For a discussion of Masaryk and the Realist fraction, see Paul Selver, *Masaryk* (London, 1940), pp. 189-207, and Alfred Fischel, *Der Panslawismus bis zum Weltkrieg* (Stuttgart and Berlin, 1919), pp. 468-9.

teen were elected. In the Lower House elected in 1901, they had only two representatives, if one excludes the representatives of the landed curia, with whom they usually were allied. The Catholic Agrarians promised to defend all Czech rights, recommended comprehensive social legislation and cooperation with all agrarian groups for the good of the rural masses, and steadfastly denounced any notions of a reform of the laws on marriage or reforms which would threaten the position of the Church. In Moravia they were the dominant party in the rural areas, and in Bohemia they cooperated with the Liberal Agrarians to defeat Social Democrats. The Young Czechs suffered most from the triumphs of both Agrarian groups. It seemed to some observers that the rural Czech masses were tired of barren quarreling over national rights and preferred to vote along economic lines; in reality, the Agrarian groups offered just as much national fervor as had the Young Czechs, with economic promises to boot. Only a supremely gifted Austrian statesman could have taken advantage of the slight hope aroused by the general results of the elections in Czech areas to secure compromise in Bohemia; no such person was to be found in 1907.

THE POLISH DEPUTIES

The Polish electorate, unlike the German or the Czech, did not generally repudiate the landed aristocrats or their representatives in the former landed curia. To be sure, many titled Poles did not bother to run for the Lower House or were defeated when they did, but about fifteen aristocratic Polish Conservatives did win their elections, among them Dzieduszycki and Abrahamowicz. The Polish Club, once controlled by the aristocrats, underwent certain changes. Though Abrahamowicz was elected its president, its tone became more democratic, thanks to professors, priests, and peasants who asserted themselves in its caucuses. The Club had not entirely freed itself from the guiding hand of aristocracy, but a process of gradual emancipation was under way. The explanation of the aristocrats' electoral success lay chiefly in their astute political maneuvering. They subsidized a willing press which warned the Polish voters to support men " who could get something for Poland at Vienna," and they formed effective anti-Socialist alliances with clerical and bourgeois elements. Most important of all, they had the active support of many bureaucrats who owed their jobs to their membership in the Polish gentry; these administrative officials, openly or by subtle pressure, influenced many Poles to vote for the aristocrats. Indeed, most of the successful Polish Conservatives were elected in urban areas; seven obviously were victorious thanks to the ballots of the Jewish population in urban districts. A " democratic " Polish spokesman sadly declared that the Jews were afraid of displeasing the administrative officials, in spite of the safeguard of a secret ballot. Should a real " democrat " be placed in charge of the administration of Galicia, the Jews would reject aristocratic candidates.[11] The absence of a strong Polish middle class in Galicia also accounted for the amazing aristocratic success in the towns.

An important fraction in the new Polish Club was the National Democratic Party, under the leadership of Dr. Stanislaus Gląbinski, the university professor. It had been definitively organized in 1905, really as a branch of the strongest party in Russian Poland. Its political platform was outspokenly nationalistic, so that its members were sometimes called Pan-Poles. The party worked for the political as well as the cultural and economic independence of Poland, though its chief activity seemed to be the denunciation of Prussian efforts to denationalize the Poles in the German Empire. It cordially supported the idea of an autonomous Galicia, enlarged by the annexation of Teschen, and was sorely disappointed that electoral reform was achieved without such a bargain. At first, its leaders had no desire to threaten the vested interests of the aristocrats in charge of the Polish Club, and the necessary machinery even

11 Michael Grek, *Neue Freie Presse*, May 31, 1907, quoted by Jaray, *op. cit.*, p. 665.

for an electoral campaign was not created until 1907. The Polish Conservatives were not displeased by the appearance of the new fraction, for it offered no real threat to their supremacy and actually gave the Polish Club a surface appearance of democracy. Relations during the campaign of 1907 remained cordial, and the National Democrats received fourteen seats, not including various independents who tended to unite with the fraction in the Lower House.[12] The party's strength seemed to be centered in Polish towns in eastern Galicia, often in territory surrounded by Ruthenes or partially populated by Ruthenes. Apart from the National Democrats and their independent allies, another party attempted to capture the allegiance of the relatively weak Polish urban middle class. This group, under the leadership of Michael Grek, called itself the Progressive Democratic Party and attempted to follow a policy of moderation toward the Ruthenes and independence of clerical and aristocratic influences. It succeeded in getting eleven mandates, but Grek decided to give up the effort to found an "enlightened" party; his followers were practically absorbed in Gląbinski's group.

The Polish rural districts were the scene of a spirited contest between the Polish Center, a Catholic Agrarian party led by Leo Pastor, which enjoyed a place in the Polish Club, and the Polish Populists, a Liberal Agrarian party led by Jan Stapinski. Generally, the former seemed to dominate Polish rural areas west of Krakov, winning fourteen seats altogether, while the latter were able to secure sixteen mandates, chiefly in districts east of Krakov. The Polish Center enjoyed the support of the aristocrats and clergy, a support which cost it some votes among the miserable peasantry of western Galicia. Distress among these peasants centered about their lack of large landholds; for the most part, they had to work for big landowners or emigrate. In the 1890's, they were supplied a spokesman in the person of a Jesuit priest, Father Stojałowski, the

12 Fischel, *op. cit.*, pp. 501-2.

parish priest of a small commune near Lemberg. Aided by other priests also of peasant stock, Stojałowski denounced the privileges of the rich landowners and the economic injustices visited upon the peasants. At the instigation of alarmed aristocrats, the Jesuit leader of peasant discontent was jailed for debt and excommunicated. Nevertheless, his party, known as the Polish Christian Populists, won six seats in 1897 and five seats in 1901; in the Lower House, it had a working alliance with three other Polish Populists. Eventually, the Polish Conservatives were reconciled with Stojałowski, who was permitted to resume his clerical duties and who moderated his economic and political criticism. Somewhat disturbed by Stojałowski's rapprochement with the Polish Conservatives, some of his followers and allies continued to reject overtures from the Polish Club and campaigned as simple Polish Populists in 1907. Their party was more radical than its Liberal Agrarian counterparts among the Germans and Czechs, for it demanded a division of land among indigent peasants at the expense of the owners of great estates and recommended the ownership of coal mines by the state. As might be expected, it paid full tribute to Polish national sensibilities by demanding complete autonomy for Galicia, whose governor should be responsible to the diet, by demanding the exclusive use of Polish in the operation of railways, postal service, and police, and a strong policy against Germany, the oppressor of Poles in Posen.

Thanks to the radical appeal of the Polish Populists, the Polish Social Democrats did not enjoy a striking success among the peasants. Considerable Socialist strength was revealed in western Galicia, where the Social Democrats assailed Pastor's party, but only six Polish mandates eventually fell to the Social Democrats. Internationalism could not compete with a party which stressed equal doses of nationalism and agrarian radicalism, particularly in a province which lagged in industrialization.

THE RUTHENE DEPUTIES

Perhaps no nationality offered as much internal cohesion as did the Ruthenes after the bitterness of the elections of 1907 had been dissipated. Normally considered the least advanced of the nationalities in Austria, the Ruthenes profited from the very fact that they were relatively homogeneous in economic and religious affairs.[13] In addition, fear of Polish oppression or machinations at court strengthened the general Ruthene desire to bury partisan differences after 1907. The willingness of a few Ruthenes to play politics with the Poles in the mixed rural districts did not modify the overwhelmingly general Ruthene desire to secure emancipation from Polish political tutelage.

Nevertheless, two factions did emerge as contenders for the Ruthene vote, and their strife actually resulted in the loss of a mandate to a Polish candidate in one district preponderantly Ruthene in population. One group, the Old Ruthenes, considered themselves to be part of the Russian nationality and they were suspected of covert allegiance to the czars.[14] The other group, known as the Ruthene National Democrats or, more popularly, as the Young Ruthenes, were wary of being treated as simple Russians and ardently hoped for the revival of a great Ukrainian state, with a capital at Kiev. Here the differences ceased, for both parties were composed of peasants and lower middle class men and were equally violent in condemning Polish ambitions in Galicia. The Young Ruthenes, it is true, were particularly vehement in rejecting all plans for greater Galician autonomy, which might deliver them into the hands of the Poles; they much preferred the idea of a separate Ruthene province, with its own diet. In the elections, the Old Ruthenes took only five seats in Galicia, whereas the Young Ruthenes captured twenty, including the five seats allotted to

13 For a discussion of Austrian efforts to "create" a Ruthene nationality as a check on possible Russian sympathies, see Gayda, *op. cit.*, pp. 138-151.

14 In 1906 Popovici made much of the general suspicion of Ruthene intentions in pleading for federalism as a guarantee that all Slavs would not go over to Russia, *op. cit.*, pp. 207-16.

the Ruthenes in the Bukovina. A third fraction, of momentary interest, the Radical Ruthenes, won five seats in some Carpathian districts; its members later cooperated closely with the Young Ruthenes in the Lower House, where all three groups formed a Ruthene Club. In the campaign, the Radical Ruthenes did stress economic grievances and significantly avoided attacking the Social Democrats, who obtained two Ruthene mandates. No conservative aristocratic party appeared, for the simple reason that there was no Ruthene aristocracy of any importance. The Ruthene Archbishop attempted to create a Clerical party, but the lesser married clergy did not respond to his pleas; anticlericalism was not an issue, for Old and Young Ruthenes were respectful of the position of their church and properly critical of the Social Democrats.

The South Slav Deputies

Among the Slovenes, the most numerous of the South Slavs, universal manhood suffrage brought smashing victories for the Populists, the party of the Clericals. Of twenty-four Slovene mandates, the Populists secured eighteen. The Slovene Liberals emphasized a continuing struggle with Germanism in their propaganda, but the Slovene voters seemed to be more interested in other issues. In South Styria, the Liberals did win two seats, possibly because of the residue of German-Slovene hostility in that area, but there were quite definite signs that many Slovenes were eager for a real understanding with the Germans. A new party of the lower bourgeoisie, though unsuccessful in securing any mandates, won a sixth of all Slovene votes on a platform which was frankly pro-German. In Carinthia, the Slovene Populist leader candidly admitted an electoral understanding with the German Christian Socialists, aimed at the defeat of the Liberal Slovenes and German ultranationalists; Slovene Liberal cries of treachery to Slovene nationalism were impotent in defeating him. In Trieste, the Slovene quarrel with Italians was not abated during the elections, but Slovene relations with Germans had very definitely improved.

The Croatians and Serbs obtained thirteen mandates, two falling by agreement to the latter in Dalmatia. Among the Croatians, two parties, divided chiefly by divergent notions of the methods to be followed in furthering Croatian self-determination, contended for power. The less successful group, the Party of Pure Right, led by a priest and enlisting the support of most of the clergy, captured only two seats; it desired to keep Croatians free of ties with either Austrian or Hungarian politicians, but expected to get more concessions from Austria than from Hungary. The other group, the Croat Party, led by Ivčević, candidly hoped for an understanding with Hungary against Austria, though it avoided the issue whenever possible during the campaign, in which it won the remaining nine seats. Economic and religious issues were clearly subordinated to nationalistic strategy by the Croats, and the victory of the pro-Budapest faction was an ominous evidence of the decay of loyalty to the Habsburgs since Jellačić's day.

THE ITALIAN AND THE RUMANIAN DEPUTIES

Among the Italian voters, Liberal candidates suffered drastically at the hands of Clericals and Social Democrats. In 1901 fifteen of the nineteen Italian deputies were Liberals; only four were returned in 1907. The foremost among them, Malfatti, was elected only because of his close ties with the Catholic dignitaries of the Tyrol; in Trentino, only one-third of the urban votes went to Liberals; and in Trieste, the Liberals were overwhelmed by men whom they accused of being traitors to greater Italy, the Social Democrats. Their fears of Italian Social Democrats were exaggerated, for one of the four Social Democrats elected in Trieste promised after the election that he would defend Italian interests and spoke of new Italian universities and a relaxation of police surveillance in a manner befitting a true irredentist.

The Italian Clericals won practically all of the peasant votes, save in some areas in Istria and Gorizia. As with other Catholic Agrarian parties in the empire, they emphasized relief for rural interests and defense of the Church; they entered the new Lower House with ten deputies.

The Rumanians of Austria seemed least affected by the variety of issues which faced other nationalities. Of their five deputies, three were independent of party ties; the two deputies who did represent definite parties were mildly nationalistic.

THE JEWISH NATIONALIST DEPUTIES

During the debates on electoral reform, Straucher, leader of the Jewish Nationalists, had begged for the recognition of a Jewish nationality in Austria, and a dozen or more Jewish Nationalist candidates campaigned for office in 1907. Despite a large Jewish population in Galicia and Bukovina, only four of these candidates were elected. In a dozen urban Galician districts Jews were in the majority, but, as has been pointed out, they seemed to prefer Polish Conservatives to Jewish Nationalists. Of nine Jewish Nationalist candidates in Galician urban districts, only one was elected. In extreme eastern Galicia, the Ruthenes and the Jewish Nationalists joined forces at supplementary elections to obtain two mandates for the latter, and there was consequently a good deal of speculation about a united Ruthene-Jewish Nationalist bloc in Galicia which would resist Polish intrigues.

Obviously, political nationalism still did not attract the Jewish minority in Austria, which tended to identify itself with the culture of the dominant nationality with which it lived, or preferred, in many cases, to vote for the Social Democrats, who offered careers to Jews of talent, or to vote for the German Progressives, the traditional opponents of anti-Semitism in Austria. Rightly or wrongly, the Jews did not seem to relish the idea of standing forth as a distinct nationality in an empire which continually shook with the impact of nationalism.[15]

---

15 For a general survey of Zionism in Austria prior to World War I, see Henry Wickham Steed, *The Hapsburg Monarchy* (London, 1919), pp. 175-180.

CHAPTER VI

THE FAILURE OF REFORM, 1907-1914

PARLIAMENTARY AFFAIRS UNDER BECK, 1907-1908

IN June, 1907 the newly elected members of the Lower House met for the first time. Would the new legislators embark upon a program of constructive work? Would they, by energy and determination, force the creation of a cabinet truly representative of the peoples of Austria, or would they, by default, permit the continuation of government by ministers who answered, in the last analysis, only to Francis Joseph? For approximately one year, the universally elected representatives gave some evidence of cooperation with Beck, though the order of business was still cluttered by motions of urgency and by sporadic outbursts of obstruction.[1] Beck, the last Austrian Minister-President of real ability, worked hard to conciliate the new members, as well as the old, but his suggestions and pleas ran into many of the traditional obstacles. It was soon apparent that bargaining with the major parties was an absolute necessity; after weeks of constant negotiation, the Ausgleich with Hungary was renewed in December, 1907, at a price. In the previous month, various groups, principally the Christian Socialists, had demanded a larger number of cabinet posts; to secure a majority for the Ausgleich, Beck reorganized his cabinet. In the new cabinet, the Christian Socialists were represented by Gessmann and Ebenhoch; Agrarian parties were recognized by the appointment of the Czech Prášek and the German Peschka as ministers. In any other country, the appointment of parliamentary deputies to cabinet posts would have been greeted with enthusiasm as a necessary step

---

1 For discussions of Beck's regime, see Czedik, *op. cit.*, III, 68-234, Charmatz, *Österreichs äussere und innere Politik von 1895 bis 1914*, pp. 82-86, *Cambridge Modern History* (New York, 1902-1912), XII, 207-209, Pierre Renouvin, *La Crise Européenne (1904-1914) et la Grande Guerre* (Paris, 1939), p. 102.

to truly representative government. Indeed, Beck was hopeful that Austrian cabinets eventually might be composed of the members of the greater parliamentary parties. Unfortunately, the entrance of party leaders into the sessions of the cabinet simply meant greater opportunities for partisan demands and more chances for nationalistic wrangling.[2]

Yet, for a year, national quarrels were fairly mild in the cabinet and in the Lower House, which not only agreed to the new Ausgleich but also passed the necessary budgets. Outside of Vienna, strife was not as well prevented. Relations between Poles and Ruthenes continued to be poor; a series of incidents between students of the two nationalities ended with the shooting of the Polish governor of Galicia by a Ruthene student in April, 1908.[3] In Laibach, in the autumn of the same year, Germans and Slovenes staged riots which troops had to put down, at some loss of life. Most ominous of all, the situation in Bohemia improved not at all, despite all of Beck's blandishments. In September, 1908 the new Bohemian diet opened its sessions, only to relapse into sterile obstruction. In the following month, Beck was forced to order its dissolution; the Czech members of his cabinet thereupon resigned.[4] The Minister-President might have surmounted this crisis, had there not been other examples of dissension within his cabinet. One Professor Wahrmund, of the University of Innsbruck, had been accused of holding and expressing views inimical to the teachings of the Church, and the Christian Socialists had called for his dismissal. The German Progressive Marchet, as Minister of Education, had steadfastly refused to accede to the Christian Socialist clamor,[5] and Beck had attempted to compromise the fight by

2 Viktor Bibl, *Der Zerfall Österreichs-Von Revolution zu Revolution* (Vienna, 1924), p. 400.

3 Theodor von Sosnosky, *Die Politik im Habsburgerreiche* (Berlin, 1912-13), I, 276.

4 Hugelmann, ed., *op. cit.*, pp. 253-6.

5 Hugo Haan, "Gustav Marchet," *Neue österreichische Biographie, 1815-1918* (Vienna, 1923-1935), II, 150-1.

ggesting Wahrmund's transfer to Prague.[6] The Christian
ocialists refused to accept the compromise, and it was com-
only believed that they echoed the views of Francis Ferdi-
and, who had violently turned against Beck, his erstwhile
nentor.[7] Unable to change Gessmann's adamant attitude, the
Minister-President resigned on November 7 and received the
customary imperial regrets on November 15.

PARLIAMENTARY AFFAIRS UNDER BIENERTH, 1908-1911

orderly parliament effort to save Beck from the attacks
motions of urgency and by obstruction. Toward did not mean that a
November, 1908, just after Bienerth presented his cabinet to
the Lower House, the Czechs in Prague underlined their resentment by attacking German students and professors and by
hauling down the imperial colors.[9] Bienerth tried to appease

6 Selver, *op. cit.*, pp. 211-14; Drage, *op. cit.*, p. 591.

7 Theodor von Sosnosky, *Franz Ferdinand* (Munich, Berlin, 1929), p. 246.

8 For discussions of Bienerth's regime, see Czedik, *op. cit.*, IV, 3-330,
Charmatz, *Österreichs äussere und innere Politik von 1895 bis 1914*, pp.
104-110, Joseph Redlich, *Austrian War Government* (New Haven, 1929),
pp. 64-68, and G. L. Jaray, " La Physionomie Nouvelle de la Question
Austro-Hongroise," *Questions Diplomatiques et Coloniales*, XXX (1910),
729-39.

9 Samassa, *op. cit.*, p. 30, Sosnosky, *Die Politik im Habsburgerreiche*,
I, 242-4.

Slavic and German critics alike by reconstituting his cabinet in February, 1909, replacing some of the "neutral" bureaucrats with deputies or experts who represented particular parties or nationalities. Two Czechs actually joined the new cabinet, but they resigned in November, as a protest against a law passed in Lower Austria which stipulated the use of German as a language of instruction in schools. Their presence in the cabinet meant little to Bienerth, anyway, for the Czech Agrarians and National Socialists continued to disrupt the sessions of the Lower House. In desperation, Bienerth attempted to coerce all of the deputies by proroguing the Lower House, thereby depriving the members of their pay. The Czechs, of course, were not alone to blame for the anarchy; whenever Bienerth gave a sign of trying to meet Czech wishes the Pan-Germans and Germans of the other ～～～～ obstruction. One could ～～～～～ ～～～～～ reform ～～～～～ Lueger that the remedy had to be swallowed, whether proposed by Krek, Kramář, or the devil. The bill was quickly accepted by the Upper House and by the Emperor, and the new law seemed to work wonderfully well for a short time. The president of the Lower House was empowered to expel fractious deputies for one, two, or three sittings; he also was compelled to relegate motions of urgency to the last hours of each sitting.[10] Decrease in obstruction did not necessarily mean greater security for Bienerth, who obtained approval for his budgets and expenditures for the armed forces only with great difficulty. The Czechs and South Slavs continually demanded representation in the cabinet, while the Poles pressed for economic improvements in Galicia which the empire could not afford. During 1910 the Polish Club suffered from internal squabbles, while the death of Lueger gave rise to unpleasant questions of succession among the Christian Socialists. Bienerth generally depended upon these two groups, and their troubles intensified his own problems. In April, 1910 his request for funds to cover the military costs of the annexation of Bosnia and Herzegovina passed by a vote close enough to threaten the continued life of the cabinet. The Social Democrats and nearly all of the Czechs and Slovenes vowed to give no support to a man who was supposed to liquidate the Bosnian problem, insofar as the problem concerned Austria alone. The Social Democrats also were embittered by Bienerth's failure to secure up-to-date social insurance for the aged and sick.

Early in 1911 Bienerth proposed a comprehensive military reform, which, at first blush, was heartily welcomed by a majority of the deputies. The new system called for a reduction of one year in the term of service for conscripted infantrymen, but such a change meant a larger annual levy of conscripts until the system was working well. Moreover, the new plan was to entail formidable expenditures, which Bienerth hoped to meet partially by effecting administrative economies and by raising the price of tobacco. The Czechs and South Slavs made it clear that their support depended on their immediate entrance into the cabinet; Bienerth seemed unable to accept their proposition or to chance his military reform without their cooperation. His advisors, the Christian Socialists, recommended that he take the question to the country in a general election,

10 H. Hantich, "Nouvelle Phase du Parlamentarisme en Autriche," *Questions Diplomatiques et Coloniales*, XXIX (1910), 158-63.

and the Minister-President acquiesced by dissolving the Lower House in March.

The elections of June, 1911 were disastrous for Bienerth and the Christian Socialists.[11] Before Lueger's death, the latter had been rent by disputes between its agrarian and urban wings and weakened by disclosures of a scandalous nature. The unseemly quarrel among the leaders after Lueger's passing added to the confusion, but no one expected the tremendous Christian Socialist losses in Vienna. Of twenty Viennese seats captured in 1907, the party retained only two; Gessmann himself was one of the losers. Thereafter, Christian Socialism in Austria was to be identified with rural interests; Vienna never again, of her own free will, would be sympathetic to Lueger's less glamorous successors. Curiously, the Social Democrats did not particularly profit from the Clerical defeats; a loose federation of former German Populists, Progressives, and Wolf's Pan-Germans, which called itself the German National Union, picked up about twenty seats. Though anti-federalist, this group was not rabidly anti-Slav, and the moderate Czech parties hoped for some improvement in relations. Bienerth had no chance of staying in power; the Christian Socialists and most of the Poles deserted him, while the Czechs and Slovenes called for his resignation. At the end of June Bienerth obliged; his successor, Baron Gautsch, asked the old cabinet to serve temporarily. This arrangement lasted until October, when the Emperor asked Count Stürgkh to form a new ministry.

PARLIAMENTARY AFFAIRS UNDER STÜRGKH, 1911-1914

Stürgkh's appointment was no great surprise, for he had served as Minister of Education under Bienerth and in Gautsch's provisional ministry. Well known for his conservatism and a certain low cunning in keeping disparate elements

11 Gustav Kolmer, "La Vie Politique et Parlementaire: Autriche," *Revue Politique et Parlementaire*, LXIX (1911), 177-87, and G. Blondel, "Les Dernières Elections en Autriche-Hongrie," *La Réforme Sociale*, LXII (1911), 218-221.

pleased, Stürgkh seemed to embody the bankruptcy of Austrian political life. His colleagues in the cabinet, who seldom were deputies, did represent the dominant German, Polish, and Czech nationalities, but essentially they were bureaucrats. Political parties continued to demand a cabinet composed of parliamentarians, but Stürgkh had no desire to repeat what seemed to be the errors committed by Beck and Bienerth. He preferred Taaffe's old system, which consisted of satisfying the most importunate deputies and parties with patronage and favors, and somehow the Lower House continued to grind out laws.[12] Baernreither, admittedly a foe of universal manhood suffrage and clearly a critic of Stürgkh's policies, commented as follows on the parliamentary scene during Stürgkh's tenure:

> It is a great asset for him [Stürgkh] that one effect of universal suffrage is to make members of Parliament perpetual beggars on behalf of their constituents. Every member gets stacks of letters by every post, and runs from Ministry to Ministry in search of favours, permits, tax exemption, exemptions from military service, etc., etc. There is hardly a person who is not deeply involved in some specific matter of great concern to his own electorate, as is not astonishing, in view of the uncertainty of conditions with us, the dilatoriness of our administration, and the destitution of our population. But good-bye to any hope of manly independence from people who are perpetually hat in hand at the Government Departments. Similar conditions, it is true, existed at the time of the old Parliament of restricted franchise, but they have grown infinitely more marked under universal suffrage, and have utterly ruined the character of the House. Moreover, this endless incursion, both partisan and personal of parties and of individual members into the administration corrupts it, too.[13]

12 For a list of laws passed by the Reichsrat from Nov. 3, 1911, to Mar. 14, 1914, see Czedik, *op. cit.*, IV, 358-9.

13 *Fragments of a Political Diary* (London, 1930), pp. 238-9.

In 1906 Hermann Bahr, the perceptive interpreter of things Austrian, had described the movement for electoral reform as an attempt to smash the clique of " Families " which dominated dynasty and populace.[14] By 1911 it seemed that the clique of the privileged and well-to-do had been partially supplanted by hungry politicians, who placed patronage above all else. It was a pity that Austria possessed no colonies, one might agree with André de Hévesy, for, in pre-1914 Austria, the spoils which might have been obtained from colonies were haggled over in the imperial bureaus.[15]

Patronage and favors often did secure favorable votes, but early in 1914 Stürgkh ran into great obstacles in getting the Lower House's consent for more conscripts. Consequently, he prorogued the sessions of the Lower House indefinitely on March 16. When the great crisis came in the summer, the Reichsrat was not in session, nor did Stürgkh favor its recall. Austria went to destruction thanks to Berchtold and apathy. No trusted advisor at court gave the slightest thought to the wishes of the members of the Reichsrat. After all, were not many of the deputies potential traitors? Most cogent reason of all, how could any sane advisor expect the Reichsrat, still the joke of Europe, to offer the Emperor useful advice without months of argument? [16]

14 *Wien* (Stuttgart, no date), p. 127.

15 *L'Agonie d'un Empire: L'Autriche-Hongrie* (Paris, 1923), p. 163.

16 Despite the Lower House's reform of its order of business, obstruction never vanished. For an eye-witness account of parliamentary turmoil as late as March, 1914, see Wolf von Schierbrand, *Austria-Hungary: The Polyglot Empire* (New York, 1917), pp. 115-18.

CHAPTER VII

CONCLUSION

THE introduction of universal manhood suffrage in Austria in 1907 was the last important step taken by the Habsburgs to reconcile the great contradictions within their empire. The Metternichean policy of restraining nationalistic and democratic forces never had a chance of survival after 1848 but Francis Joseph and Metternich's successors fought a long delaying action. The reform of 1907, though it clearly recognized the strength of nationalism and the growing demand for political democracy, was essentially the last of the delaying actions; unfortunately, it failed to create a new situation which would satisfy the masses within the framework of the historic empire. In the 1920's, commentators had no great difficulty in analyzing the errors of omission and commission which brought the empire to ruin during the first World War. In the 1940's, other commentators, confronted with the sad failure of the settlements made in 1919 and the resultant wreckage of Central Europe, may be pardoned for taking a second look at the solution attempted in 1907.

This solution was framed in terms which the nineteenth century understood and generally favored: recognition of the principles of *nationality* and of democratic government. The persons and groups in Austria who fought for reform seemed to feel that these principles were patently " good " and they exhibited surprise that anyone should question their premises. Indeed, the men who resented the idea of reforms admitted fatalistically that the chief fruits of the French Revolution could not be barred forever at the frontiers. A summary review of the attitudes adopted by the various groups and parties reveals these tendencies. The Young Czechs, who had a sort of spiritual home in the Paris of the Third Republic, expected that reform primarily would further the interests of the Czech people. They were willing to admit that new Czech voters might reject the party's middle-class orientation; the loss would be more than balanced by the gain. The Christian Socialists, increasingly respectable and dynastically minded, counted on retaining most of their urban strength while absorbing the appreciable power of the German Clericals in the rural areas. Political strategy aside, the party sensed the great peril of the monarchy and worked loyally to accomplish the government's program. Slovene and Italian Clericals, if far less interested in the ultimate welfare of the Habsburgs, saw only profit in a reform which would increase the political power of devout peasants, many of whom learned of the glory of their nationality from their parish priest. The Polish Club had no real desire to favor Polish peasants and workers with the blessings of democracy, but its members were astute enough to close the bargains necessary to make the Polish representation as crucially important to the government as before. How else could one expect to prepare for the resurrection of the Polish state? The German Liberals, whatever their party labels, were embarrassed by the reappearance of the question of the franchise. The grant of sweeping political rights to all Austrian men meant the end of the influence of middle-class Liberalism and possibly meant the doom of German predominance in Austria. Some die-hards never accepted reform, but most of the Liberals, fearful that intransigence would mean greater losses, unhappily embraced what might be considered the practical realization of much of their high-flown theory.

Middle-class parties and enlightened members of the nobility and clergy, however, might never have insisted upon, or agreed to, electoral reform, had it not been for the masterful strategy of the Social Democrats. A numerically puny group in the Lower House, the Social Democrats were able to arouse massive demonstrations which increased mightily with the news of the October Manifesto in Russia. No party was more responsible for the Emperor's unexpected support of universal manhood suffrage, and the threat of renewed popular demonstrations was a weapon which the government could not ignore. To what extent the workers who demonstrated were Marxist by conviction cannot be known; that they were willing to follow Social Democratic leaders in securing political rights cannot be denied. Adler's pointed remarks when deadlock threatened in the electoral committee were reinforced by the direct pressure exerted by the Emperor upon stubborn party leaders.

The surpassing importance of Social Democratic pressure in achieving reform poses an interesting question. Did the party, increasingly wedded to the idea of saving the economic unity of the empire, take the correct steps in sacrificing temporarily its notions of autonomy for the sake of securing votes for the masses? To be sure, Jaszi is correct in applying the phrases " too schematic and too bloodless " to the Socialist plan for " free nations in a free state "; it is not difficult to see that the seething nationalities would be impatient with doctrinaire solutions. Possibly Adler and his followers preferred first to give the vote to the masses, then persuade them to accept reasonable plans for autonomy. In view of the renewed struggles among the nationalities after the passage of reform, one might question the party's strategy while admitting that any strategy might have failed to save the empire. The Social Democrats were well aware of the limitations of the reform of 1907 and counted only on capturing enough seats to bargain effectively for social reforms and their autonomist schemes. Tragically, the party was itself split by nationalistic quarrels after 1909; in a sense, it was a victim of the universal suffrage which it helped to create. The privileged curias had been abolished, but the victory of the masses was no better guarantee of " progress " in the direction of national appeasement. The imponderables of national sentiment outweighed economic motivation decisively.

The nature and extent of Social Democratic disappointment underline the fundamental defect in the reform of 1907. Universal manhood suffrage, when imposed upon a state which insisted upon a continuing centralization of governmental functions in the face of overwhelming demands for autonomy, had no real chance to succeed. The new device admittedly could have been used as a weapon to exact federalism but only if all of the dissident nationalities first agreed upon a common program. The Germans felt they could go no further in surrendering what was left of their primacy, the Poles had no intention of accepting a plan which would give the Ruthenes real parity, the Czechs continued to insist upon the unity of the lands of the Bohemian crown. There was never any serious discussion of a program of federalism in the Reichsrat after 1907; even the Social Democrats were too embarrassed by disunion within the party to press for their solution.

The failure of the dissident nationalities to unite upon a common program had much of its basis in the uneven and unfair distribution of parliamentary strength vouchsafed by the reform. In a sense, the Habsburg policy of " *Divide et impera* " was carried on by the Germans and the Poles in the years 1905-1906, often to the embarrassment of the imperial ministry. Obviously, the Ruthenes were slighted in the distribution of mandates, though the lack of advanced political consciousness among the Ruthenes lessened the force of that injustice for a time. Much more dangerous was the German denial of an honest representation of the Slavic citizens of the empire. The onerous conditions required for any change in the distribution of strength could only inspire frustration and bitterness in the decade following 1907; by 1917, the Slavs had little desire to embrace the ideals of Austro-Slavism. The simple fact of discrimination in apportionment of parliamentary strength was hardly the dissolvent; the larger implication, that the Slavs should continue to wear the badge of inferior beings, shattered the historic ties. Some Slavs, of course, found minor irritants in the domicile provisions and in the continuing rural-urban division of parliamentary constituencies. In retrospect, one cannot honestly consider these regulations as discriminatory towards the Slavs. Undoubtedly, a majority of migrant agricultural workers were Slavs and probably were disfranchised. Yet their home districts were generally so arranged that a representative of their own nationality almost inevitably would be elected. As for the rural-urban demarcation, it was a traditional feature of government and ostensibly would limit class strife. Unfortunately, in crownlands and provinces where Germans and Slavs collided, the rural constituencies, usually Slavic, contained more voters than the German urban districts. Here was the kernel of some Slavic disaffection over the rural-urban division, and here the resentment was justified.

What groups were responsible for the failure to achieve some type of federalistic structure during the discussions of reform in 1905-1906? Undoubtedly, the German element in Austria should bear most of the blame; without direct pressure from the Emperor, the reform would have been even less favorable to the non-Germans in the empire. Francis Joseph's motives in insisting upon greater democratization within the old centralistic framework in 1905 may forever be enigmas; possibly he did feel that national quarrels might be exchanged advantageously for " class " quarrels. More likely, he realized that the suffrage had to be widened to permit at least a partial resumption of representative government. After all, he had discovered that parliamentary forms meant little real check on his authority; was there any reason to suppose that peasants' and workers' representatives would be less amenable than lawyers and counts to imperial pressure? Francis Ferdinand is credited with opposition to the reform of 1907, though his " party," the Christian Socialists, were among its chief proponents. Too much has been made of the heir-apparent's dabbling in schemes for Slavic autonomy, yet possibly he had some greater insight than the old Emperor in 1905-1906. On the other hand, his constitutional aversion to almost all of the Emperor's policies and his growing dislike for Beck may have been the real reasons for his critical attitude. At any rate, neither man seemed convinced of the need for thorough-going democracy in the empire; the Emperor was merely willing to make another stop-gap compromise while his heir, limited in influence, seemed reduced to a policy of negative criticism.

Despite the failure to create federalism in Austria in 1907, there can be no doubt that great segments of the population did benefit from the electoral reform. If the newly enfranchised citizens had been motivated solely by economic and social ambitions, they might have worked loyally for a continuation of the empire. The elections of 1907 revealed a great interest in economic affairs, to be sure, but all too often the parties which promised progressive economic policies also heavily stressed nationalistic aims. After 1909, the period of relative calm among the nationalities ceased, and the conflicts began anew. One is forced to conclude that the faith in reform manifested by many parliamentary figures in the middle of the decade was soon smashed. Indeed, did many of the friends of reform honestly feel that universal manhood suffrage was more than a last despairing gesture? Did they believe that a fair system of autonomy for the nationalities would be the panacea? Indeed, to what extent were the non-German nationalities willing to work within the framework of the empire, however liberal?

One can only point out that, for certain national groups, the empire had little to offer. Certainly the Italians and the Rumanians had homelands to which they were inevitably attracted. The leaders of the Ruthenes had no illusions about an eventual union with the Ukrainians under the Czar, yet their poorly informed followers were increasingly under the power of pro-Russian propaganda. The Ruthenes gained much as a result of the reform of 1907, yet their failure to gain all of their desires probably created more frustration than contentment. The Poles and Czechs had no ethnic state to turn to; for the time being, they seemed generally willing to remain within the empire. The greatest pull away from the empire, certainly after 1908, was to be found among the Southern Slavs. The debates on electoral reform and the elections of 1907 showed an amazing amount of cooperation between Slovenes and Germans, but, after 1908, the annexation of Bosnia seriously damaged the promising signs of reconciliation. The relatively smaller numbers of Croats and Serbs within the boundaries of Austria were more under the spell of the revived Serbia of Peter Karageorgevič than were the Slovenes, yet all these groups, confronted with the misfortunes of their fellow Slavs in Hungary and with the potent appeals of pro-Serbian societies, moved steadily away from the ideal of Austro-Slavism after 1908.

In this situation can be discerned another reason for the failure of the reform of 1907, namely, the Reichsrat's continued inability to check in any appreciable manner the conduct of foreign policy. The Czechs and Southern Slavs of the universally elected Lower House could only fume impotently over the strong policy taken by Aehrenthal toward Serbia and Russia in 1908-1909. Simultaneously, it became obvious that the Emperor had renounced his previous approval of electoral reform in Hungary; without reform, the subject nationalities in Hungary would continue to suffer political, economic, and social disabilities. The Slavs of Austria could do nothing to help their brothers in Hungary; most ominous of all, they could no longer hope to persuade the Slavs of Hungary that the empire was fundamentally a state which eventually would honor Slavic aspirations. Without control of foreign policy and without any decisive influence over the conduct of affairs in Hungary, the representatives of the citizens of Austria had ample reason to despair of the reform passed in 1907.

The narration of parliamentary activity after Beck's resignation gives a good idea of the extent of their despair and disillusionment. The attempt to remedy the faulty procedure of the Lower House was of little aid in restoring fruitful activity there. Beck's progressive notion of using representatives of the more powerful parties in the cabinet was practically scrapped by Bienerth and Stürgkh. Worst of all, as Baernreither and Joseph Redlich testified, the bureaucracy was completely demoralized by the constant demands of the deputies for favors. The deputies might continually fail to agree on larger problems of state policy; they were well-nigh unanimous in harassing and bludgeoning the bureaucrats into granting favors for their constituents. Before 1907, many deputies were practically independent of pressure from the voters of Austria; after 1907, no deputy could ignore for a moment the demands of his constituency. In a truly democratic state, popular pressure is necessary for the functioning of efficient government; in Austria, where the people's representatives could only play at democracy, the pressure of the public was soon confined to the most petty cases of patronage. The bureaucracy, one of the great props of the empire, began to collapse under the strain.

To recapitulate, the electoral reform of 1907 failed primarily because it was conceived within the old centralistic mold. Without sensible concessions to the non-Germans of the empire, orderly parliamentary government at Vienna could only degenerate into aimless grabs for patronage. The short period of relative calm which followed the reform ended abruptly with the Bosnian adventure of 1908, when the powerlessness of the representatives of the people over foreign policy was revealed once again. The failure to achieve some semblance of democratic procedure in Hungary increased Southern Slav and Rumanian bitterness and added mightily to the attractiveness of Serbia and Rumania. The male citizens of Austria showed some readiness to vote for deputies who promised economic redress, but their chief enthusiasm went to the men who swore to defend the rights of nationality. In the final analysis, the mystic ties of " blood " triumphed over the prosaic search for economic and social betterment.

APPENDIX

TABLE 1
RESULTS OF ELECTIONS TO THE LOWER HOUSE *

Political Groups	Number of Mandates Secured			
	1897	1901	1907	1911
German Progressives	47	39	19	15
German Constitutionalists	30	30	..	..
German Populists	42	51	29	21
German Clericals and Conservatives	43	37	28	..
Christian Socialists	30	22	68	76
Pan-Germans	5	21	3	4
Independent Pan-Germans	..	..	14	22
German Agrarians	..	..	19	22
German Freiheitliche	..	..	..	15
German Independents	2	1	2	13
Czech Conservatives	16	16	..	..
Old Czechs	..	..	5	1
Young Czechs	63	53	21	19
Czech Liberal Agrarians	..	6	28	37
Czech National Socialists	..	5	9	17
Czech Catholic Agrarians	..	2	17	7
Czech Realists	..	..	2	..
Czech Independents	..	..	2	1
Polish Club	59	62	..	..
Conservatives	..	..	15	17
National Democrats	..	..	14	10
Progressive Democrats	..	..	11	13
Center	..	..	14	1
Polish Populists	3	3	16	24
Polish Christian Populists	6	5	1	3
Independent Poles	..	1	2	7
Ruthene Club	11	10	..	..
Old Ruthenes	..	..	5	2
Young Ruthenes	..	..	20	23
Radical Ruthenes	..	..	5	5
Italian Club	19	19	..	..
Italian Liberals	..	..	4	6
Italian Clericals	..	..	10	10
Rumanian Club	6	5	5	5
South Slav Club	29	27	..	..
Slovenes	..	..	24	24
Croats	..	..	11	11
Serbs	..	..	2	2
Jewish Nationalists	..	..	4	1
† Social Democrats	14	10	87	82
	425	425	516	516

* Figures for 1897 and 1901 are adapted from W. Beaumont, "La Crise du Parlamentarisme en Autriche; les Elections Legislatives et la Situation Politique," *Annales des Sciences Politiques*, XVI (1901), 170-1. Figures for 1907 and 1911 are adapted from the report published by the K.K. Statistische Zentralkommission, *Summarische Ergebnisse der Statistik der Reichsratswahlen von 1911* (Brünn, 1911), pp. XVI-XVII.

† Of the Social Democrats elected in 1907, 50 were German in background, 24 were Czech, 6 were Polish, 5 were Italian, 2 were Ruthene. In 1911, 44 were German, 26 were Czech, 8 were Polish, 3 were Italian, and 1 was Ruthene.

TABLE II
TABULATION OF VOTES CAST, BY NATIONALITY *

	1907 Total	Percentage	1911 Total	Percentage
German	1,772,418	38.4	1,739,443	38.3
Czech	1,075,694	23.3	1,094,013	24.1
Polish	650,872	14.1	672,367	14.8
Ruthene	600,169	13.0	530,970	11.7
Slovene	169,021	3.7	170,356	3.8
Italian	121,906	2.6	115,905	2.6
Croatian	81,275	1.8	82,918	1.8
Rumanian	52,347	1.1	55,946	1.2
Jewish Nationalist ...	31,941	.7	31,781	.7
Serbian	11,783	.2	11,460	.3
Others	49,934	1.1	31,839	.7
	4,617,360	100.0	4,536,998	100.0

* *Summarische Ergebnisse der Statistik der Reichsratswahlen von 1911,* p. XIII.

TABLE III
RELATION OF THE NATIONALITIES IN POPULATION AND PARLIAMENTARY STRENGTH

	Percent of Population, 1900	Percent of Mandates, 1901 *	Percent of Population, 1910	Percent of Mandates, 1907 *
Germans	35.78	48.47	34.82	44.96
Czechs	23.24	20.24	22.53	20.93
Poles	16.59	16.94	17.39	15.31 †
Ruthenes	13.21	2.35	12.32	6.20 †
Slovenes	4.65	3.53	4.39	4.65
Italians	2.83	4.47	2.34	3.68
Croats and Serbs	2.77	2.82	2.74	2.52
Rumanians	.90	1.18	.97	.97

* In computing the percentages of mandates falling to each nationality in 1901 and 1907, the Social Democrats are included.

† In the elections of 1911, the Polish percentage of mandates increased to 16.09, while the Ruthene percentage dropped to 6.01. The change reflects the Polish success in capturing three Jewish Nationalist mandates and one Ruthene mandate.

TABLE IV
INEQUALITIES IN THE CURIAL SYSTEM OF REPRESENTATION *

	Number of voters per deputy 1897	1901
Great landowners' curia	64	64
Chambers of commerce	28	26
Urban curia	3,341	4,193
Rural curia	11,555	12,290
Universal curia	69,697	69,503

* K.K. Statistischen Central-Commission: *Österreichische Statistik,* Band LIX, 3. Heft, p. VII.

BIBLIOGRAPHY

OFFICIAL PUBLICATIONS

Haus der Abgeordneten des österreichischen Reichsrates
  (1) Stenographische Protokolle über die Sitzungen des Hauses der
      Abgeordneten des Reichsrates
      XVII Session 1901-1907 XXXV, XXXVI, XXXVIII, XXXIX,
      XLIII, XLIV, XLV
  (2) Verhandlungen des Hauses der Abgeordneten des österreichischen
      Reichsrates
      XVII Session 1901-1907 Beilagen, XXVII-XXVIII
Herrenhaus des österreichischen Reichsrates
  (1) Stenographische Protokolle über die Sitzungen des Herrenhauses
      des Reichsrates
      XVII Session 1901-1907
All published at Vienna, 1901-1907
K. K. Statistischen Central-Commission (Zentralkommission)
  (1) Österreichische Statistik
      Band LIX, 3. Heft (Vienna, 1901)
  (2) Summarische Ergebnisse der Statistik der Reichsratswahlen von
      1911 (Brünn, 1911)

COLLECTIONS OF CONSTITUTIONS AND LAWS

Bernatzik, Edmund, ed. Die österreichischen Verfassungsgesetze, 2. Aufl.,
  Vienna, 1911.
Dodd, Walter F., ed. Modern Constitutions. Vol. I. Chicago, 1909.
Fischel, Alfred, ed. Die mährischen Ausgleichsgesetze. Brünn, 1910.
Geller, Leo, ed. Oesterreichische Verfassungs-Gesetze. Vienna, 1896.
Scapinelli von Leguigno, Paul J. A. M. Das allgemeine, gleiche und direkte
  Wahlrecht. Vienna, 1907.

MEMOIRS AND LETTERS

Baernreither, Joseph. Fragments of a Political Diary. London, 1930.
Molisch, Paul, ed. Briefe zur deutschen Politik in Österreich von 1848 bis
  1918. Vienna and Leipzig, 1934.
Plener, Ernst von. Erinnerungen. Vol. III. Stuttgart and Leipzig, 1921.

GENERAL NARRATIVES AND SURVEYS

Bibl, Viktor. Der Zerfall Österreichs. Vol. II–Von Revolution zu Revolution. Vienna, 1924.

The Cambridge Modern History. Vol. XII. New York and Cambridge, 1934.

Charmatz, Richard. Österreichs äussere und innere Politik von 1895 bis 1914. Leipzig and Berlin, 1918.

Chéradame, André. L'Europe et la Question d'Autriche au Seuil du xxe Siècle. 4me éd. Paris, 1906.

Colquhoun, Archibald R. The Whirlpool of Europe. London and New York, 1907.

Czedik, Alois von. Zur Geschichte der k. k. österreichischen Ministerien 1861-1916. Vols. I, III. Teschen, Vienna, and Leipzig, 1917-1920.

Drage, Geoffrey. Austria-Hungary. New York, 1909.

Gayda, Virginio. Modern Austria, Her Racial and Social Problems. London, 1915.

Hévesy, André de. L'Agonie d'un Empire: L'Autriche-Hongrie. Paris, 1923.

Jaszi, Oscar. The Dissolution of the Habsburg Monarchy. Chicago, 1929.

Kleinwaechter, Friedrich F. G. Der Untergang der oesterreichisch-ungarischen Monarchie. Leipzig, 1920.

Kolmer, Gustav. Parlament und Verfassung in Österreich. Vols. III, V, VI. Vienna and Leipzig, 1902-1914.

Kralik, Richard von. Österreichische Geschichte. 3. Aufl. Vienna, 1914.

Lingelbach, William E. Austria-Hungary. Philadelphia, 1907 (based on Léger, Paul L. L'Histoire de l'Autriche-Hongrie. Paris, 1895.)

Lowell, A. Lawrence. Governments and Parties in Continental Europe. Vol. II. Boston and New York, 1896.

Ogg, Frederic A. The Governments of Europe. New York, 1913.

Renouvin, Pierre. La Crise Européenne (1904-1914) et la Grande Guerre. 2me éd. Paris, 1939.

Schierbrand, Wolf von. Austria-Hungary: The Polyglot Empire. New York, 1917.

Seton-Watson, Robert W. The Future of Austria-Hungary and the Attitude of the Great Powers. London, 1907.

——, German, Slav, and Magyar. London, 1916.

Sieghart, Rudolf. Die letzten Jahrzehnte einer Grossmacht. Berlin, 1932.

Steed, Henry Wickham. The Hapsburg Monarchy. 4th ed. London, 1919.

Taylor, A. J. P. The Habsburg Monarchy 1815-1918. London, 1941.

Wieser, Friedrich von. Über Vergangenheit und Zukunft der österreichischen Verfassung. Vienna, 1905.

STUDIES OF MORE LIMITED SCOPE

Adler, Viktor. Das allgemeine, gleiche und direkte Wahlrecht und das Wahlunrecht in Österreich. Vienna, 1893.

Auerbach, Bertrand. Les Races et les Nationalités en Autriche Hongrie. 2me éd. rev. Paris, 1917.

Baernreither, Josef M. Zur böhmischen Frage. Vienna, 1910.

Bahr, Hermann. Wien. Stuttgart. No date.

Beaumont, W. "Le Suffrage Universel en Autriche: la Loi du 26 Janvier 1907." Annales des Sciences Politiques, XXII, 1907, 618-640.

Blondel, G. "Les Dernières Elections en Autriche-Hongrie". *La Réforme Sociale*, LXII, 1911, 218-221.

Charmatz, Richard, Der demokratisch-nationale Bundesstaat Österreich. Frankfurt a.M., 1904.

——, Deutsch-österreichische Politik. Leipzig, 1907.

Fay, Sidney B. The Origins of the World War. Vol. I. New York, 1929.

Fischel, Alfred. Der Panslawismus bis zum Weltkrieg. Stuttgart and Berlin, 1919.

Hantich, H., "Nouvelle Phase du Parlamentarisme en Autriche". *Questions Diplomatiques et Coloniales*, XXIX, 1910, 158-163.

Huemmer, Karl. Der ständische Gedanke in der katholisch-sozialen Literatur der 19. Jahrhunderts. Würzburg, 1927.

Hugelmann, Karl Gottfried, ed. Das Nationalitätenrecht des alten Österreichs. Vienna and Leipzig, 1934.

Jaray, G. L. "L'Autriche Nouvelle: Sentiments Nationaux et Préoccupations Sociales." *Annales des Sciences Politiques*, XXIII, 1908, 293-310, 664-683.

——. ''La Physionomie Nouvelle de la Question Austro-Hongroise." *Questions Diplomatiques et Coloniales*, XXX, 1910, 729-739.

Kolmer, Gustav: "La Vie Politique et Parlementaire: Autriche." *Revue Politique et Parlementaire*, LXIX, 1911, 177-187.

Kosch, Wilhelm. Die Deutschen in Österreich und ihr Ausgleich mit den Tschechen. Leipzig, 1909.

Mayer, Sigmund. Die Wiener Juden 1700-1900. Vienna and Berlin, 1918.

Molisch, Paul. Geschichte der deutschnationalen Bewegung in Österreich. Jena, 1926.

Popovici, Aurel C. Die vereinigten Staaten von Gross-Österreich. Leipzig, 1906.

Redlich, Joseph. Austrian War Government. New Haven, 1929.

Renner, Karl. Grundlagen und Entwicklungsziele der österreichisch-ungarischen Monarchie. Vienna and Leipzig, 1906.

——. Der Kampf der österreichischen Nationen um den Staat. Erster Theil. Vienna, 1902.

Samassa, Paul. Der Völkerstreit im Habsburgerstaat. Leipzig, 1910.

Schwalber, Joseph. Vogelsang und die moderne christlich-soziale Politik. Munich, 1927.

Sosnosky, Theodor von. Die Politik im Habsburgerreiche. 2. Aufl. 2 vols. Berlin, 1912-1913.

Strakosch-Grassmann, Gustav. Das allgemeine Wahlrecht in Österreich seit 1848. Leipzig and Vienna, 1906.

Walsh, V. Hussey. "Through the Austrian General Election." *The Fortnightly Review*, LXXXI, new series, 1907, 977-990.

Wiskemann, Elizabeth. Czechs and Germans. London, New York, and Toronto, 1938.

BIOGRAPHICAL

Freund, Fritz, ed. Das österreichische Abgeordnetenhaus. Biographisch-statistisches Handbuch. Vienna, 1907.

Neue österreichische Biographie, Anton Bettelheim, ed. 8 vols. Vienna, 1923-1935.

Selver, Paul. Masaryk. London, 1940.

Sosnosky, Theodor von. Franz Ferdinand. Munich and Berlin, 1929.

Steinitz, Eduard von, ed. Erinnerungen an Franz Joseph I. Berlin, 1931.

Wilhelm, Artur, ed. Die Reichsrats-Abgeordneten des allgemeinen Wahlrechtes. Vienna, 1907.

NEWSPAPERS

Neue Freie Presse. 1905.

New York Times. 1905.

INDEX

A

Abrahamowicz, David von, 158, 171-72, 176, 191
Adler, Viktor, 46, 56, 70, 73, 78, 80, 84-87, 91-93, 101, 103-05, 119-20, 135, 137, 143-44, 149, 153-55, 160, 171, 174-75, 186, 209
Aehrenthal, Baron Alois, 62 note 103, 213
Age requirements, minimum, 96, 100, 104
Alcoholics, disfranchisement of, 105
Almanach de Gotha, 75
Anti-Semitism, 35 note 13, 119, 120 note 152, 121, 182-84, 198
Auersperg, Prince Adolf, 15
Ausgleich of 1867, 13, 27, 58, 105-06, 108-09, 199, 200
Austerlitz, 44
Austro-Slavism, 210, 213

B

Badeni, Count Kasimir, 24-25, 32 note 6, 182
Baernreither, Josef, 46 note 56, 51, 96, 124-25, 176, 180-81, 205, 213
Bahr, Hermann, 206
Bartoli, Matteo, 146-47, 159-60
Baxa, Karel, 52 note 71, 108, 175 note 132, 187
Beck, Baron Max Vladimir, 42 note 43, 55-56, 59, 60 note 98, 61-64, 83-84, 86, 88-89, 110-11, 132-33, 145-47, 153-54, 172, 178, 199-201, 205, 211, 213
Belgium, 78, 89, 102
Berchtold, Count Leopold, 206
Beuerle, Karl, 78, 131
Beust, Count Friedrich, 13
Biala, 157
Bienerth, Count Richard, 62, 93-94, 103, 113, 137-38, 145, 147-48, 151-53, 155, 157-61, 201-05, 213
Bohemia, 33, 36 note 23, 47, 57 note 85, 59, 61 note 98, 68, 72, 80, 97-98, 108, 112, 144-46, 149, 156, 159, 161-64, 169, 185-88, 190-91, 200, 210; diet of, 13-15, 115, 200
Borgoerizzo, 146
Bosnian Crisis of 1908-09, 201, 203, 212-14
Bozen, Bishop of, 184

Breiter, Ernest, 92, 118, 174
Brünn, 40, 42, 44, 74
Budapest, 22, 61 note 101
Budget, Austrian, 21, 109, 200, 203
Budweis, 42, 44, 163
Bukovina, 57 note 85, 60, 70 note 11, 92, 120, 124, 144-45, 150, 152, 155-56, 166, 178 note 2, 185, 196, 198; diet of, 115
Bülow, 141 note 49
Byk, Emil, 120
Bylandt, Count Artur, 50, 54, 57, 62, 89, 166, 180

C

Canossa, 169
Carinthia, 60, 70 note 11, 145, 150, 152-55, 196
Carniola, 60, 70 note 11, 114, 145-46, 150-55
Catholic People's Party, 34 note 10, 183
Catholic Socialism, 95, 99
Center, Upper House, 54-55, 62-63, 89
Chambers of Commerce, Curia of, 15-17, 54 note 78, 100, 129, 146, 181
Charles IV, 150
Charmatz, Richard, 179
Chiari, Karl, 169
Chlumecky, Baron Johann, 90
Choc, Václav, 36 note 24, 93, 102-03, 105, 148-49, 154-55, 162-64, 170, 187
Christian Socialists, 19, 21, 24-25, 34 note 10, 35, 37-39, 43, 46, 50, 86, 88, 91-92, 95, 97, 101, 107, 111, 119, 121, 124, 133-37, 149, 154-55, 157, 160, 163, 165, 178-87, 196, 199-201, 203-04, 208, 211
Cilli, 44, 150-51; controversy, 23, 151 note 75
Čípera, Josef, 149, 162-63
Clerical-Conservatives, see Right, Parties of the
Clericalism, 36, 71, 82, 151, 167, 177, 179, 182, 184-86, 189-90, 192-93
Compulsory voting, 35, 49, 60, 63, 134-39
Conci, Enrico, 161
Constitutionalists, 46, 51, 80, 136, 180, 190

221